Adriaen van der Donck

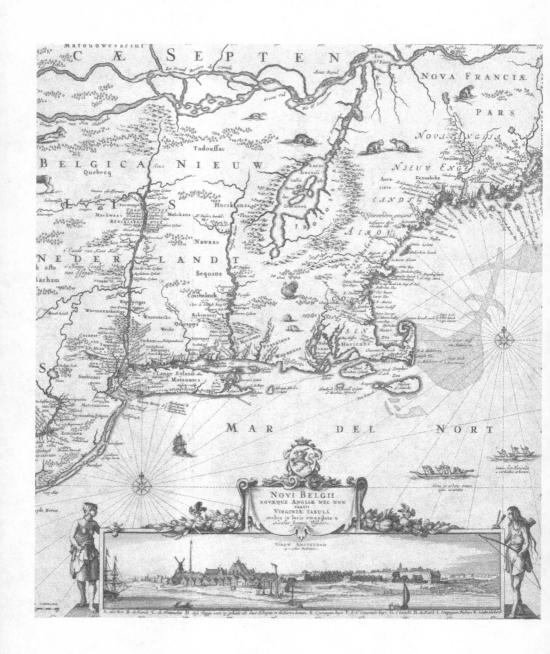

Adriaen van der Donck

A Dutch Rebel
in Seventeenth-Century America

J. VAN DEN HOUT

excelsior editions

An imprint of State University of New York Press

Cover: Portrait of a man thought to be Adriaen van der Donck. Courtesy of the National Gallery of Art, Washington. Background: Manuscript copy, *Vertoogh van Nieuw-Nederlandt*, National Archives of the Netherlands.

Back cover: The Assembly of the States General, The Hague. Courtesy of the Rijksmuseum, Amsterdam.

Frontispiece: Map known as the Jansson-Visscher map of New Netherland, 1651–1656. Courtesy of the New York Public Library Digital Collections.

Published by
STATE UNIVERSITY OF NEW YORK PRESS, ALBANY

EXCELSIOR EDITIONS is an imprint of STATE UNIVERSITY OF NEW YORK PRESS
For information, contact State University of New York Press, Albany, NY
www.sunypress.edu

Production and book design, Laurie D. Searl
Marketing, Kate R. Seburyamo

Library of Congress Cataloging-in-Publication Data

Names: Hout, J. van den, [date], author.
Title: Adriaen van der Donck : a Dutch rebel in seventeenth-century America /
J. van den Hout.
Description: Albany : State University of New York Press, 2018. | Series:
Excelsior editions | Includes bibliographical references and index.
Identifiers: LCCN 2017021795 (print) | LCCN 2017022637 (ebook) |
ISBN 9781438469225 (e-book) |
ISBN 9781438469218 (hardcover : alk. paper) |
Subjects: LCSH: Donck, Adriaen van der, 1620-1655. |
Dutch Americans—New York (State)—New York—Biography. |
New York (N.Y.)—History—Colonial
period, ca. 1600–1775. | New York (N.Y.)—Biography.
Classification: LCC F128.4.D66 (ebook) | LCC F128.4.D66 H68 2018 (print) |
DDC 973.2092 [B]—dc23
LC record available at https://lccn.loc.gov/2017021795

10 9 8 7 6 5 4 3 2 1

Contents

Contents

Illustrations

Recurring Main Characters

Jan Evertsen Bout: Delegate to the Dutch Republic with Adriaen van der Donck and Jacob van Couwenhoven

Antony de Hooges: Assistant and Under-bookkeeper of Rensselaerswyck

David Pietersz. de Vries: Sea captain and explorer; previous patroon holder of Vriessendael in New Netherland

Francis Doughty: English minister and Van der Donck's father-in-law

Mary Doughty: Daughter of Francis Doughty and wife of Adriaen van der Donck

Willem Kieft: Director of New Netherland from 1638 to 1647

Jochem Pietersen Kuyter: Danish plantation holder, member of the board of Eight Men; ally of Cornelis Melyn and adversary of Kieft

Johannes de La Montagne: Member of Kieft's and Stuyvesant's Council; Doctor of Medicine

Johannes Megapolensis: Minister of Rensselaerswyck

Cornelis Melyn: Staten Island farmer and member of the board of Eight Men; Kieft's adversary

New Amsterdam: New Netherland settlement on the southern tip of Manhattan

New Netherland: Area that is now New York, including parts of New Jersey, Connecticut, Delaware, and Pennsylvania

States General: Highest governing body of the seventeenth-century Dutch Republic

Petrus Stuyvesant: Director General of New Netherland beginning in 1647

Agatha van Bergen: Adriaen van der Donck's mother

Jacob van Couwenhoven: Delegate to the Dutch Republic with Van der Donck and Jan Evertsen Bout

Arent van Curler: Commis of Rensselaerswyck; Van Rensselaer's great-nephew

Alexander van der Capellen: Occasional chair of the States General's committee for West India affairs; brother of Hendrick van der Capellen; ally of Prince Willem II of Orange

Hendrick van der Capellen: Occasional chair of the States General's committee for West India affairs

Lubbert van Dincklagen: Vice Director of New Netherland

Cornelis van der Donck: Adriaen van der Donck's father

Kiliaen van Rensselaer: Patroon of Rensselaerswyck; former West India Company director; Amsterdam diamond merchant

Cornelis van Tienhoven: Secretary of New Netherland under Kieft and Stuyvesant; Stuyvesant's representative in the Dutch Republic

West India Company: Private Dutch trading company; administrator of the colony of New Netherland

Preface

No other figure in the compelling and colorful story of the Dutch colony of New Netherland, except perhaps Peter Stuyvesant, has attracted more interest than the young legal activist Adriaen van der Donck. His daring determination to take on the colony's top administrators in the Dutch Republic has made him a popular yet controversial figure in the history of New York. At best, he has been labeled a hero, a visionary, and a spokesman for the people. At worst, he has been branded arrogant and selfish, thinking only of his own ambitions. The wide range of opinions about him testifies to the fact that, more than three centuries after his death, Van der Donck remains an intriguing character who still strikes a chord with readers. I am not without my own opinion.

The seventeenth-century Dutch Republic was a major contender in the global rivalry for New World exploration and trade. The colony of New Netherland, encompassing what is now New York and the surrounding areas, asserted a Dutch claim on the North American continent in the early 1600s, by way of a fledgling fur trading settlement under the control of the private Dutch West India Company. The colony began to experience growing pains when, with the West India Company administration focused on its broader business and military interests, an increasing number of settlers called for a say in the colony's future. When Van der Donck left the Dutch Republic to make his mark on this new territory, he could not have anticipated that his New World aspirations would lead him into the center of the conflict in what would become a bicontinental political showdown, and the fight of his life.

Nearly two hundred years later, in 1840, the state of New York appointed John Romeyn Brodhead to procure the overseas documents relating to the state's Dutch colonial history in an effort to document this chapter of New York's past. At the time, the resulting translations focused on this "forgotten" piece of the city's history, including much of Van der Donck's story, generated a flurry of attention within the local historical community that lasted into the early part of the twentieth century. The project was set aside in 1911 after a devastating New York State Library fire destroyed or damaged many of the documents that had been preserved stateside.

In the 1970s, the wider story of New Netherland emerged anew when Charles Gehring restarted translation work with the New Netherland Project, joined later by Janny Venema. Van der Donck again caught the attention of researchers, inviting varying perspectives by scholars on his role as an instigator of change in the colony. Ada van Gastel, in her doctoral dissertation, characterized him as a spokesman for the ordinary citizenry, in contrast to later assertions by Jaap Jacobs that Van der Donck's political ambitions were largely self-serving.[1] In 2005, research and literature on New Netherland drew the story of the colony into the public arena with the breakout book *The Island at the Center of the World*, by Russell Shorto, with Van der Donck cast as one of America's enlightened but forgotten forefathers.

These earlier works presenting Van der Donck's personal story through snippets of his political career or woven throughout broader accounts of the colony left me wanting to fill in the blanks, and looking for a way to reconcile the various interpretations of his actions. It seemed that there was more to add to his story, such as the circumstances of his life leading up to New Netherland and the personal challenges he faced on his return to the Dutch Republic. None of the previous depictions of Van der Donck have looked at his life as events unfolded, in one seamless, chronological thread. As late as 1968, in a republication of Van der Donck's book as *A Description of the New Netherlands*, historian Thomas O'Donnell noted, expressing surprise, that "no biography of Van der Donck has yet been written."[2] It seems that any attempt to understand Van der Donck's ambitions would require taking a deeper look, in a complete overview of his life, in hopes of revealing insights to the motivations that shaped his role in the colony.

Building on previous writings of Van der Donck, especially on the most recent book by Russell Shorto, this cradle-to-grave narrative offers details about Van der Donck's life and his relationships before, during, and after his most visible interactions with the West India Company. The story accompanies Van der Donck from his uncertain childhood in the war-ravaged early southern Dutch Republic to his privileged education at Leiden University. It then follows him as he emerges into the fray of the New Netherland colony as a stubborn and headstrong young underling to a powerful landowner. Later, with this same willfulness and passion turned toward the volatile battle for his adopted homeland, his actions alter the course of the colony. Rather than offering a comprehensive account of New Netherland, or an in-depth look at the politics of the seventeenth-century Dutch Republic, this book aims to present an inherently imperfect human perspective, in an account that is justified for Van der Donck, whose vision for New Netherland and a willingness to fight for change made him a pivotal figure in early America.

I have come to believe that Van der Donck was driven not only to stand up for himself and the people of New Netherland but, ultimately, to pursue justice for the good of the future of the colony. Beyond any focus on individuals, his writings, time and time again, reflect an imperative to secure the country. While having the interests of the people at heart and having political aspirations are not necessarily mutually exclusive, this detailed unpacking of his life sheds light on other, possibly more nuanced reasons for his actions that are more complex than arguments of altruism versus selfishness. More personal motivations may have also come into play, such as the desire for a stable, permanent home, a disdain for authority, and an impetus to lead born of his "noble" family background and lofty education. In the end, it seems as if any or all of these underlying motivations, coupled with watching his beloved new country, with all its potential, slowly but steadily slip through the fingers of the Dutch, led to a growing frustration that Van der Donck simply could not bear, and a cause he would not concede, whatever the cost. It is my hope that new information continues to be discovered that will bring more information to light on Van der Donck's contribution to one of America's foundational colonies.

For those familiar with the story of New Netherland, this chronological narrative offers the opportunity to experience the colony through the perspective of Adriaen van der Donck's life, with new details not found in other histories of the colony, while adding to an understanding of New Netherland, as a whole. For readers without prior knowledge of New Netherland, this spotlight on a fascinating figure in America's early Dutch history can serve as an introduction to the colony. For those who, like me, wanted to know more about Adriaen van der Donck, this thoroughly researched stand-alone biography aims to provide clear and concise information and a reliable resource.

Many different pieces of evidence from archives in New York and in the Netherlands, as well as input from secondary sources, were puzzled together to create this whole picture of Van der Donck's life. Improved access to records, including expanding work in digitization, continues to make new

information available. However, there are still gaps in what we, as researchers, know about the colony. Many West India Company documents in the
Netherlands, dating before 1700, were sold for scrap paper, much to John
Romeyn Brodhead's surprise and mortification. Records that remained in
the colony suffered in storage during the English period, and some of these
eventually fell victim to damage or complete destruction in the 1911 state
library fire. Personal letters, valuable as crucial insights when there is no one
left alive to give an interview, often survived as only one side of the story,
as in the case of the letters between Van der Donck and his first employer,
Kiliaen van Rensselaer. Van der Donck's letters have not been found.

In this process of creating a comprehensive timeline of Van der Donck's
life, I have chosen to include many quotes that have been translated from
original documents of the colony. While I provide context for these accounts,
the translations act as a voice from the past and, in many cases, express the
sentiment of a situation more directly than any interpretation I could offer.
It has been my goal to stay true to the facts of the story while providing a
readable, interesting, and informative narrative. As much as possible, I have
provided my own translations from original manuscripts. In some cases, however, such as when the manuscript was inaccessible or too damaged by fire,
smoke, or water to be clearly legible, I have relied on published translations
for quotes. The source of each translation is reflected in the citation. In the
case of a manuscript, I have also attempted to provide a reference to a previously published, accessible English translation of the document. Spelling
variations that occur in the context of quotes have been left unchanged.

I owe many thanks to the various archives and their representatives that I visited in the Netherlands during research for this book. The
Nationaal Archief in The Hague is an efficient, state-of-the art facility with
a knowledgeable and helpful staff. Thank you to the Stadsarchief Breda and
the Regionaal Archief in Tilburg for helping me find documents on the
Van der Donck family in Breda and Oosterhout, as well as to the Special
Collections librarians at the University of Leiden who, over several visits
and emails, helped me sort out the circumstances of Van der Donck's legal
training. Special thanks to Diederick Wildeman of the Scheepvaartmuseum
in Amsterdam for securing naval clearance for me to look at Kiliaen van
Rensselaer's letter book, and for facilitating the digitization of this invalu-
able resource on New Netherland. Thanks, also, to the Stadsarchief in
Amsterdam for helping me find many of the legal contracts that Van der
Donck recorded while he was in the Dutch Republic. I owe Joris van den
Tol and Tom Quist for their assistance in procuring additional documents
for me from the Dutch National Archives.

The work that has been done by Charles Gehring and Janny Venema at the New Netherland Research Center, and supported by the New Netherland Institute, is not to be underestimated. Without their translations, finding much of the information needed for this book would have been an insurmountable task. I owe them many thanks for the valuable work they have produced, and I have also appreciated their encouragement. The recent addition of the colonial manuscripts to the New York State Archives' Digital Collections has also been immensely helpful. Many thanks, also, to Steve McErleane at the New Netherland Institute, who pointed me to resources I would not have found without him, for helping me untangle the many volumes of nineteenth-century authorship on New Netherland, and for his general camaraderie during my work on this project.

I would never have come this far in my research without the support of mentors at UC Berkeley, especially Jeroen Dewulf, who has been an un-wavering source of support throughout this process. My appreciation also goes out to Alison Field, the history professor who first connected me to the colony of New Netherland and gave me the freedom to dive in, head first. Thank you to Wijnie de Groot and Frans Blom for making seventeenth-cen-tury Dutch fun, and for helping me with paleography and sticky translations. Thanks, also, to Els van Boldrik, a great reader, for her proofreading and hon-est feedback of my first draft, and to Karen Tarver, who graciously reminded me that Dutch names can be confusing. I have also appreciated many rounds of encouragement from friends. I am grateful to the skilled editors at State University of New York Press, especially Amanda Lanne-Camilli for shar-ing my interest in Adriaen van der Donck and for supporting this project. I also want to thank the anonymous reviewers who took the time to provide thoughtful and constructive feedback, though any errors or omissions remain my own. Most of all, thanks to my family, who listened patiently to count-less stories about Adriaen van der Donck when I did not want to talk about anything else.

It was "Hartgers' View," an engraving of the first view of Manhattan, that excited my interest in New Netherland.[3] Something about the centuries-old print of Manhattan, with its Dutch merchant ships and Native canoes gliding past the fortressed island, pulled me into the story in an almost otherworldly attraction. I had lived in Breda, the place of Van der Donck's birth, for four years, but it was many years ago. In those days, I would walk home through the city center along the Spanjaardsgat, the water gate to the entrance of the turreted Castle of Breda, while listening blissfully to the sound of the eve-ning bells toll from the tower of the Grote Kerk. As I passed the shops that lined the Havermarkt, the shopkeeper's bells would chime in, one by one, as doors closed for the night and the late afternoon sky began to darken. It was far from my imagination, back then, and little did I know what those places would come mean to me in the distant future, in the name of Adriaen van der Donck.

I

Breda

If one looks from a distance across the low horizon to Breda, there is an openness about it that is palpably different from the bigger cities to the west. The skies are expansive in a palette of hues ranging anywhere between a heavenly blue and a mournful gray that might, at any time, give way to a muddle of clouds. This blissful opulence seems to rest atop an uninterrupted low-lying earthly landscape of farms, roofs, and treetops, dotted with the occasional steeple. In town, the moist air presses down, blanketing everything in insular intimacy, as if while walking down the street one could make out a barely audible whisper coming from the opposite side. It somehow feels provincial.

This description of Adriaen van der Donck's hometown would have also fit Breda when he lived in the seventeenth century, when countless artists were famously inspired by those same skies. Once part of the heart of the Low Countries commercial region that included Antwerp and Brussels, Breda was situated in the predominantly Catholic territory below the two great rivers, the Rijn and the Maas, which divided the region from the mainly Protestant northern Dutch Republic. While the town remained a welcome respite and active hub on the road between the Southern and Northern Low Country provinces, Breda's central location, though strategic in many ways, had also made it a liability. As the boom of the Dutch Golden Age was generating unprecedented growth in the western cities of the Dutch Republic, Breda was continuously exposed to conflict as part of the Dutch-administered province of North Brabant that bordered the Spanish-controlled territories. A century earlier, Breda had been turned into a battleground when the relentless push for control by the Spanish from the south, and resistance by the Dutch from the north, left it caught in the middle in a tug-of-war. The fighting that ensued eventually ignited the Dutch Revolt in 1568 and the Eighty Years' War that followed. The ongoing hostilities exposed the area to so much trauma and violence that a cleric would later write, "Almost every hand's breadth of ground in Brabant is stained with blood."[1] Even after the formation of the Dutch Republic, North Brabant and Breda remained unsecured in the turbulent strife between the two forces. While the northern Dutch provinces prospered, North Brabant and Breda continued to be pulled apart, held hostage by the volatility between the Catholic Spanish Low Countries and the Protestant Dutch Republic. The road to peace would be long for Breda.

Breda, named for the wide (*breed*) river Aa just to the south, was a city with a fifteen-bastioned fortification, four gates, and a castle surrounded by a moat. It was one of the oldest fortresses in the province of North Brabant and one of the original cities belonging to the Nassau aristocracy. Willem of Orange, a descendant of the Nassau family, fought for Dutch independence from Spain during the Eighty Years' War. In spring of 1590, in one of the most famous battles that is still a source of pride for Breda today, Willem's son Maurits, who had succeeded him as Prince of Orange, called on the owner of a *turfschip*, or peat boat, to aid in a daring military tactic.[2] In a ruse reminiscent of the Greek legend of the Trojan Horse, the peat boat operator who was contracted to deliver the dried, boggy vegetation commonly used for fuel secretly stowed seventy-two Dutch soldiers in the boat's cargo hold. Packed tight in the fake compartment, the soldiers waited for the opportune moment to enter the fort, stifling their coughs in the damp and leaking boat for fear of giving themselves away.[3] In the dark of night on an ice-cold Shrove Tuesday that March, the boat operator smuggled the soldiers past the Spanish guards and through the fortress of the Castle of Breda. The dauntless Dutch company battled the Spanish soldiers, who were caught unprepared in the surprise attack, and won control of the city back for the House of Orange. In his gratitude, Maurits rewarded the peat boat owner generously, deeding him a house and an honorable official city function in Breda as harbormaster. The peat boat owner, from the nearby village of Leur, was Adriaen van Bergen, Adriaen van der Donck's maternal grandfather, and his namesake.

Breda prospered under Prince Maurits who, like his father Willem, ruled with a tolerance for both Protestants and Catholics. This approach not only benefited the community socially, it also aided commercial expansion as a by-product of the cooperative climate. By the early 1600s, Breda, which had also recovered from a devastating fire in the previous century, was growing into a provincial city. The river Marck meandered idyllically through the city

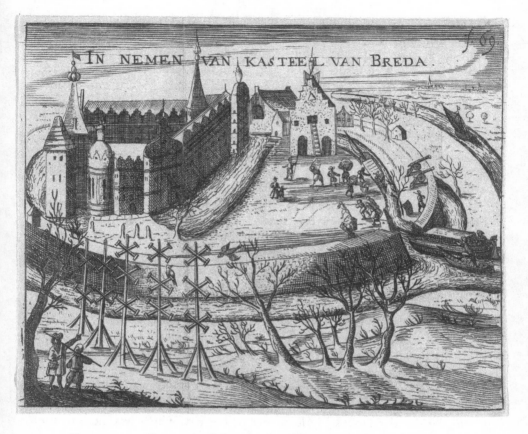

FIGURE 1.1. Capture of the Castle of Breda, 1590. Courtesy of the Rijksmuseum, Amsterdam.

from the north, facilitating transportation from outside areas into the center of town. Though still much more of a pastoral setting than a big city like Amsterdam, Breda nevertheless bustled with local merchants in lively public markets like the Vismarkt, Veemarkt, Houtmarkt, and Havermarkt, selling fish, livestock, wood, and grains.[4]

From all indications, the decorated military history of the peat boat victory had propelled the Van Bergen family into the class of the socially privileged. The family had a coat of arms, which, itself, was a sign of wealth or status, featuring three lions rampant, or forelegs raised in profile, over a peat boat on the water.[5] However, when Adriaen van der Donck's mother, Agatha Adriaens(dr) van Bergen, from Breda, married his father, Cornelis Ghysbrechts(z) van der Donck, from Dordrecht, she married into a family that had some social standing of its own.[6] Originally from the central province of Gelderland where an estate named Donkersgoed in Putten was likely named for them, the family were landowners and also had a coat of arms, featuring three castles in red against a gold background.[7] The Van der Donck family names were recorded with titles, a sign of status at the time. *Sr.*, short for *Sieur*, was used for the men in the family and *Jo^e*, for *Joffrouwe*, or *Jonckvrouwe*, addressed the women. After the death of Cornelis van der Donck's own father, his mother remarried another man of high social ranking, Artus Pels. This marriage made Pels, a steward in the House of Orange, stepfather to Cornelis. Records show that Cornelis later sold two houses, with their lots, in Breda, which may have come from Pels.[8]

Adriaen van der Donck was born into his Protestant family between 1618 and 1620 during the Twelve Years' Truce with Spain that had begun in 1609, after forty years of war.[9] This was a time of welcome and hopeful respite from years of conflict when the people of Breda could finally go about their lives, living peacefully together in a community that was roughly two-thirds Catholic and one-third Protestant. Agatha and Cornelis van der Donck had settled there, in a posh area in the northeast part of town, and had at least three children, Agatha, Adriaen, and Balthasar, and possibly a fourth, Ghysbrecht.[10] The family home stood on the north side of the Gasthuyseinde (now the Boschstraat) at the corner of an alleyway called Duivelshoek. These residences just inside the Gasthuyseinde Poort, one of the four gates on the edge of the city, made a welcome presentation of Breda's prosperity to visitors entering from the north.[11] There would have been plenty to do and see in the Van der Doncks' little corner of the city, which was close to the center of activities and apparently quite diverse. Just down the street stood the Gasthuis, or Guest House, a care center for foreigners and anyone of lesser means, with its own church on the property. A couple of hundred yards to the north lay the serene twelfth-century brick Begijnhof, a walled complex where the Beguine order of Catholic laywomen lived quietly and independently, insulated from the religious conflicts because of their long-standing relationship with the Nassau family. In their enclosed courtyard, the Beguines' gardens flourished with the color and aroma of hundreds of varieties of plants and herbs, grown for medicinal purposes in their calling as caregivers. From the Begijnhof, the Castle of Breda was an imposing sight as a noble and monumental brick structure, with its main building forming a quadrangle around an inner square. Home to family members of the House of Orange, the castle, as well as all of its ancillary buildings, was contained within the surrounding moat. The entire formation held a gracious but formidable presence in the city.

From Adriaen van der Donck's house he could look up and see the majestic steeple of the Grote Kerk, or Great Church, rising more than three hundred feet toward the heavens. Built in the 1400s from lightly colored local natural stone in the Brabant Gothic Style, the church's dramatic and elaborate architecture dominated the Grote Markt, the largest and most prominent marketplace in Breda. The affluence of the Orange-Nassau family was reflected in the church's ornately decorated structure, and the remains of some of the family members are still encrypted there under intricately carved monuments. In the volatile period of the Eighty Years' War with Spain, control of the church fluctuated between Catholic and Protestant authority, but it was in Protestant hands from the time of the peat boat victory of 1590 through the time of Van der Donck's birth. He would have had to walk past the church on the way to visit his grandfather, who lived just on the opposite side in a house on the Havermarkt named De Zwaan.

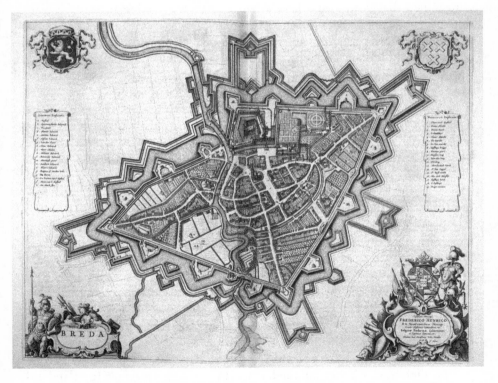

FIGURE 1.2. Map of the bastioned city of Breda. Courtesy of the British Library, London.

The peaceful and undisturbed existence that Adriaen van der Donck enjoyed as a young boy in Breda was short-lived after the Twelve Years' Truce with Spain ended in 1621. It had become more and more likely that war would resume after the truce ended, and that Breda would be one of Spain's next targets, in part to make up for an earlier, failed attempt to take the neighboring village of Bergen op Zoom. Control of Breda and the province of North Brabant would give the Spanish command of the rivers that bordered the Dutch Republic, positioning them to disrupt the trade that had grown in these regions. In 1624, the Spanish, no longer bound by the armistice, made plans to assault the city from the south in a siege offensive. In May of that year, city leaders got wind of a plan to attack, and the people of Breda braced themselves for what was likely to come. The city stockpiled warehouses with grain and other provisions, while strengthening their defense levels by adding soldiers and munitions. The Spanish, knowing it would be difficult to penetrate Breda's stepped-up fortification, tactically determined that they would have a better chance of taking Breda by isolating the city than by a traditional weapons attack. Under decorated officer Ambrogio Spinola, the Spanish plan was to cut off supplies to Breda until its citizens would literally be hungry enough to surrender.[12]

By the end of July, a growing number of Spanish troops were assembling just two miles away from the city. A month later, the Spanish were successful in securing the first area, just south of Breda. Local leaders encouraged the farmers living outside of the city to move their families into town for safeguarding. To help fund their own defense, all citizens, especially those like the Van der Doncks who had the means, were ordered to declare under oath all the money, gold, and silver they had and then turn it in to the city on loan. The metals were melted down and made into coins to pay the additional soldiers that were there for their protection.[13] The military in Breda cut through forests of trees and burned down houses in the southern part of town to get a clear view of Spinola's activities as he positioned his companies of soldiers into four quarters around the city. By September, Spinola's army had succeeded in erecting a fortification around the city, as troops moved closer into makeshift forts to cut off any channels by which food could reach the city from the countryside. The Spanish, whose patience was waning, began firing on the city with cannons and grenades, destroying some homes in the barrage. Food supplies that, until then, had been able to move throughout the city with some ease, were becoming more difficult to access. Bread, a staple for the Dutch, was being rationed. Little by little, shortages of food and especially medicines worsened. By February 1625, catastrophic diseases such as scurvy, dysentery, and the plague were spreading among the despondent community.[14] The soldiers were suffering from fatigue. After several attempts by the army of the Dutch Republic to come to Breda's aid failed to get through the Spanish defenses, the city began to concede that there would be no relief from the Spanish hold. Finally, in June 1625, a debilitated and depopulated Breda had no choice but to surrender.

While Spinola was praised for capturing Breda with a minimal amount of bloodshed, the conflict had taken a heavy toll on the citizens of Breda in turmoil and suffering. By the time the Spanish moved into the city, approximately five thousand residents, a third of the population of Breda, had lost their lives to starvation and disease. The people's attempt at defense from within Breda had been valiant, however. In a feat of clever Dutch water engineering, a system of defensive locks had been deployed, damming the rivers Aa and Marck to create a moat around the city. The resulting flooding not only affected areas along the rivers, but also inundated the western and northern parts of the city that would have included the area where the Van der Doncks had their home.[15] The despair and flooding might not have been enough to drive the family away. But, though the Spanish had agreed to many of the city's conditions for surrender, there would be no concession on religious divergences. The Catholic Spanish denied the freedom of conscience for Protestants, the right to follow their own religious beliefs, even disallowing Protestant burials in the church in Breda. Occupation by the Spanish meant that most of the Protestants would be expelled from the town, regardless of their rung on the social ladder. After the devastating loss of their hometown, the Van der Donck family fled north to the smaller village of Oosterhout. Rather than growing up in Breda, basking in a privileged childhood playing marbles or leapfrog, spinning tops or jumping rope, and enjoying the innocence of his youth as has heretofore been assumed, Adriaen van der Donck witnessed firsthand the inescapable inequities of war, the death and suffering of friends and neighbors, and finally, the loss of his very community. While the family's affluence likely positioned him better than those in lower socioeconomic classes, he was forced to leave the only home he had ever known, as a boy of about seven years old. For a child who had not known the adult construct of war, the prospect of death, or another home for that matter, this flight must have been a terrible upheaval, wrought with uncertainties. He probably wondered, as children often contend when they have no voice in a matter, how this could possibly be fair.

While Oosterhout was not home, it was at least nearby, being less than a day's walk from Breda. And it was not a bad refuge, as towns go. Many of the bigger farmhouses in the area had been expanded into modest castles during the late Middle Ages. Belgian history professor Jean Baptiste Gramaye

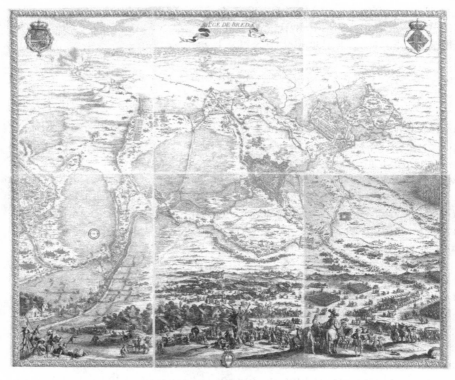

FIGURE 1.3. Spanish Siege of Breda *(detail below)*. Courtesy of the Rijksmuseum, Amsterdam.

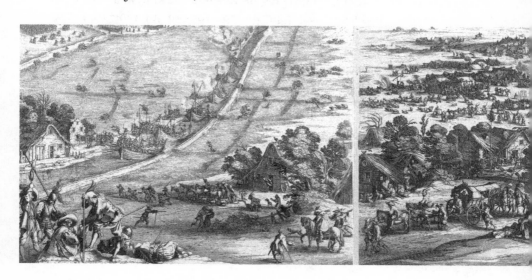

praised Oosterhout in the seventeenth century as one of the most beautiful villages in the Barony of Breda. He was so taken by it that he wrote, "If the Barony would be a ring, then I would call Oosterhout the gemstone."[16] And, apparently, the family was not alone in seeking sanctuary in Oosterhout. By looking at the statistics, it seems that others from their Protestant community likely did the same. After the Spanish siege on Breda, the Protestant population in Oosterhout, which numbered only seventy to eighty in the years before the takeover, grew to two hundred by the following year. By 1637, ten years later, the Protestant community counted approximately five hundred people. It appears that the Van der Donck family weathered the Spanish hold on Breda by staying in Oosterhout for quite some time. In 1626, Van der Donck's father received permission to transport a horse to his home in Oosterhout. The following year, probably realizing that their refuge was not as temporary as originally thought, he received additional approval for the transport of two mares and two cows. Five years later, records of a debt paid by Cornelis van der Donck and his wife, Agatha, still show an Oosterhout address.[17]

Fortunately for Adriaen van der Donck, his new community included access to schooling. The seventeenth-century Dutch Republic emphasized education. The growth in trade and the push for accessibility to the lessons of the bible had spurred the need for competency in arithmetic and reading, resulting in higher than average literacy rates compared to the rest of Europe. In the bigger cities, schools were often subsidized. In the smaller villages,

learning was prioritized through private lessons, if there was money, and through the trades, if not. The village of Oosterhout was an exception among smaller villages in that it had a Latin school, dating from 1594. The curriculum at the Latin school was taught in the classical language, as the name implies, and was among the highest level of elementary schooling available in the Dutch Republic. The Latin schools were specifically aimed at preparing students for entrance into one of the universities and often included not just Latin but Greek and Hebrew, along with a range of other general scholarship such as religious studies, mathematics, logic, and planetary sciences.[18] This was exactly the kind of education that the Van der Doncks would have wanted for their son.

Eleven years after the dark days of the surrender to Spinola, the army of the Dutch Republic recaptured Breda in October 1637. The Protestants who had been displaced slowly began returning to their homes in Breda to reconstruct their city and their livelihoods. Though the Van der Donck family also eventually returned, documents place them in Oosterhout as late as 1638.[19] They seem to have fared well enough to maintain an upper-class standing for the upcoming generation, however. Van der Donck's sister Agatha went on to marry an officer of the Dutch East India Company. His brother, Balthasar, later moved to the northern province of Friesland, possibly to attend the University of Franeker there, and became a regional administrator.[20] But Adriaen van der Donck never returned to his childhood home to stay. In May of 1638 he enrolled, at about age twenty, at Leiden University. His Latin school education had given him the foundation he needed to further his education. When he registered, however, he gave his place of origin as neither the city of Breda nor the village of Oosterhout, but as the region of Brabant.[21] Through no fault of his own, a permanent home had been kept out of reach for most of his life, when he had been too young to do anything about it. He would more than make up for any feelings of helplessness in the future. Though his life would not be long, his path forward would be filled with resolve, determination, and the pursuit of justice. He was about to embark on a new opportunity at one of the foremost learning institutions in Europe, leave the uncertainties of the past behind him, and finally be in control of his own life.

2

Leiden

When Adriaen van der Donck arrived in the city of Leiden in 1638, he stepped into the midst of a burgeoning mecca of the textile industry. The cloth workers who had fled the Catholic Spanish from the prestigious linen-producing region of Flanders in the Southern Low Countries had brought their expertise to the more tolerant northern Dutch coast. The bustling and densely populated trade center of Leiden was more typical of the urban environment of big cities in the Dutch Republic, like Amsterdam, than of the rural areas of North Brabant. The energy and diversity of this thriving hub of activity must have felt like quite a contrast from the rural village of Oosterhout, or even a provincial city like Breda, still trying to pull itself out of the trenches from years of conflict. And this contrast was probably exactly the reason why a city like Leiden would appeal to a young man like Adriaen van der Donck, ready to leave the instabilities of his past behind to see what the more cultivated provinces had to offer.

Besides being highly regarded for its expert cloth industry and superior textiles, Leiden was also known for its top-notch university. Founded in 1575, Leiden University was well established by the time Van der Donck enrolled on September 24, 1638, under Juris Studiosus, the study of law.[1] It was the first university in the northern provinces, and a gift to the city of Leiden from Willem, Prince of Orange, for its courage and perseverance in two earlier Spanish sieges. In partnership with the city of Leiden and the States of Holland, the university saw its institutional role as a mediator of conflict in the fledgling republic, offering words and debate in contrast to weapons, in the spirit of the classic maxim of the pen versus the sword.[2]

More importantly though, the university provided a way for academics in the Protestant Dutch Republic to assert and distance themselves from the prominent Catholic University of Leuven in the Southern Low Countries, still distinguished, but controlled by Spain.

At Leiden University, Van der Donck had signed on for a world-class education, one destined to put him on a trajectory for a life in the spotlight. The trustees of the university had recruited leading scholars to build the university's reputation, top professors who had already established the intellectual culture, long before Van der Donck's arrival. In 1578, the trustees had scored an academic coup when they wooed the esteemed humanitarian professor of history and law, Justus Lipsius from Leuven, and then leading French jurist Hugo Donellus from Heidelberg. Just three years later the trustees recruited Austrian Rembertus Dodonaeus, author of *Cruydtboeck*, the authoritative book on herbs and their medicinal uses, for a chair in the medical faculty. Later, the trustees pushed hard to get the great Latin professor and man of letters French Huguenot Josephus Justus Scaliger, even going as far as transporting him under the protection of warships for safe delivery from France to the Dutch Republic.[3] Among the university's prestigious alumni were innovators like theologian Justus Arminius, known for his discussions on religious tolerance, celebrated mathematician and physicist Simon Stevin, philosopher René Descartes, and law prodigy Hugo Grotius. These men, like watchful portraits hanging in the hallowed halls, would indirectly mold and influence Van der Donck, as well as other impressionable young minds, with their innovative ideas and teachings.

Out of the four courses of study offered by the university, law, theology, medicine, and philosophy, Van der Donck's choice of law was the most popular. The law study was sought after not only by students interested in legal work but also for those with their sights set on a career in public office.[4] The courses encompassed as many different topics as there were docents to teach them, ranging from statesmanship to commentary on Tacitus, or on the ethics of Aristotle.[5] The law students took classes on Justinian's Institutes; contracts, wills, and oaths; canon and civil law; ethics and rhetoric; and even feudal law.[6] At least once, Van der Donck had debated this last topic with his professors, to which they reportedly concluded, in an example of forward-looking instruction, that "instances in Holland rarely occur and are useless to spend time on."[7]

An encyclopedia of the larger body of law, the Corpus Juris Civilis, stood as the basis of the curriculum and, especially in the early years of the university, Roman law was held up as the gold standard of the law study.[8] The prevailing belief, led by Hugo Grotius, was that this was where the "purest expression of wisdom and justice could be found."[9] Grotius' treatise, *The Introduction to the Jurisprudence of Holland*, had hit the shelves just a few years before Van der Donck began his law studies and met with such popularity that it had already been reprinted four times.[10] Like Dodonaeus' *Cruydtboeck*, Grotius' book was written in Dutch, rather than in the traditional scholarly Latin of most textbooks, to make it accessible to the broader public. This groundbreaking work of Roman-Dutch law ushered in a new school of thought, an application of natural law where rules were not interpreted literally, but taken and applied as practical standards.[11] Van der Donck's later attempts to apply the intent of the law to the heart of a problem would reflect his exposure to these contemporary teachings.

This new theory of law fit well within with the general teaching approach of the university, which was fundamentally centered on post-Renaissance humanism. Humanism was the belief that "human beings' complexity gave them the potential capacity to fathom the world and to strike a balance between opposing elements."[12] In other words, it was within the capability of the human mind to make judgments through rational thought, rather than by a dependence on outdated belief systems. This ideology played out as a focus on more general knowledge, scholarly debate, and a renewed interest in classical subjects such as rhetoric and ethics. It simultaneously addressed academics and training as well as logic and reasoning, under Christian morals, in a sort of practical wisdom. Overall, the university curriculum was demanding and the standards were rigorous. Van der Donck would have been expected to "be able to distill and explain the 'argument' of a text, its structure, and the gist and consequences of a particular line of reasoning."[13] A student "had to have his knowledge at the ready, stored in his memory or in a kind of scholarly apparatus . . . to be able to use his skills for the benefit of Church and State: to speak up in administrative bodies, or to address political assemblies or religious gatherings . . . to be, in the words of Cato the Elder, '*vir bonus dicendi peritus*,' a good man and an able speaker."[14] The idea behind an education at an institute like Leiden University was to shape a new generation of young mediators who were capable of influencing the society at large.

Alongside their normal courses of study, the students' activities were supplemented by the extraordinary intellectual and cultural offerings of the university's four institutions, the library, the anatomy theater, the botanical garden, and the fencing school. The university library, the first library in the Netherlands, housed maps and globes in addition to books. This rich repository was made accessible to the broader community of booksellers, printers, and scholars in a commitment to intellectual exchange. The anatomy theater, the setting of Rembrandt's famous 1632 group portrait, *The Anatomy Lesson of Dr. Nicolaes Tulp*, hosted dissections in the winter, a time of year when human remains could be preserved by the cold weather, which slowed decomposition.[15] These presentations were so popular that they would sell out the three-hundred-plus capacity of the theater and regular classes would be cancelled. Experiments to confirm William Harvey's theory of the blood-stream were also done here, as well as research on animal glands, knowledge that Van der Donck would put to use later.[16] In the summer, when the warm weather would not permit the laying open of cadavers, the anatomy theater and the covered passage of the botanical garden would be filled with "curiosities" such as skeletons, seeds, dried plants, exotic imports such as shells, and prints, all on display for visitors and local audiences, "in the service of scholarship."[17] The botanical garden, originally built for the study

BIBLIOTHECÆ. LUGDUNO-BATAVÆ. CUM PULPITIS ET ARCIS VERA IXNOGRAPHIA.

Figures 2.1. to 2.4. The four institutions of Leiden University. Courtesy of the Rijksmuseum, Amsterdam.

Figure 2.1. The library.

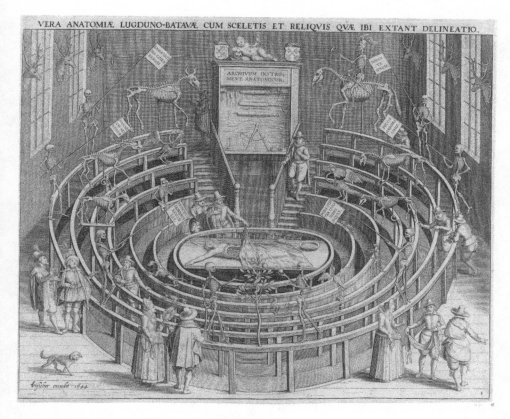

VERA ANATOMIÆ LUGDUNO-BATAVÆ CUM SCELETIS ET RELIQVIS QVÆ IBI EXTANT DELINEATIO.

FIGURE 2.2. The anatomy theater.

of medicinal herbs, eventually widened to collect exotic specimens. Fragile plants, raised in handmade greenhouses, were kept alive in winter with warm stoves attended by devoted guards.[18] The fencing school included instruction not only in fencing, but also in riding as well as shooting, with the goal of exercising the mind in the contrast of violence and control. Additionally, the school taught banner waving based on mathematical principles using geometric formations, intended to instill the civic duties of militiamen.[19]

The humanistic philosophy of the school allowed plenty of time for extracurricular activities. Classes were typically held five days a week, with no lessons on Wednesdays or Saturdays, and with time allotted for church on Sundays. Breaks were frequent, with two weeks off at Christmas and Easter, time off for Pentecost, and six weeks leave during summer.[20] Among the most important intellectual activities outside the classroom were the

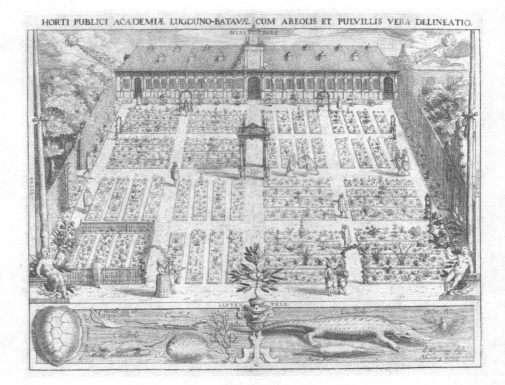

FIGURE 2.3. The botanical garden.

disputations, formal academic discussions aimed at weighing both sides of an argument. These debates, often held in small private groups led by the docents, were considered essential for practice in public speaking, the practical application of knowledge, and in preparing for exams. Numerous other private classes were offered outside the regular curriculum ranging from Italian, to dancing, and horseback riding. Besides providing a social outlet, these activities aligned with the pedagogical theory that studying involved gaining knowledge and discipline, "in a physical as well as an intellectual sense."[21] The year before Van der Donck enrolled, the school installed a lane next to the university building to encourage sports like *kolf*, similar to golf, and *pall-mall*, comparable to modern croquet.

Van der Donck's 300-plus student community was extremely diverse and, like student life at most colleges, very social. While the students were expected to work hard at their studies, one bundle of favorite Leiden student songs from the era titled *nugae venales*, Latin for "nonsense for sale," suggests a

DELINEATIO IVDI PVBLICI GLADIATORII VRBIS ET ACADEMIÆ LVGDVNENSIS APVD BATAVOS.

FIGURE 2.4. The fencing school.

spirited student life.[22] Several large residences close to the university provided housing, where students often lived and socialized with their fellow country-men. Others, like Van der Donck, stayed in private residences.[23] University professors also often took in students for lodging, which offered the op-portunity to extend learning into evening discussions, many times over a meal. Although the student body was primarily upper class, the school was not exclusive. It admitted sons of noblemen alongside the sons of plumbers and local cloth workers, as well as those from families in other trades such as carpentry and cobblery. Half of the students came to the university from foreign countries, including Switzerland, Germany, France, and England.[24] This diverse student body provided invaluable life experience for Van der Donck, who would cross paths with people from a wide variety of cultures and social classes.

The privilege of attending an institution of higher learning like Leiden University could only be topped by one thing—more privileges. These

FIGURE 2.5. Leiden University, seventeenth century. Courtesy of the Rijksmuseum, Amsterdam.

liberties were one of the most attractive benefits that the university had to offer and included such perks as exemptions from tolls and taxes on beer, as well as dispensation from serving in the local militia. In addition to these desirable benefits, the students had access to an exclusive tribunal, outside of the normal civic judiciary, to sort out any disagreements that occurred between the students and the city or townsfolk.[25] Student privileges at Leiden University were so prized that, in the early years, locals clamored to register just to have access to the privileges, and foreign students who studied for only a few months could find a lucrative secondary market selling their year's worth of exemptions to ordinary burghers or citizens.[26]

For most students, the stress on theory over practical training at Leiden University translated to "a kind of initiation into a cultural elite, a form of socialisation that placed more emphasis on formal discipline than acquiring

EEN STUDENT IN SYN KAMER.

Ik ben een Heremijt en altyd in 't gewoel:
Ik sit meest stil. en ga door zee en aarde lopen.
Die doot sijn spreke my. die levenloos. verkopen.
Voor arbeyd wetenschap. waar op ik stadig doel.
Wat Koning is soo rijck: de weerelt is mijn sot.
De wijsheyd is mijn goed. mijn seden sijn gebreken.
Mijn kisten niet vol gelt. mijn armoe vol van streken.
Mijn leven vol geneugt. mijn heer de wijngaard God.

STUDIOSUS IN CUBICULO.

Pone supercilium totus mihi desipis orbis.
Insanumq aliud nil nisi vulgus habes.
Utilis en omnem solus studiosus in usum
Pallada Pieria claudit utramque domo:
Nam capiat calamos. meus es sapientia cultor.
Si gladios. Mavors. tu meus. inquit. eris.
Ai quis tam Superum variorū Mysta premuntur
Vina. Lyæe. manu. docta Lyeæa pede.

FIGURE 2.6. Student in his room, ca. 1650. Courtesy of the Rijksmuseum, Amsterdam.

specific skills and knowledge."[27] This meant that students did not always study with the intent on entering a specific profession. The degree was not the most important thing about attending the university. In fact, few students stayed long enough to complete their course of study and earn a formal degree. While this would seem surprising by today's standards, it was the rule rather than the exception in the early years of the university. Between 1625 and 1649, which includes the years that Van der Donck studied, only eight percent of students earned doctorate degrees, the only degree awarded at the time, and in the period that followed, only sixteen percent earned degrees.[28]

It is unknown exactly how long Van der Donck stayed at Leiden University. There was no set amount of time required for the law study, and, while his registration in fall 1638 is documented, annual reenrollment records for the surrounding years are missing from the archives.[29] Considering that the university's original recommended minimum age for the doctorate was twenty-five, it is possibile that he was not yet eligible for a degree.[30] Letters from early 1641 place him in Breda, however, and indicate he had stayed in Leiden just up to taking his exams.[31] Regardless, the fact that he did not obtain his degree at this time does not mean that he did not get something out of his education in Leiden. In fact, he got something almost more important. He had attended of one of the world's most progressive universities at a time when intellectual history was being made, when only four to five percent of Van der Donck's age group went on to university studies at all.[32] He would walk away as part of the up-and-coming generation of movers and shakers, having been groomed "for public life—'in the market and in the Senate.'"[33] And he would leave with a mindset indoctrinated by the university's ideal to produce "an administrative and professional elite to take up their rightful positions in society."[34] This seemed like a role well suited for someone like Adriaen van der Donck, who was obviously already smart and ambitious, with roots in a family of privilege. His time in Leiden had given him the knowledge and the impetus to seek out a position of leadership in his community.

The Dutch Republic in the latter half of the seventeenth century offered plenty of opportunities for students coming out of the university with an eye on entering the field of law, or for those seeking public office, for that matter. But, considering the inquiries he was making from Breda, it appears that Van der Donck wanted something different, something more. Perhaps he was enticed by tales of travel he had heard from the Walloons in the textile community of Leiden, some of the first settlers to voyage to New Netherland, or from others who had been to the New World.[35] Or maybe the idea of a life in provincial Breda seemed boring after living in the city, and it did not feel like home anymore, anyway. It could be that he simply saw the chance to make his mark in the wide-open space of uncharted territory. He had been exploring opportunities to go abroad, armed with both a sword and a pen.

3

Kiliaen van Rensselaer

From his home office in his large and well-appointed house on the Keizersgracht in Amsterdam, Kiliaen van Rensselaer conducted his jewelry business, wrote his many long and detailed letters, and received his guests.[1] He was a smart and prosperous businessman, demanding, devoutly religious, and highly principled. His years as a former director of the West India Company had made him politically savvy and when he saw the opportunity to invest in the New World, he, along with several of his business associates, wanted in. That January, Van der Donck approached Van Rensselaer, patroon and proprietor of the colony of Rensselaerswyck in New Netherland, about opportunities for settlers. Van Rensselaer, always on the lookout for good people to help populate his fiefdom, was clearly intrigued. In the postscript of a letter dated January 25, 1641, to Toussaint Muyssart, one of his business partners and a cloth merchant in Leiden, Van Rensselaer wrote, "Please find out through Mr. de Laet or someone else, about a young man who studied law in Leyden called Van der Donck, from the Barony of Breda, who is interested in trying something in our colony that has to do with farming."[2] Though much older than Van der Donck, De Laet was also an alumnus of Leiden University, and another of Van Rensselaer's business partners.

The Dutch colony of New Netherland had been founded in 1614, five years after the Englishman Henry Hudson sailed into the mouth of the Hudson Bay in the service of the Dutch East India Company, searching for the fabled Northwest Passage to the Orient. Although the rivers Hudson explored did not lead to westward waters, he traded with the Natives for furs and claimed the area of what is now approximately New York to Delaware

for the Dutch Republic. The availability of furs captured the attention of
Dutch business interests. The demand for beaver skins, used to make the
waterproof felt hats favored by affluent Dutch merchants, was high, while
supplies of Muscovy furs from present-day Russia were limited, and import
duties heavy.[3] Possession of land in North America would mean new and
cheaper sources of furs. A small fur trading post was established by the New
Netherland Company in this new Dutch territory, on Castle Island in the
upper Hudson River or the Dutch-named Noord Rivier.

In 1621, the governing body of the Dutch Republic granted a mo-
nopoly on fur trade within the Dutch claim along the Hudson River to the
newly formed West India Company, modeled after the established Dutch
East India Company, but with both business and paramilitary functions. In
1624, the first colonists arrived in support of a small trading post established
at Fort Orange, in present-day Albany.[4] While most of the trade continued
in this upriver area, a year later, a second stronghold, Fort Amsterdam, was
established on the southern tip of Manhattan Island to receive incoming
ships and to protect the entrance to the river. The settlement surrounding
the fort was populated by both administrators and colonists. While trade was
the initial focus of the West India Company, increasing the population of the
colony soon become a practical necessity. Providing an agricultural base was
fundamental to supporting the community, and a stable physical presence
was essential to discouraging encroachment from the nearby English colonies
and offensives by the local Natives. In an attempt to increase colonization,
the West India Company directors initiated the granting of patroonships in
1629, land tracts deeded to private investors, which allowed the establishment
of private trading colonies under the umbrella of the company. Kiliaen van
Rensselaer, as one of the original founders and directors of the West India
Company, took advantage of this opportunity from the ground floor up. He
was given a patent for a colony approximately two hundred kilometers, a
three-day sail, north of New Amsterdam, near present-day Albany, which he
called Rensselaerswyck.[5]

Van der Donck's inquiry had unquestionably caught Kiliaen van
Rensselaer's attention, and for good reason. For one thing, it was not easy
in the prosperous days of the mid-seventeenth-century Dutch Republic to
attract people away from the comfort of family and friends to settle in faraway and unknown lands. And of those who could be persuaded to go, most
came from trade backgrounds or even from the lower classes of society with
few other opportunities to choose from. From Van Rensselaer's perspective,
someone with the background and credentials of Van der Donck did not
come along every day and, he probably reasoned, would surely be an asset

to the colony. So much so, that he was already thinking ahead as to how he could best use Van der Donck, assuming he would get a good reference. In his letter to Muyssart, he wrote, "And there being no outstanding charges, as one can not always get the best to go over there, one could also use him in some other way."[6]

Maintaining a suitable population in the colony was an ongoing concern for Van Rensselaer. The West India Company guidelines for patroonships stipulated that each colony settle fifty inhabitants within four years, and it had taken twice that amount of time for Rensselaerswyck.[7] When Van der Donck approached Van Rensselaer again just six days later, having no reservations about calling on someone of Van Rensselaer's status, he raised the stakes in an offer that would have been difficult for Van Rensselaer to refuse. Van der Donck requested, with power of attorney in hand, to contract for "two or three families of farmers" to sail to Van Rensselaer's colony in New Netherland.[8] This must have been music to Van Rensselaer's ears, especially since, as he reported to Muyssart in a second letter, the terms of the contract that Van der Donck was suggesting were "better or at least as good as our previous."[9] Van der Donck's offer was not open-ended, however. It appeared he had made up his mind to go, with or without Van Rensselaer's approval. Alongside Rensselaerswyck, he was also considering another colony, Achter Col, started by Godard van Reede, Lord of Nederhorst.[10] Moreover, he had plans to take another potential colonist from Breda, merchant Louys Saulmon, with him. With the pressure on Van Rensselaer, their negotiations seemed to take on a new sense of urgency. In his letter, Van Rensselaer pressed Muyssart to respond quickly on his background check of Van der Donck. "If you have heard about him . . . please advise me citto citto," urging speed in Latin, and then doubling that.[11] Within a week, Van Rensselaer got the thumbs up from Muyssart that he was hoping for, still, nonetheless, appealing to Muyssart to warn him, should he hear "anything to the contrary."[12] Muyssart's "good testimony" had come as a relief. Van Rensselaer was continuing to move forward with his plans in anticipation of securing a contract, already discussing details with Van der Donck, such as the condition of his animals in the colony. In an apprisal and assurance that all was going according to plan, Van Rensselaer asked Louys Saulmon, in a March letter to Breda, to tell Van der Donck that a company ship was "being made ready."[13]

In mid-April, Van der Donck sent an update to Van Rensselaer that the people he represented in Breda were getting ready to go, and further, recommended a wheelwright he had managed to recruit. Yet by early May, it was Van Rensselaer who was putting pressure on Van der Donck. "The skipper makes great haste and several people have already boarded the ship with their goods, so that neither you nor they must tarry any longer," he responded.[14] Van Rensselaer also did not hesitate to inform his new employee that he was late. "Our resolution was that you would come back at the end of April," he reminded Van der Donck, in this first show of annoyance at not adhering to his instructions, before the contract was even signed. It was a forewarning of things to come.[15] "Therefore," he added, "do not be neglectful any longer, as your commission and instructions must still be written up, which already takes time for me to do."[16]

Van der Donck would go to Rensselaerswyck, but not as a farmer. Van Rensselaer had only one officer in the colony at the time and must have realized that he could use someone with Van der Donck's pedigree and education in a position of authority. Van Rensselaer had offered him the position of *schout*, an officer of the colony similar to sheriff and prosecutor, a position that had remained open since the contract for the previous *schout* had lapsed in 1637.[17] On May 13, 1641, amid preparations in Amsterdam for the long journey ahead, and less than a week before Van der Donck left for New Netherland, Kiliaen van Rensselaer commissioned him, in a signed document, Schout of Rensselaerswyck.[18] The commission was accompanied by a separate document outlining instructions for Van der Donck, "according to which he must faithfully conduct himself."[19] "First of all," it began, "he shall promote the true and pure service of God, in conformity with the Christian Reformed religion."[20] The full instructions for Van der Donck's commission are not among Van Rensselaer's pages, but detailed expectations were set forth several years earlier in instructions for Rutger Hendricksz van Soest, the first *schout* of Rensselaerswyck. Besides the expectation that officers conduct themselves "in all faithfulness and sincerity," Van Rensselaer's orders attempted to instill a sense of solidarity and loyalty among his personnel.[21] They required that the *schout* offer "all favor, assistance, and neighborly friendship" to the commis, in charge of all merchant transactions, "to mutually assist each other, not only with advice, but in time of need, with body, against common enemies."[22] Second, the instructions reflected Van Rensselaer's religious standards. "On all occasions when Council is held," the orders read, "[they] shall not neglect to invoke the name of the Lord, and every Sunday or customary holidays, congregate to read aloud some chapters from the Holy Scripture."[23] Only after these most important overriding commands were delineated did Van Rensselaer describe the actual day-to-day duties, which included keeping an eye on the behavior of other members of the colony's administration, such as the *schepens*, or council members. The directives were especially aimed at controlling all business enacted within the colony, including, "the trade in beavers, otters, minks and similar peltries," goods such as "the seawan, the pearls, mineral, crystal or the like," as well as the discovery of "any gold, silver, copper, marble, or similar mines, also, pearl fisheries and whatever might be of importance."[24] That about covered any unforeseen futures. It was the job of the *schout* to make clear and enforce these rules. Van Rensselaer left no stone unturned in outlining his expectations, even covering, preemptively, "And that no one has to claim any ignorance, the aforesaid officer shall summon before him all the inhabitants of Rensselaerswyck, in addition to all those in my service, old or young, man or woman, master or servant, no one excepted, in order to notify them of this, my intention."[25]

Van Rensselaer's very specific instructions were his way of trying to maintain a tight rein, from a formidable distance, over the many moving parts of his organization. He had a lot of money invested in his colony, though he also understood it would take time to see some return on his long-term venture. What came through time and time again in Van Rensselaer's communications was his expectation that his officers, in every undertaking, should "seek [his] advantage and to protect [his] losses."[26] And he expected his *schout*, as the colony's chief watchdog, to make sure his business interests were guarded. To go along with the office, Van Rensselaer had sent "a silver-plated sword with a belt and a black hat with a plume" for his first commissioned *schout* in 1632.[27] Perhaps he wanted to provide an ensemble that would give his *schout* an air of command and set him apart from the others, lest any doubt be cast upon his authority. It was a small perk. This ceremonious sword and plumed hat must have appeared a little pompous in the primitive world of the fledgling colony. Although on a practical level, the sword could serve as a weapon, it is difficult to imagine that Van der Donck would have ever actually donned this attire, except possibly in the context of an official ceremony. In fact, this is exactly the kind of display of authority he would later criticize. And he would soon make it very clear that he preferred to gain the allegiance of the people of Rensselaerswyck as their champion, rather than as an autocrat.

Sliding into a leadership position as *schout* seemed like the perfect next step for Van der Donck, with the added opportunity of journeying on an adventure to the New World. His new appointment would allow him to practice the administrative and leadership skills he had acquired among a diverse group of internationals in the heady environment of Leiden University. He knew the law, and his education had given him the credentials to be recognized as a member of the upper class in his own right. He would bring with him the confidence of a firm handshake, the onus to change society for the better, and a little bit of a sense of entitlement. Perhaps these were not the best qualities for an underling matched with an employer as micro-managing and controlling as Kiliaen van Rensselaer would turn out to be. Still, Van Rensselaer had been willing to take a chance on someone like Van der Donck, who had studied law at Leiden and stood out as "a young, learned man."[28] Van der Donck had, and he was. When he would finally set sail for New Netherland on the ship *Den Eyckenboom* on May 17, 1641, he would have his back to the Dutch Republic and his whole future ahead of him. His face would be damp from the salty spray of the North Sea mist as he looked out toward the vastness of the ocean, and flush with that combination of youthful ambition and fearlessness that transcends generations across time.

4

Den Eyckenboom

The brisk business of preparing for a journey across the Atlantic began in the weeks leading up to the voyage, and was never less than a major undertaking. As much as possible needed to be anticipated in advance, as oceangoing vessels had to serve as self-sufficient floating little cities, alone at sea, for up to several months at a time. They would have to be prepared for any number of unpredictable circumstances, not limited to bad weather, unforeseen course changes, and the possibility of enemy or pirate attacks but also onboard threats such as food or water shortages, disease, or even mutinies, all subject to the judgment and competence of the captain. At a minimum, ships had to be readied at the docks, meaning "well caulked and provided with anchors, ropes, tackle, sails, running and standing rigging, victuals and other necessaries."[1]

Personnel for the voyage also had to be assembled. Besides the captain, or skipper, and sailors to man the rigging, crews also called for a surgeon, boatswain, carpenter, ship's steward, cook, sailmaker, cooper or cask maker, and various "mates," to assist in all these functions. The West India Company ships were first loaded with goods at their warehouses on the Oude Schans, a waterway on the edge of Amsterdam. In addition to the cargo and the personal effects of the crew and the passengers going to the New World, the ships also needed to store food in the way of meat, cheese, vegetables, dried fish, and grains, for the people as well as any animals it was carrying.[2] Once supplied and ready, the ships moved to the sandy island of Texel, to the north of Amsterdam. There, barrels of water hauled from the iron-rich *wezenputten*, or "orphan wells," were loaded on board. The iron in the water from these wells, named for the orphanage that owned them, acted as a preservative. Thoroughly outfitted and ready with goods, passengers, and supplies, the ships then waited in the harbor at Texel, adjacent to the North Sea, for a window of opportune tides and east winds that would carry them out to sea.

Den Eyckenboom (The Oak Tree), was most likely a fluytschip, a versatile vessel belonging to the West India Company's fleet of carriers, commonly used for transporting passengers and goods to New Netherland.[3] Developed in the late sixteenth century as an innovation in nautical design, the Dutch fluytschip was mass-produced as "cheap to build, easy to sail, and having a large cargo capacity."[4] Its design as a square-rigged merchant vessel with three masts was conceived to carry the highest load possible with a minimum crew. Ships passing through waters under threat of attack could be outfitted with cannons, shot, and gunpowder, although a fluytschip full of cargo could only be lightly armed. The fluytschip had a wide hull and a high, narrow stern, giving it its trademark pear shape. The wide front hull, in addition to creating more space for cargo, also allowed the ship to have a shallow draft, making it a highly functional craft for sailing into the river tributaries throughout Europe.[5] This combination of features widely credited the fluytschip with pushing the seventeenth-century Dutch Republic ahead of its European rivals into trade dominance. The lowest cargo deck typically held ballast and goods for transport in addition to the ship's stores and supplies. Passengers lived midship. The top deck included a forecastle, a small structure at the forward mast, sometimes used for the kitchen, and a high stern deck, often the officers' quarters. Den Eyckenboom was an average-sized fluytschip: "length 122 [feet], width 25 and a half, hold 11 and a half, above that 5 and a half and 6 feet, with a half deck and forecastle on the other side."[6]

Den Eyckenboom would serve as a temporary home on the water to several groups of men, women, and children traveling to New Netherland, including twenty in the party bound for Rensselaerswyck with Van der Donck and another group of about forty people bound for Staten Island.[7] The cargo of Den Eyckenboom, "of about 100 lasts," included goods in fulfillment of orders that had gone out from New Netherland months earlier.[8] These included carpentry nails and ships' supplies such as cables, tow line, flags and pennants, as well as caulking supplies of tar, pitch, oakum, and moss. For sailmaking, the ship had French canvas, bales of sailcloth, and two hundred pounds of yarn. For the locksmith, it had coal, and iron. In its general provisions, the ship would bring welcome casks of brandy, French wine, oil, barrels of beef and pork, fine salt, starch, candles, winnowing baskets, and stationery.[9]

When the passengers of Den Eyckenboom drifted away from the safe haven of their homeport that spring of 1641, an uncertain two-to-three-month voyage lay between them and their new beginnings. Typically, the

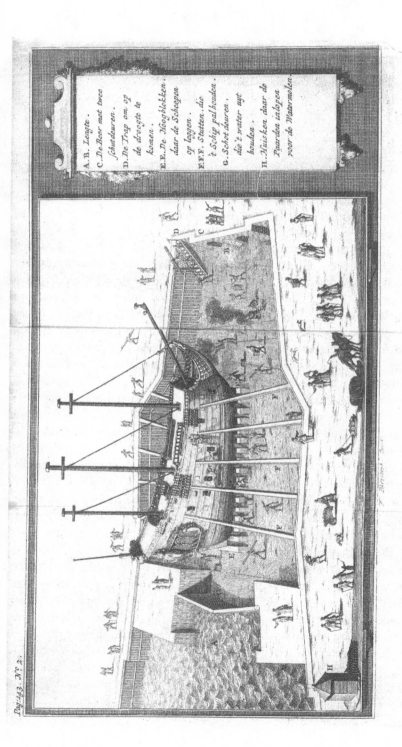

FIGURE 4.1. Ship in the dry dock of a wharf.
Courtesy of the Rijksmuseum, Amsterdam.

route to New Netherland would take ships past the coasts of England and Spain before heading out to open waters, but the trip was hardly a straight shot. The path as well as the pace of the journey was at the mercy of the direction and strength of the prevailing winds, as well as any weather they would meet underway such as rain or fog. On board, there were few amenities. Passengers ate and slept in close quarters, with the inescapable sounds and smells of farm animals, housed in nearby stalls, percolating through the fresh salt air. Compared to the *Mayflower*, a *fluytschip* that carried over a hundred people on a similar route some twenty-odd years earlier, the number of crew and passengers traveling to New Netherland on *Den Eyckenboom* was not excessive. Yet, the time spent on the ocean was long, even in the best of circumstances, to be cooped up in close quarters with the same crowd, day in and day out. In this restricted space of little privacy and close communal living, personalities sometimes clashed, and friendships were often forged.

One of Adriaen van der Donck's shipmates on board *Den Eyckenboom* was fellow settler Cornelis Melyn, originally a leather dresser, or tanner, from Antwerp, in the Southern Low Countries.[10] Melyn was old enough to be Van der Donck's father, but the two found some things in common. Like Van der Donck's hometown, Melyn's larger city of Antwerp, just thirty-five miles south of Breda, had also suffered under a Spanish siege. While this had taken place shortly before Melyn was born, it had directly affected his Protestant family. Similar to the situation in Breda, Protestants had been ousted after the capture of Antwerp though first offered a grace period for deciding whether to leave or convert to Catholicism. Despite the grace period, intended to stabilize the population, approximately thirty-five thousand inhabitants of Antwerp fled to the Dutch Republic in a mass exodus. The Melyn family had apparently decided to stay, most likely because of business ties to the area, and three of the Melyn children, including Cornelis, were among the many abrupt Catholic baptisms that took place at the end of the grace period. Melyn's father had been a successful carpenter and lumber dealer, sometimes serving as the president of the carpenters' guild, which gave the family a strong socioeconomic standing. Though both of Melyn's parents died while he was still a boy, his guardians placed him, at age twelve, as an apprentice in the tailors' guild, where he worked himself up to an apprenticeship with a master tailor. Unlike Van der Donck, Melyn did not have a university education or the clout that goes along with it. But he found the patronage he needed for going abroad in a written character testimony from his godfather, who, like his father, had also held the position of president of the carpenters' guild. Later, inheritances from the estate of his parents as well as from the properties of other family members may have provided the funding for his New World ventures.[11]

Now a seasoned traveler, Melyn had been to New Netherland a few years earlier, looking around while working as supercargo, also in Van Rensselaer's employ, in charge of goods on the West India Company ship *Het Waepen van Noorwegen*.[12] He had attempted to return to New Netherland earlier but, his ship was taken during the passage by Dunkirk pirates, the Spanish-backed privateers operating from the French and Flemish coasts.[13] He was eventually released and made his way back to Amsterdam, but the whole fiasco delayed his plans for New Netherland by almost a year.[14] This time, Melyn was returning with his wife and daughter in a commitment to establish his own colony on Staten Island. Partnered with Gerard van Reede, son of Godard van Reede, Lord of Nederhorst, for a patroonship there, he had brought a group of settlers with him to start working the land as soon as they arrived. Incidentally, the Lord of Nederhorst's colony was the other offer that Van der Donck had been considering while in negotiations with Van Rensselaer. This suggests that Melyn and Van der Donck had most likely been acquainted even before their voyage together on *Den Eyckenboom*, potentially, even, through Melyn's brother, Isaac, who lived in Leiden. Regardless, if Van der Donck had gone to the Staten Island colony with Melyn, he probably would have gone as a farmer. The position as *schout* in Rensselaerswyck had surely sounded a lot more appealing to Van der Donck and, moreover, better use of his skills and law training. Chances are, the opportunity on Staten Island was never any competition for Van Rensselaer's offer.

Contacts were being formed for Adriaen van der Donck in his new capacity before he even set foot on land. Among his belongings was a letter entrusted to him by Van Rensselaer for delivery to New Netherland director Willem Kieft, which included an introduction of Van der Donck as Van Rensselaer's new officer in Rensselaerswyck. Kieft, an educated man with a merchant background, had been appointed director of the New Netherland colony three years earlier, in 1638. It may have been family ties that were responsible for his appointment, as his background did not include experience in administrative circles.[15] Though Kieft himself was not wealthy, his family network included some of the most prominent families in Amsterdam, which secured a place for him among the noble class. Van Rensselaer had made an effort to cultivate a relationship with Kieft before Kieft had left for New Netherland. He depended on Kieft to be of assistance with the trade and to represent him fairly in the business dealings of Rensselaerswyck, always walking a fine line of preserving his rights as patroon while ensuring an amicable relationship with the director. Likewise, Van Rensselaer seemed to have high expectations of Van der Donck's skills as a diplomat. Pointedly describing Van der Donck in his letter as "a young, learned man," he appeared to be leaning on Van der Donck's academic standing to ensure favorable transactions with Kieft's West India Company administration. "Certainly he will maintain good relations with you and not treat you so impolitely as you complain that others of my people have done," Van Rensselaer wrote, confidently.[16] If only he had known how contrary this relationship would later become.

A second letter from Van Rensselaer introduced Van der Donck to Arent van Curler, Van Rensselaer's great-nephew and now his *commis* in charge of trade for Rensselaerswyck.[17] Van Curler had grown up in Nijkerk, Gelderland, where the Van Rensselaer family originated, and, from his writings, it is clear that Van Curler, like Van der Donck, had also attended a Latin school, possibly in the nearby city of Harderwijk. Van Curler had not gone on to university studies but had opted for the path of a merchant instead, in the footsteps of his great-uncle. He had arrived in Rensselaerswyck three years earlier, at the age of eighteen, and begun his commission the following year, initially as secretary and bookkeeper. Though he had not chosen a scholarly vocation, he appeared to enjoy putting to use what he had learned in school, making notations in his account books in both Latin and Greek. He also seemed to possess a bit of a sense of humor. Next to his name on the cover of one of his account books he had written, in Latin, "Est nomen meum Cato & inquit Rem Tuam," meaning, "My name is Cato and I inquire into your affairs," in a satirical reference to the Roman statesman and moral guardian.[18] Unfortunately, Van Curler's playful notations were lost on Van Rensselaer, who complained more than once that Van Curler should forego extraneous verbiage in lieu of actual accountings, which he had yet to receive.[19]

Van Rensselaer's introduction to Van Curler was, in some ways, more critical than the introduction to Kieft, because his two officers would have to work so closely together on the everyday administration of the colony. In his letter, Van Rensselaer expressed assurance to Van Curler, who would have seniority, that Van der Donck had been instructed to respect him. He clarified one of his prime objectives, that the two "offer each other a hand," referring to specific instructions he had given Van der Donck regarding the manner in which he expected them to conduct the fur trade. He defined his plans for the twenty people coming to the colony, specifying the location of their farms, the division of animals for each farm, and exactly where to plant two cases of grapevines he had shipped, with which he hoped to start a vineyard. No matter how much detail Van Rensselaer's instructions provided, which was almost always exhaustive, he knew he was ultimately dependent on his officers to carry out his plans according to his wishes. It was in everyone's best interest, especially Van Rensselaer's, if his subordinates would get along and unite in the common goal of the colony's advancement. "Discuss everything with Van der Donck, how it will work out best," he instructed Van Curler[20] Like a good businessman, Van Rensselaer had ensured, as best he could, that Van der Donck's contacts would be in place and his work cut out for him by the time he would arrive at his new locale.

On board *Den Eyckenboom*, with Van Rensselaer's introductory letters safely stowed among the possessions accompanying him to the New World, Van der Donck's duties had, in a sense, already begun. As sworn officer of the colony, he would have already been acting as point person for the families going to Rensselaerswyck, especially the people he had brought with him from Breda. He had also likely been charged with watching out for Van Rensselaer's cargo, especially Van Rensselaer's valuable animals. Guarded optimism would have been the spirit of the day, every day, as soon-to-be neighbors bound for New Netherland exchanged hopes and aspirations for their new lives in an exotic new country and returning settlers, like Cornelis Melyn, sang its praises. In late July or early August 1641, the sights and sounds of New Netherland lay before the ship as it entered the mouth of the Hudson River, nearing Manhattan. Judging by its relatively short passage across the Atlantic, the voyage of *Den Eyckenboom* had been as uneventful as one could hope for. As the ship approached the waterfront, the passengers, weary but relieved, would have been anxious to get their feet on dry land and explore the new environment they had been anticipating for so long. New Netherland's legendary, sweet smelling air would fill their lungs in the intoxicating realization that they were truly in another world, far from home. In due time, Van der Donck, as well as the other passengers bound for Rensselaerswyck, would continue their journey from Manhattan northward up the river to their new posts. Van der Donck arrived in Rensselaerswyck by early September. The river would have glistened idyllically in the late summer sun as a calm, wide waterway with thick foliage along its banks that yielded to rocky, rising, bluffs and smoky green hills in the distance. Wildlife would have been abundant, the rivers teeming with fish and graced by white swans, as families of beavers played along the water's edge and deer and elk timidly approached the shores to drink. Birds, ordinary and majestic, would have been taking to the air between treetops, or soaring overhead against a crystal clear blue sky. It was like a dream.

5

Schout of Rensselaerswyck

In late summer 1641, Rensselaerswyck was a small settlement located just south of the interchange of the Hudson River and the Mohawk River Valley, where Fort Orange stood built along the shores of what is now Albany. The settlement had been growing steadily since Kiliaen van Rensselaer purchased his land near Fort Orange from the native Mahicans in 1630 and then contracted with one of the first settlers, Wolfert Gerritsz, to begin farming.[1] Out of necessity, Rensselaerswyck had evolved to be fairly independent. It was cut off from Manhattan for several months out of the year in winter, when the rivers iced over and access by boat became impossible. By 1639 the colony counted eight farms, along with dwellings, that dotted the riverbanks—the homes of more than eighty settlers, including carpenters, sawyers, blacksmiths, farmhands, brewers, and bakers.[2] Pine trees supplied a working sawmill. A year later, construction of a gristmill was completed. By then, the number of colonists numbered one hundred and growing, principally through Van Rensselaer's extensive influence and network of family and friends. In 1643, two years after Van der Donck's arrival, a memorandum by French missionary Father Isaac Jogues described "25 or 30 houses built along the River," in a growing, but still primitive settlement.[3] "All their houses are merely of boards, and are covered with thatch," he wrote. "There is as yet no masonry, except in the chimneys." Jogues' memorandum also described scattered farmlands. "[The colonists] have found some very suitable lands, which the [Natives] had formerly prepared, on which they plant corn and oats, for their beer, and for the horses, of which they have a great many. There are few lands fit to be tilled, as they are narrowed by hills, which are poor soil; that obliges them to separate from one another."[4]

At about the same time that Van der Donck arrived in Rensselaerswyck after his long voyage, twenty-year-old Antony de Hooges stepped aboard the trade ship *Den Coninck David*, leaving the Dutch Republic as a third, soon-to-be administrator of the colony. De Hooges had come into the Van Rensselaer dynasty, not by blood, but via other close family ties linked to his father, Johannes, who was also a West India Company shareholder and book-keeper. After De Hooges was orphaned in Amsterdam at a young age, he was cared for by families woven into the Van Rensselaer network either through their merchant relationships or West India Company connections.[5] The use of Latin in De Hooges' writings indicates he had received a Latin school edu-cation, but, like Van Curler, De Hooges did not continue on to the university. Van Rensselaer had given him a job as his secretary in Amsterdam, and now, De Hooges was leaving behind the love of his life to serve Van Rensselaer as

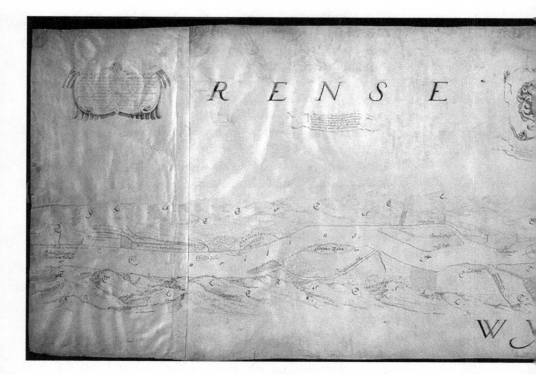

Figure 5.1. Map of Rensselaerswyck.
Courtesy of the New York State Library.

assistant and under-bookkeeper of Rensselaerswyck. Frustrated by the spotty record of Van Curler's reporting and bookkeeping, Van Rensselaer had tasked De Hooges with maintaining copies of Van Curler's letters and accounts, in hopes of ensuring better oversight in tracking the colony's expenses and earnings, enabling him to keep closer tabs on his business there. Indeed, De Hooges seemed to be good at record keeping, beginning with a journal of his voyage to New Netherland, in which he recorded an entry for every day of his four-month passage on a cargo ship, by way of the West Indies.[6] This pleased Van Rensselaer greatly. In his advice to De Hooges, Van Rensselaer recommended, "in the beginning, hear and see, notice and learn, obey and make yourself friendly and pleasant; with that you will come to accomplish much."[7] He had sent along the newest edition of Grotius' law book, yet unbound, destined for Van Curler for use in administration of the colony but surely meant for Van der Donck.[8] De Hooges would complete Van Rensselaer's administrative team.

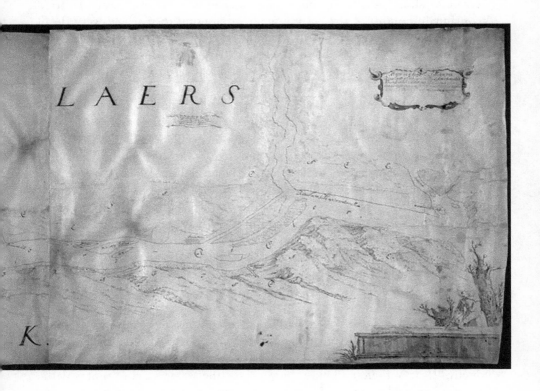

In contrast to De Hooges and Van Curler, Van der Donck was being dropped into the latticework of Van Rensselaer's well-established relationships, in a prominent position, as a glaring unknown. Expectations were high that he would fall into step as a complement to the administration in Rensselaerswyck. Even though the new management was not yet firmly established, Van Rensselaer already had a history with De Hooges in Amsterdam, and an even longer one with Van Curler. Moreover, while roughly the same age as Van der Donck, Van Curler had already been working in Rensselaerswyck for three years and was familiar with everyone in the colony. While Van Rensselaer often complained about Van Curler's record keeping, he at least knew and trusted his great-nephew, whom he referred to as *mon cousin*. Van Rensselaer seemed to have attached enough credibility to Van der Donck's exceptional educational status that he was willing to take a chance on him as an outsider.

Van Rensselaer's expectation that his employees would follow his rules, remain loyal, and adhere to a chain of command was one of the ways he tried to maintain control of the colony while attempting to manage every detail from *patria*, an ocean away. While this model might have been reasonable in a traditional master-apprentice relationship, where novices work their way up the ranks under close supervision, it was difficult to enforce remotely, to say the least. Considering it would take up to three months to receive a letter by ship from New Netherland, and another three months before any response would be read, this long-distance management was neither the most practical nor satisfying arrangement for someone as detail oriented and exacting as Kiliaen van Rensselaer. He often expressed his frustration and repeatedly complained that his instructions were not being followed. There had already been problems with some of the farmers who were bypassing their agreements with Van Rensselaer by employing workers from outside the colony as well as by selling grain and trading furs elsewhere for higher takes. This all undercut Van Rensselaer's share of the profits, which were rightly his after investing so much in establishing the farms, and clearly outside of the farmers' contract stipulations.[9]

Van Rensselaer had sent letters and memorandums along with De Hooges for Van Curler and Van der Donck, instructing them to look into these transgressions. In his letter to Van Curler, Van Rensselaer directed him to "speak about it with Officer Vanderdonck to put it in order, if it is right and justness required."[10] His indignation was clear when he deduced succinctly, "[Is it not] after all pure thievery that the farmers sell to others without my knowledge, grain of which half should go to me, or that they trade with the residents the furs that they ought to deliver to me?"[11] He included strict instructions on how he wanted Van der Donck to handle the offenders. "The officer is ordered to summon all such farmers before the commission-ers of the patroon, and if necessary also before the councilors of the colony (with the exclusion of those who may themselves be guilty thereof), in order to take proper action in this matter by further rule or ordinance and to pun-ish the delinquents with such penalties and fines as the law provides."[12] Van Rensselaer also ordered Van der Donck to investigate a farm from which he had expected grain yields but whose farmers could not come up with any traces of them. "They surely cannot hide that in their sleeves," Van Rensselaer concluded sarcastically.[13] To crack down on transgressions against the colony's interests was exactly what Van Rensselaer had hired Van der Donck to do, but, not surprisingly, this did not serve to make the new official very popular. Even the farmers Van der Donck brought with him from Breda complained about him after they realized that enforcement of their contracts would pro-hibit them from getting as much for their grain as the established farmers were getting by going around Van Rensselaer. Van der Donck was caught in the middle. Yet, to Van Rensselaer, Van der Donck's job was to protect his interests, which meant being on the lookout for offenders. "Officer vander-donck can watch out for it—he can catch some of them," he wrote to Van Curler, hoping Van der Donck's presence would mean the illegal practices would end.[14]

On a softer and more personal note, Van Rensselaer expressed a heartfelt lengthy greeting in a separate letter to Van der Donck, wishing him well. "[Of] your honor's safe arrival, as well as the other people and goods, and especially that of the animals, I hope to hear with joy in due time, and even more so, that not only have you arrived at your place of destination in the colony, but also that you have surely settled down to, on the one hand, your pledge, and, on the other hand, your farming, which the Lord our God, by the loving blessings, will have already taken charge of with faithfulness and perseverance." In this same memorandum, Van Rensselaer introduced tailor Johan Verbeek, with his wife, as being "from breda, directed to me by your mother, subsequent to the conditions sent over to the Secretary Arent van Corler."[15]

Van der Donck's involvement with Rensselaerswyck had become a bit of a family affair. His father, Cornelis, had contacted Van Rensselaer shortly after the departure of *Den Eyckenboom* to offer that he knew of two ad-ditional families in Breda who were interested in going to the colony. Van Rensselaer was undoubtedly interested, asking to be advised "of the number of persons, their ages and how many sons, daughters and servants there are among them; also whether they understand farming and whether they know any trades besides, which in those countries is very convenient."[16] A ship was due to leave for New Netherland in two weeks, Van Rensselaer advised, asking his new intermediary to let him know, "citto citto," whether the families could be ready by then.[17] He also suggested, perhaps in a gesture of friendship, that Cornelis van der Donck had addressed him too formally. "In addressing your letter you give me the title of '*welgeboren*;' such titles belong to princes; I shall be satisfied if you give me a lesser title," he wrote. "Instead of 'formerly councillor of the West India Company,'" Van Rensselaer instructed, "put 'ex-director of the West India Company,' this being the way in which in this city the retired gentlemen, each in his capacity, are distinguished from those who are in office."[18]

Several weeks later, Van Rensselaer contacted Cornelis van der Donck to give him an update on the voyage of the tailor and his wife from Breda. He also took the opportunity to mention that he was looking for a smith's helper and a brick maker, presumably hoping the elder Van der Donck might have more leads.[19] In other correspondence, Van Rensselaer personally provided details and advice to Cornelis van der Donck about a shipment to his son, suggesting he wait until spring, "as the winter is at hand, such that the goods cannot get to the colony before the frost this year."[20] Moreover, he wrote, the current ship was scheduled to take a longer route to New Netherland, via Curaçao, and not "a droiture," or directly. His reference in French indicates his assumption that Cornelis van der Donck was of a high level of education or class. Adriaen van der Donck's parents continued to support their son's endeavor by way of this personal business relationship with Van Rensselaer. Later, Van der Donck's mother would write Van Rensselaer about two boys from Breda who would go to Rensselaerswyck as servants.[21] Of course, their son would get the opportunity, first, to employ the helpers his family helped recruit.

In December, the first letters from Van der Donck arrived from New Netherland, one for his father, and the other for Van Rensselaer, carried by a young man traveling on to Breda. When there was a delay in unloading the ship's goods, including a small box and squirrel coat that Van der Donck had sent for his father, Van Rensselaer expedited delivery of the letter to Breda, having it sent personally, while the young courier waited for the ship to be unloaded.[22] This was the first news Cornelis and Agatha van der Donck had received from their son, including the consolation that he had arrived safely in New Netherland, almost seven months after he left on an uncertain transatlantic voyage.

The work had indeed begun almost immediately for Van der Donck after his arrival, as Van Rensselaer tried, with his new administration, to restore a waning command over the colony and shore up the profits leaking out around the agreements he had made. Van der Donck's first proclamation as *schout* seems to have been a joint one, probably dictated by Van Rensselaer in Amsterdam and carried to New Netherland.[23] The "Ordinance of the colony of Rensselaerswyck regulating trade," issued by "We, Adriaen van der donck, chief officer, with the commissioners and councilors of the colony of Rensselaerswyck," was written in De Hooges' handwriting and signed by Van Curler. The first order, that the colonists should not buy or trade with foreign residents, reflected Van Curler's knowledge of local business dealings, types of furs, and common shipping vessels. It prohibited the exchange of "any beavers, otters or other furs, directly or indirectly, upon fine and forfeiture." Exceptions would be made with permission of the officer, meaning Van der Donck, for buying if "any shallops or vessels of the Company or any one else come up the river." Peppered with legalities, the second part of the ordinance declared that no one be allowed to send any furs down the river "or cause them to be sent down, without handing in a true inventory." Certainly influenced by Van der Donck, the proclamation was bolstered with statements such as, "Herein we dispose as above," and in the case of non-company vessels sailing without inspection, "Everything on forfeiture as above."[24]

Despite the new authority and the official decrees in Rensselaerswyck, the problems persisted, prompting three stricter ordinances later. All three were issued by "We, the commissioners and councilors of the colony of Rensselaerswyck" and prohibited trade between the colonists and private traders, including banning traders and goods from coming into or out of the colony without special consent.[25] The punishments for infractions were severe. Foreign traders risked "forfeiture of ship and lading" and colonists who traded with the foreign residents were subject to the loss of "200 guilders Dutch, and, the second time, of life and property, everything subject to immediate execution, without defense or contradiction."[26]

Even if the new rules succeeded in putting an end to illegal trading, there were still other problems with the settlers that made Van Rensselaer insecure about the future of his undertaking. Workers were often unreliable. Though new colonists were provided with passage and advances to help them get started, there was no guarantee they would complete the terms of their contracts after arriving in New Netherland. Some of those Van Rensselaer had sent to the colony had abandoned their commitments, others never even venturing north to their posts in Rensselaerswyck from Manhattan once the ship arrived. Still others returned to the Dutch Republic before completing their terms of service or left after finding different work, moving, or getting married. Van Rensselaer called on Van der Donck to "charge these people in writing, each and every one, and the husbands of the married, that they shall satisfy their advanced monies and expenses for their obligated time in the place where they should have remained with the Patroon."[27] Any recourse was doubtful, however. When Van der Donck did manage to track down one of these deserters, Jannitje Teunis, not only had she gotten married, she was, by then, quite pregnant. Her case was postponed on the condition that she repay her advance and provide surety for the contract.[28] Van Rensselaer was counting on Van der Donck to enforce these rules, whether he agreed with them or not.

On top of the multilayered problems Van Rensselaer had with the business of the colony, his own health was beginning to fail and he was unsure whether his young administrators would be able to work together effectively without his consistent direction. With these things in mind, he selected a mature man, thirty-nine-year-old Johannes Megapolensis, "a very pious and experienced minister," as a religious leader for the colony.[29] Megapolensis arrived in New Netherland on August 4, 1642, with his wife and four children, along with various other workers destined for Rensselaerswyck, including a brewer, surgeon, and the two boys Van der Donck's mother had enlisted in Breda. With his choice of clergy, Van Rensselaer intended for Megapolensis to act as arbiter and voice of reason as an older, established, respected man of the cloth. He gave this authority to Megapolensis, outright, in a memorandum wherein he clarified the structure and hierarchy of the colony's leadership. "Concerning the business of the administration of the colony as it is presently conducted, resting chiefly on the person of Arent van Corler, and Adriaen van der Donck represents the chief officer in case of need, so Corler represents the directorship thereof, likewise, in case of need." This left no question as to Van Curler's seniority over Van der Donck; however, Van Rensselaer made it clear that Megapolensis would have the final say in differences that the administrators could not settle among themselves. In the case of a disagreement, according to Van Rensselaer, both parties should present their arguments to Megapolensis. After hearing both sides, he resolved, "the decision of Rev. Megapolensis shall take effect without contradiction, until the lord patroon, after being enlisted, sends over his written resolution thereof."[30] The last thing he needed was for his two top officers to end up in a stalemate that would paralyze progress.

Perhaps this memorandum was simply another example of Van Rensselaer following his usual protocol of detailing procedures, this time, one for Megapolensis to use in mediating disagreements. However, in his lengthy and thorough missive, Van Rensselaer confessed, "it grows very confusing in the administration of my colony, which could easily cause some trouble among the chief principals."[31] On some level, he seemed to be acknowledging that he was asking a lot of his inexperienced administrators in charging them with restoring order to the colony in a complex situation, even taking into consideration his unreasonably lofty standards. On the other hand, it might have simply been that his basic tendency toward distrust and suspicion was starting to get the better of him in light of the lack of sure signs of improvement. If he was anticipating problems, however, it appears his instincts were not unfounded in a series of events that looked to be evolving into a self-fulfilling prophecy. His young team was giving him cause for concern.

6

The Beginning of the End in Rensselaerswyck

Sometime before Megapolensis left for New Netherland, Van Rensselaer learned that Van der Donck had deviated from his agreement almost as soon as he had arrived in Rensselaerswyck, and this did not sit well with him. While Van Rensselaer had ordered Van der Donck to take up residence in one of three farms at the entrance to the colony in Bylaers Dal, he had apparently chosen a different spot, "the utmost upward," poles apart from Van Rensselaer's instructions. Van Rensselaer's frustration and indignation were evident in his words to Megapolensis. "I very much resent that Officer Van der Donck, knowing my intentions in placing him at the entrance to the colony, which I communicated to him orally along with many reasons, excluded himself from it."[1] Instead, his officer had moved to what Van Rensselaer considered "the furthest from my intent, the furthest from all the people, and the furthest from the entrance to the colony where the key ought to be." Adding to his displeasure was the fact that Van der Donck had made his decision without the consent of the other officers and "with the simple mention that there was room for only two farms." In Van Rensselaer's opinion, Van der Donck had not only gone over his head, but over Van Curler's as well. "If below there was only room for two farms, he ought to have been one of them most of all," Van Rensselaer surmised sharply. He was willing to let Van der Donck keep his farm as long as he would also have an inexpensive house built in the more central church neighborhood, to be nearby and available, conceding that "at times he can also inspect his farm." However, he was also skeptical of Van der Donck's request that there only be one farm built in his selected location, suspecting it was motivated by the idea of having the

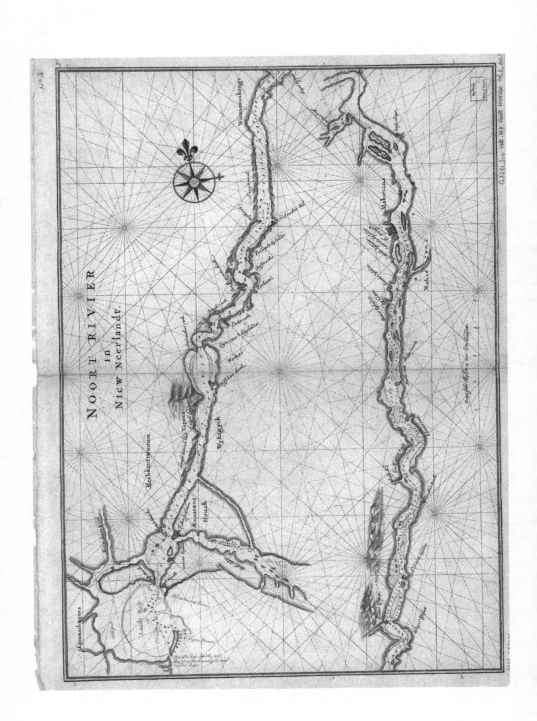

NOORT RIVIER in Niew Neerlandt.

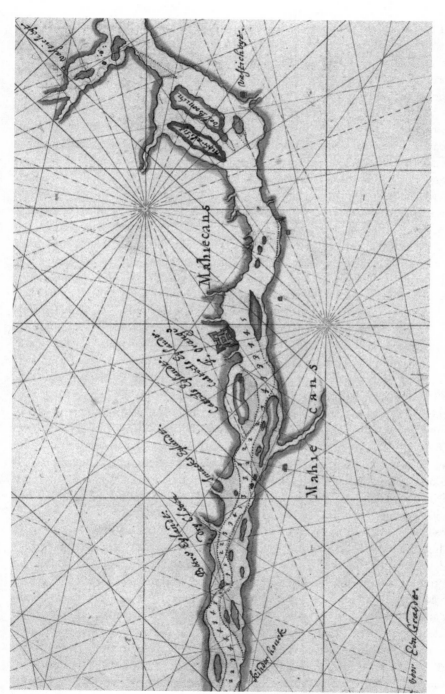

FIGURE 6.1. Map of Castle Island, Rensselaerswyck (*p. 48, detail p. 49*). Courtesy of the Library of Congress.

land all to himself. He directed Megapolensis to have Van Curler and others investigate how many farms could, in their unbiased opinions, be established in the area. "I do not exclude Officer Van der Donck but only in that he himself is interested in the matter," he directed wisely, "for no one may be judge in his own case."[2]

Van der Donck's failure to follow what were, in Van Rensselaer's opinion, explicit instructions, only added to an already mounting dissatisfaction. Apparently, Van der Donck had been writing complaints that, in the unpredictable timing of seventeenth-century transatlantic vessels and the limited accessibility of Rensselaerswyck, had crossed Van Rensselaer's in the mail. On March 9, 1643, more than a year after Van der Donck began as *schout*, Van Rensselaer answered three of Van der Donck's letters all at once, one dated September 7, 1641, written shortly after his arrival; and two, dated June 21, and August 19, 1642, from the following summer. Part defense, part counterattack, part advice, and part warning, Van Rensselaer's displeasure was dramatically blatant as he replied with pent-up emotion to the complaints in one long, if not rambling, admonition that took him four days to compose.

The letter began ominously: "On the occasion of this extraordinary ship and for fear of delay of the one of the Company, I can not postpone communicating to you these lines in reply to three [letters] of yours."[3] One of the first grievances Van Rensselaer addressed was Van der Donck's accusation that he showed preference for his relatives, namely, Arent van Curler, over others. On the contrary, Van Rensselaer responded, "[i]t is not only blood that I have looked at, as I prioritize the carrying out of my commission and instructions, alongside my advantage and profit, far above blood."[4] In light of the criticism he regularly dished out to Van Curler, this may have very well been true. He inserted a compliment between this and his next criticism, in what seemed like an attempt to emphasize how he liked things done. "What now pleases me in you is this zeal and diligence that I detect in your honor in the expediting of several things," referring to an agreement that had been reached between the colony's carpenters.[5] However, he wasted no time in returning to his disparagement, scolding Van der Donck for acting too independently, and underlining his words for emphasis. "But what especially fails me," he continued, as he had already complained to Megapolensis, is that, "without the consent of the commissioners, you had chosen the place so far apart from my intention and instructions."[6] Second, he went on, "complaints have been made to me that, from the beginning, your honor has conducted himself not as officer but as director," and in a note of sarcasm added, "I had more faith in your honor's prudence . . . that instead of procuring a premature advancement, to have granted me the time that I might have been allowed to find out by experience, in order to have the honor of my advancement myself."[7] Next, Van Rensselaer pointed out what he felt was Van der Donck's lack of gratitude. "I urge your honor, give me grounds upon which I could have advanced you more than I have." He continued, "If instead of putting up your own smokescreen, you had advised me, from the articles, what you had accomplished on one point of my instructions, which is the only way to your honor's advancement and ought to be your sole objective, it could have moved me to take further notice of your honor's person."[8]

Van Rensselaer's letter continued to counter Van der Donck's complaints, dismissing them one by one, while pointing out that the problems lay in Van der Donck's failure to carry out his instructions, rather than in any over-sight of his own. "On the contrary," Van Rensselaer continued, "I find great boldness therein, to charge me with several things beyond reason."[9] Van der Donck had contended, for example, that "the council was without esteem," but Van Rensselaer, once again, turned the tables.[10] "Answer," he began, "this was not strange because they had never had an able leader and consequently I sent your honor to bring the council into good esteem with the people."[11] When Van der Donck claimed that Van Rensselaer's letter about the farmers provided "quite some cause for dissatisfaction," Van Rensselaer considered the allegation absolutely without foundation. Instead, he insinuated Van der Donck's lack of judgment as the source of the problem since, "besides that such words were written to my commissioners who must handle them with discretion and confidentiality, they stand in great fairness and justness."[12]

Van Rensselaer hit below the belt when he expressed disappointment in Van der Donck's legal work, dispensing his own advice in Van der Donck's supposed area of expertise. "What disappoints me most in you, of which I had quite the opposite expected of you," he began," is that you bring forth a great many difficulties and do not show me any legal procedures against any of them, the legality existing not in discourses or words, but in formal and judicial actions and procedures," admonishing and counseling at the same time.[13] Although this might have been the best advice Van Rensselaer ever gave him considering what he would be up against in the future, it probably felt like the ultimate insult at the time. The seemingly endless rant must have been hard for Van der Donck to swallow as Van Rensselaer attempted to put him in his place over and over again, clarifying his already explicit instruc-tions and prevailing upon his officer not to act on his own. "I am not with-out suspicion that you have yielded too much to ambition . . . he who goes slowly gets further than he who goes fast," Van Rensselaer warned, sagely.[14]

What appeared to strike the biggest nerve with Van Rensselaer was Van der Donck's accusation that he had sent informers into the country, which

Van Rensselaer took very personally. "It does not suit you and you go far outside your bounden duty in criticizing my administration, and again on offensive statements that I would send informers into the country, seeking to make determinations under a confidence that was blind and deaf," he chided, adding, "Indeed you do not increase your trust thereby, but diminish it."[15] Perhaps Van der Donck had underestimated with whom he was dealing. This charge had pushed Van Rensselaer too far, and he had no problem letting it show. "I shall answer for my actions to whom I have granted it, and you take care to do as much for me as I do for you," he warned, then asked sarcastically, "Do you want that I should have to trust you whether you do good or bad, or do you imagine that you can do no wrong?"[16]

Despite Van Rensselaer's vehement defense of this last allegation, it is not entirely unfounded that Van der Donck would suspect him of using informers. One of the ways that Van Rensselaer tried to keep watch over his personnel's behavior was to have them report on each other. In an earlier letter, Van Rensselaer had specifically instructed Van Curler that if the court refused to sentence outsiders who traded in the colony illegally to "send it over to me and write me especially how Van der Donck behaves in the matter."[17] And ironically, the very letter he wrote to Van der Donck, chastising him for his accusation of using informers, he had placed, unsealed, within another letter to Megapolensis, in a ploy to expose a possible indiscretion. Van Rensselaer's crafty plan was an attempt to uncover the truth about something Megapolensis had overheard about Van der Donck and reported to him, something so dissenting that, according to Van Rensselaer, "if it were true . . . and all this not [said] in a flood of passion, he would not be worthy to live and be unfit for his office."[18] Van Rensselaer's strategy for getting to the truth was for Megapolensis to bring the situation up to Van der Donck under the pretext that Megapolensis had read Van Rensselaer's unsealed letter. "Tell him this has been done on purpose and that I had understood things [to be] as you wrote to me, without naming anyone," Van Rensselaer schemed, and, "in the event these things are true, [I] have given you orders not to hand him his letter, but that what it concerned would be kept in suspense until further advice. This will cause him to excuse himself or, in case of admission, if any of the charges are true, to humble and justify himself."[19]

Van Rensselaer summed up his letter to Van der Donck by unleashing a final scathing, almost threatening, condemnation, again in underlined script. "I trust that you will respect your oath, my instructions and advice, but time will tell. They are nothing but spiteful words that you give me about hating or loving; you must first have proof of it. If you have in mind to take the directorship away from me, you will be much deceived, for that is not the way to do it; neither did you have reason to break off your last letter that way after having no letter from me, moreover, to point out my duty to write in good time."[20] He put the onus for change on Van der Donck in a clear and concise statement, leaving no question as to where they stood. "If it seems contrary to you, I cannot help it; I mean well with you, but you will have to adapt to me, and not I to you, though I gladly hear what opposes me, if it is done in reason, without passion, without ambition, and without selfishness."[21] Yet, after all of his disparaging remarks, he closed his letter in a conciliatory tone, mentioning that he forwarded goods sent by Van der Donck's father "as his own" and enclosing a letter he had received from him that very day. Maybe Van Rensselaer felt he had been too harsh or just felt relieved after four days of venting his irritation. In the end, he offered his excuses for the letter, though not for its content, but for its being "somewhat prolix and poorly arranged."[22]

As cutting as Van Rensselaer's words were, his tone seemed more aimed at remediation than a complete dismissal, as if he held out hope that Van der Donck would take his tough-love lessons to heart, realize the error of his ways, and rise to the occasion. His frustration was clearly palpable, however, and he may have simply been trying to salvage a less than ideal situation without a lot of options. If Van Rensselaer was not then ready to throw in the towel on Van der Donck, whom he felt was, at the very least, a little too big for his britches, he would be soon. He was about to receive more criticism of his *schout* in a long June report from Van Curler to his great-uncle on the affairs of the colony, which probably went out on the very next ship. In answer to criticism of his lack of record keeping, Van Curler blamed many of his difficulties on Van der Donck for failing to help and, moreover, accused him of stirring up even more problems. In his very first paragraph, Van Curler explained that the reason he had not sent the account books over was that he could not get the accounts from the farmers and "Van der Donck does not even speak to them about it, according to his instructions, nor has he done anything about it as long as he has been in the colony."[23]

Van Curler also defended a report Van Rensselaer had heard from Van der Donck, that he had placed one of the carpenters, Jean Labatie, on a farm with a salary of twenty guilders per month. "Those who wrote that to your Honor lie like rogues, for I never thought of doing so," Van Curler countered.[24] He chalked it up to a vengeful case of sour grapes. "But I suspect that this report was sent to your Honor by van der Doncq, who is much troubled by this undertaking, because he is not allowed to live there and who still daily, in my absence, goes about finding fault, saying that we expect much profit from it for the masters, but that it will fail."[25] There appeared to be no love lost between Van Curler and Van der Donck. In response to a complaint Van der Donck had made to Van Rensselaer about the "impertinence of Lebatie," Van Curler summarized his opinion. "This will serve for answer. Van der Doncq is very [selfish and greedy]."[26] According to Van Curler, "several times," while he was absent from the colony, Van der Donck had "gruffly" told Labatie to give him goods. Labatie had refused, saying that he did not have orders to do so. "By and by hatred became so deeply rooted that they challenged each other with rapiers," Van Curler reported. "The same he has also done to De Hooges, whom he called an informer and moreover has struck, and thus he also acts toward me, spreading false reports about me to your Honor and among the colonists, in order to render me suspected."[27] It looks as if those fencing lessons in Leiden had come in handy. That Van der Donck could be a bit of a hot head, or "passionate," had been alluded to before. In Manhattan, at about the same time he was there to prosecute Jannitje Teunis, the pregnant deserter, Van der Donck had apparently gotten into an altercation with a cooper that resulted in a lawsuit for slander brought by both parties. However, by the time the court date came along, things had cooled to the point that the court ruled both men, "abiding by their affection and friendship, acknowledge of one another to know nothing but honor and virtue," and the case was dismissed.[28]

Van Curler also complained that rather than supporting him and the Rensselaerswyck administration, Van der Donck seemed to be aligning himself with the farmers, against the council. When illegal trade was driving up the cost of furs, Van Curler could not get help from Van der Donck. "The order was that the officer should enforce it, but he has never attended to it, nor been willing to do so, and when he was told to look into the frauds and abuses, in order to prevent them as far as possible, he gave for answer that he did not wish to be the most hated man; secondly, that he did not care to make himself distrusted by the colonists, as his term of office was short," he griped to Van Rensselaer.[29] The colonists were complaining about the crackdown, and understandably so. They had been doing business however they pleased with little oversight and, from their point of view, a new officer had appeared seemingly overnight, enforcing old rules and making new ones. At one point, Van der Donck had even been threatened.[30] Though the tightened control should not have come as a surprise, the farmers did not welcome the fact that they were now being held accountable to all regulations, and the changes were restrictive. With the new ordinance that shut independent traders out of the colony, the colonists questioned how they would get the goods they needed. The council's solution was a promise to procure goods for the farmers. This way, all payments would go through the colony and Van Curler as the "sole merchant." Though they agreed to this initially, when a sloop with goods appeared in Rensselaerswyck a few days later, the colonists bought from the merchant anyway after Van Curler refused to allow debits to their accounts as payment for the goods purchased through him.[31] Van Curler and Megapolensis sent for Van der Donck to search the houses of the offenders but, according to Van Curler, the search was halfhearted and preferential. He related the event, exasperatedly, to Van Rensselaer.

> First, he went to Reyer Stoffelsen's house. There he chatted, without once making a search. Then he went to Willem Juriaensen's in the same manner, and so forth. Further, he went to Dirck Jansen's, at the mill, where he was told that there were three pieces of duffels and, as he had a hatred for him, he took them. Then he went to the house of Cornelis van Merkerck. There he also had a little chat, without once making a search. Likewise, at Broer Cornelissen's, he never made a search, but only asked: "How are all your cows?" and looked at them and went away, although he knew perfectly well that there were duffels there. Returning thence and going home, he stopped at the house of Claes Jansen van Nyckerck who, he knew, also had duffels, and said: "Claes, I shall come here tomorrow to make a search. If you have any duffels, put them in the cellar, which I shall not search." Claes himself told me this and promised to give me an affidavit of it, which I shall send your Honor by the next ship.[32]

The last straw, and what seemed like a betrayal to Van Curler, was that Van der Donck sided with the local carpenters after they objected to Van Curler's purchase of a house for Megapolensis from someone outside the colony. Van Curler explained that he had good reason for the outside transaction, since delays and neglect had necessitated breaking the contract he had made with the colony's carpenters for the original house.[33] According to Van Curler, Van der Donck had instigated the carpenters in challenging him on the basis of the recent ordinances forbidding trade outside the colony, suggesting, "those whom this concerned should mutiny," and telling them that Van Curler "sought to steal the bread out of the mouths of the colonists too." Much division ensued. "This protest having been drawn up, some were for driving me out of the colony as a rogue; others wished to knock me in the head," Van Curler wrote.[34] But while Van der Donck "promised [me and] the council to assist us in this . . . when it came to the point, he was to desert me and the council and to support them." "So," he concluded, "that your Honor will please consider for yourself what kind of an officer you have here, who would cause the ruination of the whole colony." And while Van Rensselaer was, theoretically, contemplating this last question, Van Curler's next charge against Van der Donck was cocked to push Van Rensselaer's ailing health over the edge or to at least generate a sizeable spike in blood pressure. "He intends, next year, to return home," Van Curler began. Moreover, "He has been to Catskill with some colonists to [inspect] that place and your Honor may be sure he intends to look for friends to plant a colony there. Burger Jorissen, the smith who heretofore has been in your Honor's colony, will live there also. He has let his farm to Brant Pelen for [200] guilders a year, on which Brant Pelen intends to settle his son-in-law. This will not happen with my consent."[35] For Van der Donck to scheme to take Van Rensselaer's colonists and become his competition, behind his back and on his payroll, would amount to the ultimate act of dishonor and betrayal.

These accounts of Van der Donck in Rensselaerswyck paint a negative picture of him, though Van der Donck was likely just as frustrated with Van Rensselaer's overbearing management style as Van Rensselaer was with Van der Donck's insubordinate behavior. And Van Rensselaer's criticism was not just reserved for Van der Donck. Van Curler had also been on the receiving end of his sharp and cutting words. It is very likely Van Curler's complaints about Van der Donck were, at least, partially motivated by competition, fueled by Van Rensselaer's suspicious and accusatory manner that pitted his officers against each other. Much maturity was still ahead for Van Curler, Van der Donck, and De Hooges, who were all still in their early twenties. Even though they were considered adults in seventeenth-century Dutch society and heavily entrusted with the administration of Rensselaerswyck, the men were at an age of peak testosterone production and a developing prefrontal cortex that we now know is important for thinking through the consequences of our actions. Even keeping in mind that these reports only provide one side of the story, it would be hard to argue that, above all, the Van der Donck–Van Rensselaer relationship was a terribly bad fit. Van Rensselaer was used to being in charge and expected his junior administrators to abide by his rules and detailed orders. Van der Donck, on the other hand, was not bound by ties to Van Rensselaer's extended network. He was independent, headstrong, and willing to challenge Van Rensselaer's authority. Having just come off his student days in Leiden where he was taught to think critically and to take charge, he might have had unrealistic expectations about his role in the colony's administration, the people he would work with, and the duties that would be required of him. He was most certainly ambitious, and it was not uncommon for settlers to take advantage of incentives such as free passage to the New World, or to take a position in order to test the waters, much like Cornelis Melyn had done several years prior. At the very least, Van der Donck's position as *schout* would be a way to gain experience in New Netherland and support himself in a position of privilege until he found his own footing there. If this was the case, it could explain Van der Donck's choice to align himself with the farmers and carpenters of the colony as the beginnings of a following, rather than to act as an extension of the authoritarian administration under the thumb of Van Rensselaer, which was how he viewed Van Curler and De Hooges. He had said that his term of office was short, and politically, he was already separating himself.

In early September Van Rensselaer wrote, then had printed, a "Redress of the Abuses and Faults in the Colony of Rensselaerswyck," aimed at restoring order while redefining the duties of his agents, including Van der Donck.[36] Though this supports the idea that he had not written Van der Donck off entirely, a few days later it appeared that he had had enough, after all. On September 10, 1643, Van Rensselaer issued an order for Peter Wyncoop, *commis* on his recently purchased ship, *Wapen van Rensselaerswyck*, "to purchase for a reasonable price from the natural owners and inhabitants, and from their chiefs, their lands lying about Katskill, in consequence of certain information which he had that Adriaen van der Donck, his sworn officer, dishonestly designed to purchase . . . the said lands lying under the shadow of his colony."[37] In the event that the purchase had already been made, Van Curler and Wyncoop were to "constrain" Van der Donck from the transaction, surrendering anything he had acquired to the patroon. If it had not yet been purchased, he was to swear under oath "not to proceed therewith."[38] Either way, Van Rensselaer was not planning to let Van der Donck out from under the lease on his farm. He wrote, "In case Van der Donck should prove obstinate, he shall be degraded from his office, and left on his *bouwerie* to complete his contracted lease, without allowing him to depart, and his office shall be conferred, provisionally, on Nicolaus Coorn," Van Rensselaer's upcoming defense officer.[39]

Kiliaen van Rensselaer died in October of that year, before the ship carrying the order even reached Rensselaerswyck the following spring, in March of 1644.[40] However, his attempt to thwart Van der Donck's acquisition of land in Catskill apparently met with success because Van der Donck did not begin a colony there and, instead, stayed for the time being on the farm he had leased from Van Rensselaer. Court records are few during this period and sources of written documentation about Rensselaerswyck diminished substantially without Van Rensselaer's letters. Van Rensselaer's son, Johannes, became heir to the colony, although, because he was not yet of legal age, jurisdiction fell to Johannes' guardians in Amsterdam.[41] Van Curler went back to the Dutch Republic for three years beginning in the fall of 1644, leaving De Hooges immediately in charge of the colony.[42]

It is unclear when Van der Donck stopped functioning as *schout*. Statements in Van Curler's letter point to a three-year commission that Van Rensselaer had extended to previous *schouts*, which would have ended mid-1644. However, the lease on Van der Donck's farm was contracted until 1649, leaving open the possibility that the original intention might have been for a longer period in Rensselaerswyck.[43] Regardless of the contract, Van Rensselaer's death likely spelled the end of Van der Donck's official admin-istrative duties in Rensselaerswyck. Nicolaes Coorn, the man who would have taken over Van der Donck's office if he had not backed down from his Catskill plans, had arrived with the ship *Wapen van Rensselaerswyck* in the spring. Coorn had been commissioned as commander and *commis* of Rensselaersteyn, a new defense fortification Van Rensselaer had ordered erected on approach to the colony on Beeren Island, and his duties may have overlapped with those of *schout*.[44] As early as April 6, 1644, Coorn's name was on a court action in Manhattan, discharging two men from their contract with the patroon.[45] The following year, another court document recorded Coorn's name as "officer of the Colony of Rensselaersw[yck]."[46] As late as May 1646, however, Van der Donck along with fellow Rensselaerswyck set-tler Abraham Staets offered testimony in a legal action as "officers of the court."[47] While Van der Donck may have been enjoying some status in the colony, officially or unofficially, after Van Rensselaer's death, he had long ago made up his mind that his future would not be confined to the boundaries of Rensselaerswyck.

7

Manhattan

Although Van Rensselaer had put an end to his surveying for land in the Catskills, Van der Donck's later writings indicate that he had been spending a fair amount of time there. Alongside talking to the Natives for the purposes of negotiating a land deal, he had also been enjoying an up-close and intimate view of their lives, traditions, and the environment. And these were not just day trips on horseback. Some Native settlements he visited, such as Mohawk villages, were as much as forty miles away.[1] His curiosity displayed a level of interest toward the Natives and openness that was unusual at the time, when Europeans commonly dismissed Native peoples as heathen and uncivilized "savages." The knowledge Van der Donck was acquiring of Native languages and customs, as well as the observations he was making of flora and fauna in his wanderings throughout the land, was all information he would later put to good use.

When he was not roaming the Catskills, Van der Donck was minding his farm, which had become productive, yielding 28 *schepels* of oats that fall of 1643.[2] He was also busy sowing crops for the future, probably with the help of the boys who had come from Breda, enough to yield 112 *schepels* of wheat the following year. Various legal proceedings were drawing him downriver, where he was gaining some visibility in the administrative circles there. In one court case that began in the summer of 1644, Van der Donck was named in a Manhattan appeal by former council member Symon Pos, over earlier actions originating in Rensselaerswyck, which dragged on for almost a year.[3]

In this same period, a bigger drama was unfolding in the heart of Manhattan. The area was reeling from the threat of revenge by local Natives in a series of attacks and counterattacks initiated by Director Kieft, which had escalated into nothing less than a full-fledged war. In February 1643, Kieft, against the recommendation of his appointed advisory board of Eight Men, had ordered a retaliatory attack on the nearby Lenape Natives when the tribe refused to name the murderer in the killing of a colonist. David Pietersz. de Vries, sea captain, explorer, and now New Netherland council member, had argued with Kieft directly against an attack. Respected in the colony as one of its early settlers and patroon holder of short-lived Vriessendael on the west bank of the Hudson River, De Vries had seen firsthand the devastation that could follow. His two previous attempts at colonization in New Netherland had both ended in violent conflicts with the Natives, and, like Van der Donck, he had made an effort to form relationships with local tribes. In the end, however, he was unable to sway Kieft away from his decision for a surprise offensive. The attack was particularly brutal, carried out at night while the Natives were sleeping. Later, in his journal, published in 1655, De Vries reported having heard "a loud cry" about midnight.[4] Walking out on the wall of the fort, he "looked out toward Pavonia, saw nothing but shooting, and heard shouting that the Natives were being murdered in their sleep."[5] Later accounts reported young children "torn from their mothers' breasts and hacked to pieces in view of the parents, and the pieces thrown into the fire and into the water," and infants, "bound to wooden boards . . . massacred [so] miserably that it would weaken a heart of stone." Others described children thrown into the river, "and when the fathers and mothers tried to save them, the soldiers would not let them come back on land, but drowned both old and young."[6]

By that fall, the colony's men, women, and children who had not fled altogether were reduced to living in and around the fort from areas such as Pavonia and Long Island, "deserted of both people and cattle," and with little resources with which to face the coming winter.[7] Kieft's board of Eight Men sent an urgent request for help in late fall 1643, to the Amsterdam Chamber of the West India Company, the branch of the company that oversaw the administration of New Netherland. The threat was looming. "The houses have, for the most part, been destroyed and burned; those that still exist stand to be burned," the board wrote, urgently pleading the colonists' grievous predicament.[8] "The Fort lies in a heap without defense, more like a mole-hill than a fortress," they lamented.[9] In contrast to their vulnerability, they reported, the Natives "have moved all of their women, children, and aged into the interior; the rest of the most warlike lay down our lives daily with murder and fire, [and] threaten to attack the Fort with all their force (which consists of about 1500 men), which we also expect hourly, for all the outside places are mostly in their power."[10] A few days later, the Eight Men sent a second letter, a formal remonstrance addressed to the States General in The Hague, the highest governing body of the Dutch Republic. They reported the same situation while appealing on political grounds. "And should suitable assistance not speedily arrive (contrary to our expectations), we shall, through necessity, in order to save the lives of those who remain, be obliged to betake ourselves to the English at the East, who would like nothing better than to possess this place."[11]

The West India Company responded by dispatching a ship, *De Blauwen Haen* (The Blue Cock), carrying soldiers and supplies, but even after the immediate threat dissipated, the conditions in the colony did not improve. There was very little gunpowder available for defense. Most of the soldiers were dismissed shortly after they arrived, while relations with the Natives remained tentative. The people had been unable to return to the business of reconstructing their homes in areas that remained abandoned and unsecured, or even harvesting what remained in the fields for food. On top of the overall anxiety that the colonists were feeling about their future, instead of heeding their concerns, Kieft continued to act unilaterally in his actions, including imposing new taxes without consulting his council. Frustration was mounting that their leader was neither trustworthy nor effective. A year after the board had sent their two letters asking for help, tensions between the colonists and Kieft's administration had only worsened. In October 1644, the Eight Men sent another letter to the Amsterdam Chamber of the West India Company. This third letter, though, had a different intent. It bypassed Kieft, smuggled out of the country by independent Flemish trader Govert Loockermans. The letter outlined the dissatisfaction of the Eight Men, again describing the deteriorating conditions that continued to plague their everyday livelihoods and hamper recovery. Most pointedly, though, it criticized a series of administrative actions leading up to the current state of affairs, by this time placing the blame for the colony's despair squarely onto Kieft and asking for his removal.[12]

Van der Donck had to have been acutely aware of the dire situation in Manhattan. Although the fighting was taking place far to the south of Rensselaerswyck, he had been traveling to Manhattan for court appearances. He would have seen, firsthand, the deserted and burned-out settlements along the shores of the river as he sailed south. Moreover, the community in Manhattan had become relatively compact. Being in the courts would have positioned him amid both those who were suffering and those who were debating the matters at hand. The cases involving Symon Pos also place him there during the time the Eight Men were holding their secret meetings, desperately conspiring to get rid of Kieft. And if that were not enough, the board of Eight Men included Van der Donck's shipmate on *Den Eyckenboom*, Cornelis Melyn. Van der Donck had undoubtedly heard that Melyn had been on the receiving end of harassment by Kieft, along with Melyn's friend and political ally, Jochem Pietersen Kuyter, a German-speaking Dane with his own plantation in northern Manhattan. The third, secret, letter from the Eight Men had been signed by all eight. However, when the West India Company decided, in December, to recall Kieft to defend his actions, Kieft focused his blame on his most vocal opponents, Melyn, as president of the board, and Melyn's friend Kuyter, later arguing that they had written "nothing but slanders and lies."[13]

Besides the recall of Kieft, the West India Company had drawn up a redress for the colony in response to the complaints from the Eight Men, weighing out the suggestions of both the administration and the commonalty. Director Kieft had proposed "[t]o bring peace and calm to the land, the Natives who have, through the force of weapons, been at war with us, must be completely destroyed and exterminated," estimating the number of Natives "would not be above three hundred strong." The commonalty, on the other hand, believing the Natives to be "some thousands strong," thought a better idea would be "to promote the customary quiet through a general peace." Wisely, the West India Company decided to adopt the advice of the commonalty, and, "in no way," that of the director.[14]

Peace talks began slowly, with some tribes accepting peace offerings, but the truce often only lasting until one or another faction of colonists or Natives provoked another violent eruption.[15] Fortunately, springtime, with planting season at hand, had the effect of incentivizing peace negotiations, and some tribes near Manhattan agreed to a cessation of the violence. In early summer 1645, Kieft traveled north in search of a friendship treaty with the Mohawks residing around Fort Orange, whom Van der Donck later described as "then and still the strongest and most feared Nation in the country."[16] The hope was that a treaty with the powerful Mohawks, who claimed sovereignty and imposed tribute over several nearby tribes, would extend to all the tribes under their dominant influence. A group of men assembled at Fort Orange for talks, including Director Kieft, his Manhattan council member Johannes de La Montagne, and agents of Rensselaerswyck, including Adriaen van der Donck. Van der Donck was in a good position to assist with peace negotiations. Not only was he familiar with the New Amsterdam administration of Kieft and the problems of the war, after living in Rensselaerswyck for four years, he was also familiar with the customs and languages of the Native tribes surrounding Fort Orange, including the Mohawks. This familiarity became critical to the success of the treaty when it appeared that Kieft had underestimated the importance of gift exchange in the pending negotiations and had come to the table low on funds. Understanding the good faith in offerings that this ritual represented to the Natives, Van der Donck lent money to Kieft in the form of *sewant*, "in order to secure the agreement."[17] He wrote about this Native tradition later. "All their treaties, accords, peace negotiations, reconciliations, proposals, requests, contracts, and covenants are all sealed and reinforced with gifts or offerings. Without this, their actions and promises do not mean much," he reported, describing the ceremonial protocol. "While the subject, article, or point is stipulated, established, or reiterated for the last time, the one making the request or speech has the offering in front of him, or in his hand, and at the end of the discourse, lays it down in front of the one for whom it is intended. What is decided this way, with or among them, they will remember very precisely and exactly, as well as observe, and revere, in every possible manner."[18] With this decisive ritual, the peace treaty allegiance the group negotiated with the Mohawks at Fort Orange was secured and, in effect, spoke for any of the tribes under their command.

An interesting aside to the peace negotiations that Van der Donck recounted later was an event that took place before the deliberations began, still in his "fresher memory." A Mohawk interpreter, who had been employed by the Dutch for the occasion, had come downstairs that morning and begun applying a shiny paint coloring to his face. "Watching this," Van der Donck recalled, "the Director appealed to me to ask him for the material he was applying to himself, which he passed to me, and I to the director." After inspecting it for some time, and suspecting the shiny material might be "some precious mineral," Kieft arranged to have the Mohawk compensated for it. The heavy substance was then placed in a crucible and heated according to the instructions of La Montagne who, as a doctor of medicine, was "a wise man who also had some familiarity or knowledge about it." When it was taken from the fire, the material "produced two small pieces of gold, together worth about three guilders." Van der Donck maintained that further tests confirmed these findings, though his report was later contradicted by a West India Company account of the specimens, which concluded they were most likely pyrite, now commonly referred to as fool's gold.[19]

On August 30, 1645, the sachems, or chiefs, of the surrounding tribes gathered in Manhattan for a formal end to the war. The New Amsterdam court messenger was ordered to notify the citizens to come to the fort "when the flag shall be hoisted and the bell rung," inviting all the colonists to hear the terms of the treaty.[20] Subsequently, the court messenger returned with the good news, announcing that he had notified "all the burghers around the

Manhatans from the highest to the lowest, no one excepted."[21] Once every-one was assembled in the fort, the peace was concluded in the presence of the sachems, the director, his council with negotiators and translators, as well as the entire commonalty, "under the blue heaven."[22]

Kieft was appropriately grateful for Van der Donck's assistance in obtain-ing the treaty, in an end to the disaster he had begun, and he repaid the favor nicely, granting Van der Donck his own tract of land, on the east side of the Hudson River, about sixteen miles above New Amsterdam. This 24,000-acre parcel, "bounded on the north by the Saw-kill, which the Indians called Maccakassin, and ran south to Nepperhaem; thence to the Shorakapkock kill and to Papirinimen Creek, called by the Dutch 'Spuyten-duyvel,'" encom-passed what is now Yonkers and part of the Bronx. From north to south, it included the area along the Hudson River between present-day Saw Mill River and Spuyten Duyvil Creek, just north of Manhattan, then "stretched eastward to the river Bronx."[23] Van der Donck was one of the select few, be-sides Jonas Bronck and David Pietersz. de Vries, to have received a land grant beyond the original West India Company patents. The grant gave Van der Donck all the rights and privileges of a patroon outlined in the West India Company Charter of Freedoms and Exemptions of 1629, including the right to establish a local government within the boundaries of his colony, install officers and magistrates, establish churches and schools, and engage in fishing, fowling, and milling, in perpetuity, on his own little piece of heaven on the Hudson.[24]

Van der Donck would finally get his wish to lead his own colony after his earlier foiled attempt in the Catskills. It had initially appeared as if he would have been happy to have his own property further north near Rensselaerswyck, or probably anywhere in New Netherland. This location would put him closer to Manhattan, though, and in the long run, give him better access to the heart of the affairs of the colony, including the admin-istration and the courts. Besides the action of the local politics, however, something else had been drawing his attention to Manhattan. Her name was Mary Doughty.

8

Mary Doughty

Mary Doughty was different. She was English, several years younger than Van der Donck, and she was a woman of status as a preacher's daughter.[1] Most of all, she was no stranger to controversial men. Mary Doughty's father had come to New Netherland as a minister, originally from the area of Old Sodbury, in Gloucestershire County, England. Francis Doughty began making waves early on when, while preaching a sermon, he used noncanonical wording when referring to the King of England. This "blazing indiscretion" did not go over well, since it amounted to, in essence, an insult to the crown.[2] The whole affair was taken seriously enough to make its way through the local courts all the way up to the Bishop of London, to whom Doughty finally submitted a humble and remorseful apology. Warned "to beware how he let slip any undutiful speeches against his Majesty's church or state," he was eventually released from his post as vicar of Sodbury in 1637.[3] Shortly thereafter, he left England with his wife and children for Cohannet, Massachusetts, now Taunton, in search of a more accepting community in New England. Unfortunately, this move did not spell the end of his problems. On a more personal note, trouble followed him across the Atlantic in the form of his sister, Elizabeth. Elizabeth and her husband had emigrated as well, only to engage Doughty in family litigation for several years stemming from disagreements regarding the settlement of their father's estate.

The biggest problem for Doughty, though, occurred in New England when he began preaching to his new congregation in Cohannet and instigated uproar in the church. Openly objecting to the church's practice of excluding nonmembers, he argued that, "according to the Covenant of Abraham, all men's children that were of baptized parents, and so Abraham's children, ought to be baptized."[4] The daring public declaration of this controversial opinion ignited such a disturbance that Doughty was subsequently dragged out of the assembly by the constable.[5] At the time, and in the context of adopting a "covenant" for the Cohannet church, Doughty seemed only to wish to contend, in a theological argument, that all children of Christians, whether church members or not, should be allowed to be baptized. His punishment, however, for speaking openly against the wishes of the congregation was that, while he was not banished, he would not be recognized in the office of minister, nor even allowed the privileges of a church member. This latest fiasco spelled the end of Doughty's career in the Plymouth colony, where his flight to New England felt like he had, as Van der Donck would write later, "gotten out of the frying pan into the fire."[6] Again, Doughty packed up his family, sold his land, and, sometime around 1640, sought refuge in Newport, Rhode Island, bringing a group of his followers with him.

Rhode Island had the unfortunate reputation of being a place for outcasts and refugees from New England, considered by some English "the *latrina* of New England" and, therefore, not a place that Francis Doughty would be likely to call home.[7] Before long, he, along with his family and followers, found their way to Long Island, looking to settle among a more tolerant citizenry where Doughty could, once and for all, preach undisturbed. He thought he had finally found the security he was looking for when Kieft's administration, in the interest of increasing colonization, issued him a patent for 6,666 acres at Maspeth, later part of Newtown, present-day Queens County, on March 28, 1642. The patent for the colony in Newtown specified his right to hold worship services, "with power to build on the aforesaid land a village or villages, a church or churches, to exercise the Reformed Christian religion."[8] The Doughty family had barely settled into their new neighborhood when Kieft's War began, and in September of 1643, Doughty's Long Island community, counting as many as eighty people, was attacked and burned.[9] The family and what was left of his flock had to relocate to Manhattan for protection. Doughty purchased property directly outside of the fort, obtaining permission to resume preaching to the English congregation in the church inside the fort.

It is not known exactly how Adriaen van der Donck and Mary Doughty met, although, by this time, there would have been any number of opportunities for their paths to cross. Most of the activities in the now relatively small community of Manhattan were happening within the confines and security of the area around the fort. Moreover, Francis Doughty's position as the leader of the English congregation that had moved from Long Island gave the family some visibility and social standing. In the summer of 1645, when an Englishman of Doughty's church, William Gerritson, wrote "a scandalous" song about Doughty and his daughter, Mary, the administration considered this no laughing matter. In a hearing, the court ordered the presumptuous songwriter to "stand in the fort tied to the Maypole, with two rods around his neck and the said libel over his head," threatening that he would be "flogged and banished" if he should sing the song again.[10] Van der Donck's administrative activities in Manhattan at the time would have certainly brought him into contact with community leaders like Francis Doughty and, by extension, his family, whose social position was similar to his. And he would have found something else in common with Mary Doughty. The persecution and displacement she had suffered on religious grounds would have been reminiscent of the experience in his own youth, of the expulsion of his Protestant family by the Spanish, from their home in Breda. The years of adversity had made Mary Doughty confident and capable, far from the stereotypical picture of a passive and submissive preacher's daughter. In Adriaen van der Donck, she would see someone like her father, a man with strong opinions who was not afraid to stand up for what he thought was right, a man by whom she could stand tall.

Adriaen van der Donck and Mary Doughty were married in the Dutch Reformed Church in New Amsterdam on Sunday, October 22, 1645.[11] Upon their marriage, Mary Doughty's father conferred his Maspeth farm on his daughter, although Van der Donck did not obtain a patent for it until 1648. For the time being, Mary Doughty accompanied her new husband back to Rensselaerswyck to live in his home on Castle Island. The contentment of the Van der Donck's new marriage would have to warm them as they faced the upcoming winter, which, in what became known as the Little Ice Age, was one of the coldest in recent history. Nonetheless, the fall they moved in together as husband and wife, their farm produced a healthy crop of oats, a small amount of peas, and even more wheat than the year before.[12]

The prospect of a bright future would not keep an unwelcome chain of events from interrupting the newlyweds' first year together. At the height of that cold winter, on January 18, 1646, the house they shared as honeymooners caught fire and was destroyed.[13] Antony de Hooges, the former work associate with whom Van der Donck had mostly butted heads while Van Rensselaer was alive, generously offered to take the couple into his home. This was especially charitable of De Hooges, considering he was already living in tight quarters in Van Rensselaer's storehouse.[14] However, what started as amicable neighborliness did not last long before old feelings started to surface again. A disagreement erupted as Van der Donck began negotiations to transfer his farm for the remainder of his lease. When the new lessee wanted it stipulated that everything would be conveyed "clear" of the recent damages, the conversation turned to the question of the liability for the loss of the house in the fire. Van der Donck asserted that the liability for the house fell completely on the patroon of Rensselaerswyck, which he endeavored to substantiate "by the laws."[15] De Hooges, who was acting as the colony's administrator, disagreed, however, referring to the contract, which he contended took precedent and "subsequently exhibited."[16] His argument might have had some precedent. Although there is no known copy of Van der Donck's contract, the agreement Van Rensselaer had with the farmers, at least, stipulated that a farmer "must also bear half of the [expense of] fire to his house and what belongs to it."[17] In any event, from there, the argument escalated and the two fell into a full-fledged quarrel, which De Hooges later recorded in his memorandum book. Things heated up when De Hooges brought up accusations that, he asserted, Van der Donck had made behind his back. Van der Donck then accused him of lying, he wrote, "in the presence of some honorable people."[18] Tempers were running high, according to De Hooges, until, finally, in his words, "the wolf came out of the sheep's clothing." This served as confirmation to De Hooges that Van der Donck, "without a doubt—long before now—had fostered his ingratitude in his heart."[19] De Hooges felt doubly insulted since, from his point of view, he had always treated Van der Donck well. Furthermore, after the fire, he had sent over "almost a *tonne* of meat" and then taken the couple in, sharing whatever else he had.[20] Having been called a liar, especially in public, after all he had done, had pushed him too far, and, as he put it, "his blood was starting to boil."[21] Infuriated, he gave Van der Donck an ultimatum to get out of his house within the next two days, and to take his chest of belongings with him or, he threatened, he would put the chest outside himself. Despite having lost all credibility with De Hooges, Van der Donck approached him before leaving, "playing the downtrodden," according to De Hooges, and asking for an accounting of whatever he owed him. De Hooges was suspicious, however, that Van der Donck was feigning sorrow with the objective of using the debt to his advantage, perhaps as a deduction from what he might eventually owe for the house. De Hooges, not being willing to play the fool, refused the request while accusing Van der Donck of his familiar "craftiness." By this time, things had settled down enough that De Hooges, perhaps in an attempt to appear reasonable himself, enumerated some pragmatic and more tactful reasons for asking Van der Donck to leave. First, he wrote, he hoped "to avoid arguments," and second, "his supplies were almost gone." He also cited his freedom, "because sometimes I have things to write or to say that I do not want everyone to know."[22] And to give his actions even more legitimacy, he added that he had notified Van der Donck twice previously that he should go but had not seen him make any moves toward leaving.[23]

De Hooges recorded the quarrel in his notebook sometime between February 22nd, when the Van der Doncks moved out, and March 10th, the date of the following note. At some point in those two weeks after the confrontation, he must have felt it might not be a bad idea to document his side of the story. He was wary, and perhaps rightly so, that Van der Donck would talk about him behind his back and distort that the facts. The two, who had never truly been on the same page with their goals in Rensselaerswyck, would still have to work together to sort out the liability for Van der Donck's farm and De Hooges needed to maintain his authority in the community. He wanted his bases covered. Using an old Latin proverb, describing a hypocrite, to explain his reasoning, De Hooges wrote, "I know his nature well: *mel in ore, fel in corde,*" meaning "honey in the mouth, bitterness in the heart."[24] What seems to have finally compelled him to put pen to paper was what to him seemed like Van der Donck's determination to get the last word, even after having been kicked out of De Hooges' house. "No one would consider it strange that I have now recorded these things so exactly, if they were familiar with his cunning and craftiness," De Hooges defended.[25] "A small example of this," he related, was that he had offered Van der Donck and his wife lodging in the house that Nicolaes Coorn had occupied. But, rather than accept the offer, Van der Donck chose to make a dramatic demonstration instead, going from De Hooges' house to the house of "Master Harmani," in Fort Orange, "and crept there into a shack, or hovel, where one would hardly want to enter . . . all for show."[26] Van der Donck seemed to have declined De Hooges' offer out of spite while trying to making it appear, for the public, that he had been turned out. Even though De Hooges could see what Van der Donck was trying to do, he still could not believe that Van der Donck would rather stay in a "shack" under the auspices of the West India Company than in a perfectly good Rensselaerswyck house, just to prove a point. This, "apparently has its reasons," De Hooges acquiesced.[27] "God only knows."[28]

By April 1646, Van der Donck decided to cede his farm to his neighbor on Castle Island, Cornelis Segersz van Voorhout. Segersz, the only other resident of the island, would take over the remaining three years' lease on the farm, and in return, he would get the whole island to himself.[29] Van der Donck would still take responsibility for any pending liability on the damages that happened before the transfer, but the agreement allowed him to use the small house, even if only for his workers, until the ice melted and he and Mary could move south. With the farm, Segersz got the grain standing in the fields as well as in the hay barracks, the haystack adjacent to the barracks that survived the fire, the farmstead, the garden, the fences surrounding the land, all the unsawn wood on the property, as well as the use of a small sailboat. He also acquired the mares, geldings, cows, and pigs that belonged to the farm.[30]

Van der Donck also agreed to arbitration for a resolution on the liability for the house fire. The two sides were still fairly far apart. By Van der Donck's accounting, rather than owing for the house, after subtracting his debts from his credits, the patroon owed him money.[31] De Hooges laid out Van der Donck's calculation in the agreement, which they both signed. However, he expressed his doubt about the proposal, this time unemotionally, "because the house is burned down and some other things, which add up to a large amount of his credit, which, in my opinion, should go to his debts."[32] In an effort to be clear, but primarily as an explanation for the request for arbitration, De Hooges also noted, "On the contrary, Van der Donck finds, that he believes himself to be exempt from damages and charges."[33] On the one hand, Van der Donck stood to lose a lot of what he had invested by walking away from his farm after almost five years in Rensselaerswyck. But it would also mean he would be out from under his commitments there, leaving the volatile relationships as well as many of his own mistakes behind him. With no house of his own in Rensselaerswyck, and no career opportunity to speak of, all signs pointed south. He would be free to start over with his new wife north of Manhattan, closer to her family and his work in the courts, to develop his land there, be his own boss, and lead his own community the way he saw fit.

9

Colendonck

Sometime after May when the cold winter snows finally thawed and the rivers became navigable again, Adriaen and Mary left Rensselaerswyck and traveled south with their plans to establish themselves closer to Manhattan.[1] Van der Donck purchased the land from the Natives licensed by the grant from the West India Company by Director Kieft, making him officially "Adriaen van der Donck of Breda, Patroon of the Colonie of Nepperhaem, called by him Colendonck."[2] But Van der Donck was beginning to be known by another formal designation. As a landowner, or perhaps through the status of his law school education, his experience in the courts, or the respect he had gained in the peace negotiations, he was beginning to be referred to as "the *Joncker*," adapted from the Dutch word *jongeheer*, which translates to "young gentleman." At the time, *Jonckheer*, or *Joncker*, though not a title of official standing, was an honorific given to those belonging to nobility or of other higher social status.[3] The first documented reference to Van der Donck as "the *Joncker*" came on January 2, 1646, in an administrative complaint, against the Manhattan minister Everardus Bogardus, in which he had acted as mediator.[4] A second reference to Van der Donck as *Joncker* was made a few months later, in May 1646, as Van der Donck was wrapping up his business in Rensselaerswyck. In De Hooges' memorandum book, a carpentry bill for charges, still in dispute for Van der Donck's burned house, made reference to "the farm of the *Joncker*."[5] Adriaen van der Donck's colony of Colendonck gradually became known as "de Jonckheer's Landt," then later "Ye Youncker's land" under the English. This name remains today as the city of Yonkers, just north of Manhattan, in a contemporary reference to Van der Donck.

Van der Donck began developing his colony of Colendonck on the Zaeg Kill, the waterway named for the sawmill he erected, where the creek intersects the Hudson River near present-day Van der Donck Park. He also established a grain mill and plantation on the nearby meadows, where he farmed the former Native cornfields in the area that is now the Van Cortlandt Park Parade Ground. His house would be built on the southern end of the property facing Manhattan, across the Spuyten Duyvil Kill. Although this area might seem quite separate from Manhattan today, in the seventeenth century the waterway was not the wide estuary it is today, but small and winding, and there are several references to this area being likely passable during low tides, potentially on foot or on horseback.[6] From his house, Van der Donck had his eye on Manhattan, both literally and metaphorically. He was beginning to work himself into more and more of the affairs of the colony. The summer after leaving Rensselaerswyck, and again in December and January, he was making appearances in the courts of New Amsterdam and acting as legal counsel in a variety of capacities, including as an impartial witness in another complaint brought by Kieft and his council against Reverend Bogardus.[7]

Kieft was still acting as director of the colony. It had taken quite some time for the administrators in the Dutch Republic to agree on an appropriate replacement after their recall decision. While Kieft still hung on to his role, the knowledge that he was on his way out and had lost all support from the community was bringing out the worst in him. Though he could not, at this point, expect cooperation from the bulk of his constituents, as a "lame duck" official he also had little to fear by pushing the limits of his power. He had become increasingly unreasonable and tyrannical, targeting those he considered disloyal. In his long-running feud with the Reverend Bogardus, he was reduced to attempting to disturb the church services by whatever means possible. He, along with those who did not dare to cross him, went as far as childishly interrupting the sermons with stomping, singing, dancing, even resorting to drum rolls and cannon fire.[8]

For Van der Donck, Kieft's antics hit a little too close to home when Kieft took on Francis Doughty, now his father-in-law. A conflict arose when Doughty's partner patentees on his Long Island settlement brought suit against him, charging him with asking for down payments and quit-rent for land. The administration accused Doughty of restricting population there.[9] But Doughty felt that Kieft's accusations had a different agenda, borne of his decision to stay within the security of Manhattan after the war instead of going back to Long Island right away, "because the peace was doubtful."[10] He believed that Kieft's administration wanted him out of the way so that it could make the land available to other potential colonists, such as to his business partners. In April 1647 Kieft rescinded Doughty's patent and con-fiscated his possessions, leaving him only his *bouwerie*. Doughty was not in a good position to argue considering the administration had already lent him money and supplies, and he was in debt to them.[11] When he tried to appeal the decision, however, Kieft, who had already publicly terminated the right of appeal to the courts in the Dutch Republic, punished Doughty for his request by sentencing him to twenty-four hours in prison and fining him twenty-five guilders. Van der Donck considered Kieft's act "tyrannical."[12] If he did not already dislike Kieft for all the missteps of his administration, he certainly did now.

The West India Company knew that the new director of New Netherland was going to have to be able to restore order to a messy situation that had the potential to get even worse. They needed someone who was authorita-tive, unafraid, and loyal to the company. After some consideration, they settled on one from their own ranks, Peter Stuyvesant. Stuyvesant, who went by the Latinized name of a scholar, Petrus, had studied at the University of Franeker in his staunchly Calvinistic northerly Dutch province of Friesland, where his father was a minister. He had worked his way up the West India Company ladder from supplies officer to commander of a company of Dutch soldiers, defending the company's interests in Brazil and the Caribbean. During his last battle against the Spanish on the island of St. Martin, Stuyvesant's right leg was struck by a cannonball while his troops advanced on the enemy fort. Against all odds, Stuyvesant survived the rescue and subsequent amputation.[13]

It is not surprising that the West India Company directors liked Stuyvesant, a quintessential company man. After he lost his leg and braved the recovery, not only did he report for work in whatever managerial capac-ity he could, he even apologized for losing the battle. When his leg would not heal in the tropical humidity of the Caribbean, Stuyvesant was reluc-tantly sent home to the Dutch Republic to convalesce, where he lodged at the home of his sister and brother-in-law in Leiden. While there, he met his future wife, his brother-in-law's sister, Judith Bayard, who had been living there since her father passed away, and who helped nurse Stuyvesant back to health. Coincidentally, Bayard's Huguenot family was from Breda, where her father was also a Protestant minister in the Walloon church there.[14] According to the baptismal records that survived from the church, Judith Bayard was at least ten years older than Adriaen van der Donck.[15] Nevertheless, consider-ing she was the oldest of eight children, it would be difficult to imagine that the families did not know each other. Moreover, this Walloon church, where Bayard and Stuyvesant married in August 1645, was part of the Beguine property, a stone's throw away from the Van der Donck family home.[16]

On July 13, 1646, the West India Company sent a memorandum to the States General asking for the commission of Petrus Stuyvesant as Director of New Netherland.[17] The ship that would transport the new director to his post, the *Prinses Amelia*, along with its companion ship, was held up in port while the West India Company directors waited for the States General to approve Stuyvesant's commission. Finally, on July 28, 1646, Stuyvesant appeared before the Assembly of the States General of the United Netherlands to receive his commission as "Director on the Coast of New Netherland," together with "the Islands of Curaçao, Buenaire, Aruba and their dependencies."[18] He would not have to relinquish control of his territory in the Caribbean while New Netherland was added to his command. Stuyvesant's ship left the North Holland harbor of Texel sometime in early August, making its first stop at the island of Curaçao in November. After remaining several months in the Caribbean, a squadron of four ships set sail for New Netherland in April 1647, carrying Stuyvesant and his newly pregnant wife, as well as a cargo of 200,000 pounds of Brazilian red dyewood it had picked up while there.[19]

FIGURE 9.1. New Amsterdam.
Courtesy of the New York Public Library Digital Collections.

When the new director arrived in New Netherland on May 11, 1647, he was courted by the full fleet of ships that had sailed together out of Curaçao.[20] Van der Donck must have immediately been put on guard by all the ceremony, later describing Stuyvesant's first arrival as "like a peacock, with great posturing and pomposity."[21] Stuyvesant let it be known, Van der Donck reported, that he wanted to be addressed as *Heer Generael*, the equivalent of "Lord General."[22] He kept his audience, including some of the most prominent citizens who had come to greet him, standing for several hours without their hats, while keeping his own hat on, "as if he were the Grand Duke of Muscovy."[23] And if the entire spectacle was not surreal enough, Stuyvesant's leg had been replaced with a wooden one, reinforced with shiny silver nails.

After the colonists' success in getting rid of Kieft, their collective feeling was that the West India Company had listened to their complaints. Not only their hope, but also their expectation, was that its directors, having understood the gravity of the situation, would do their best to send over an effective leader. But for Van der Donck, the bar was set even higher than that. He was in a unique position. He was one of the few people in the colony with a university education. And after almost six years, his experiences had brought him into contact with nearly everyone in New Netherland, Manhattanites, Long Islanders, the people of Rensselaerswyck, as well as the Natives of the surrounding tribes. He knew the history of their relationships, had seen the changes, and he had plenty of his own ideas about what the colony needed. He was probably beginning to feel like he knew more about the workings of the colony than almost anyone. Not only that, he was as smart as anybody the administration could throw at them. At this point, just about anyone the West India Company would have sent would have felt like a corporate outsider. It must have then been disappointingly sobering for all the colonists when one of Stuyvesant's first actions was to add a wine tax to Kieft's already unpopular beer tax, which they had hoped the new director, who was "very much longed for," would abolish.[24]

Aside from any apprehensions he might have had about Stuyvesant, Van der Donck seemed to be trying to put his best foot forward to try to get along with the colony's new leadership. Shortly after Stuyvesant's arrival, Van der Donck enlisted Cornelis Segersz to promise to deliver, on his account, 300 *schepels* of wheat and 150 *schepels* of oats, from his old farm in Rensselaerswyck, to the Stuyvesants, after the fall harvest.[25] A resolution on Van der Donck's farm holdings was still pending, though he had been pushing for full settlement and De Hooges signed as security on the note. In the process of arranging this transaction it became apparent that De Hooges still had not sent over the accounts to be arbitrated in the Dutch Republic, and

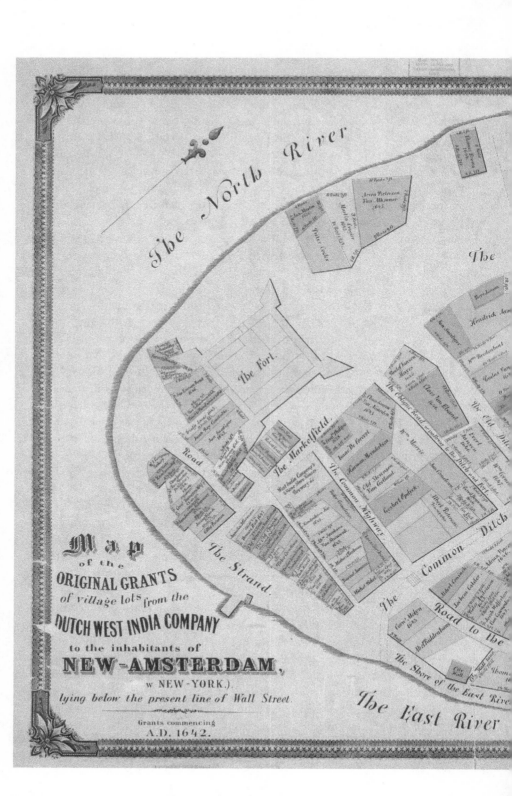

Map
of the
ORIGINAL GRANTS
of village lots from the
DUTCH WEST INDIA COMPANY
to the inhabitants of
NEW-AMSTERDAM,
(w NEW-YORK.)
lying below the present line of Wall Street.

Grants commencing
A.D. 1642.

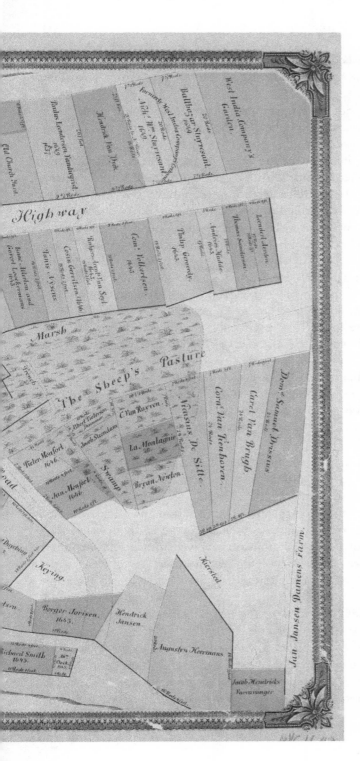

FIGURE 9.2.
Map of original
West India Company
Land Grants,
New Amsterdam,
beginning in 1642.
From the collection
of the New York
Public Library.

he was ordered by the court to do so "at the first [opportunity]."[26] It would not give Van der Donck very much credibility with Stuyvesant to be making promises he could not keep.

All relationships aside, Stuyvesant had plenty to keep him busy as he settled into his new position, not the least of which was attempting to re-establish a sense order to the colony after the fragmented administration of Kieft. One of the first items he had to face was the one that that had pro-duced the defamatory letter from the Eight Men, prompted Kieft's removal, and became, indirectly, the whole reason for his coming to the colony in the first place. A commission was called to investigate the conflict between Kieft and his two targeted opponents, Melyn and Kuyter. Much to Stuyvesant's surprise however, instead of subordinating themselves to the council by pro-viding an excuse, Melyn and Kuyter dropped off a long and detailed draft of interrogatories on events leading up to the war, directed at Kieft's adminis-trators. It is said that the best defense is a good offense. The questions were specifically devised to expose Kieft's transgressions and included such queries as, "Did we Dutch, here in this country, not live in peace with these Natives before that cruel deed over at Pavonia and the Island of Manhatans was ex-ecuted on them?" and, "Is it also not true that, through this act, the general war between us Dutch and those Americans here around the Manhatans first arose?"[27] The style of examination, as well as the level of pointedness and detail of the interrogatories, suggests they were crafted by a skilled writer who also had some knowledge of law.[28] Stuyvesant had underestimated who he would be up against.

The new director was beside himself with indignation at this attempt to turn the tables; just over a month into his new post and his authority was already being tested. He submitted the petition and the accompanying interrogatories to his commission for their consideration and advice, but not without some questions of his own to consider. "First, if it was ever heard or seen in any republic that vassals and subjects conceived, forged, and submitted to their magistrates, self-proposed points—interrogatives to examine them with—without authority from their superiors?" Stuyvesant had no intention of entertaining the idea that this type of questioning would be permitted, much less render his administration under any obligation to answer to "two private malignant subjects."[29]

In this process, Kieft formulated a defensive response to the accusations made against him in the earlier letter of the Eight Men, which he still main-tained Melyn and Kuyter had sent without clear consent of the others. He enumerated the accusations made in the original complaint, arguing that he and his administration were "well prepared to prove these are complete false

slanders and lies," and demanding the two plaintiffs "prove said letter" and
"their falsehoods [be] punished."[30] The administration then made its next
move, delivering the demand by court messenger to Melyn and Kuyter, who
were "expressly commanded to answer thereon within two times 24 hours."[31]
In other words, the two had precisely forty-eight hours to put together a
defense.

Within two days, not only was the explanation from Melyn and Kuyter
ready, but it also read like a professionally and finely composed legal defense,
not like something that could have been scraped together by two farmers
on short notice. Here again, it seems clear that someone with a knowledge
of law had had a hand in this document, addressing each of Kieft's points
thoroughly and meticulously, while invoking the names of philosophers and
the wisdom of ancient sages.[32] The writer of this rebuttal would have to have
been someone with a sound understanding of the complex events at stake
as well as the ability to quickly compose a concise administrative document
that would be capable of standing up to Stuyvesant's council. It would have
to have been someone like Adriaen van der Donck.[33]

The argument, clearly expressed, allowed Melyn and Kuyter to essentially fight back on the level of what they were being served up by the administration, rather than being pushed into a corner of complete submission.
Their action did not succeed in getting them off the hook entirely, though
the reasoning did, at least, seem to influence Stuyvesant in handing down
a lighter sentence and, more critically, left the door open for an appeal in
the Dutch Republic. After the deliberation of the commission, Melyn and
Kuyter were still found guilty of the charges, but punishment was moder-
ated from Stuyvesant's initial ruling, which had been a death sentence for
Melyn.[34] On July 25, 1647, Stuyvesant's council formally pronounced Melyn
guilty of *laesae majestatis*, or high treason, fined 300 guilders, and sentenced to
banishment from the colony for seven years, "to depart with the first ships."[35]
Jochem Kuyter, whose charges were determined to be less serious, was fined
150 guilders and sentenced to banishment of three years.[36]

Van der Donck was straddling the fence on his stance toward Stuyvesant,
at least outwardly. In assisting Melyn and Kuyter, his contempt seemed mostly focused on Kieft. In siding with Kieft against the two farmers, however,
Stuyvesant had allied himself with at least some of Kieft's views, even if his
allegiance only extended to the defense of the West India Company administration. And Stuyvesant was that same construct of authority figure that
Van der Donck had rejected in the past. It remained to be seen whether
Stuyvesant would be willing and able to pull together the necessary resources
to turn the colony around from the ruinous path that Kieft had set them on

and appease a dissatisfied constituency. If Van der Donck had any problem with Stuyvesant, he did not let it show publicly, but it would not be long before the two would have to face off. As much as possible, though, he knew that he would need to remain in Stuyvesant's good graces if he wanted to advance his own standing in the community.

In September, Stuyvesant and Van der Donck seemed on good enough terms that Van der Donck was asked to help on an unusual case as one of three impartial witnesses, "all understanding the English language."[37] A Scotsman had shown up in the colony, claiming Long Island, its surrounding islands, and part of the mainland for "Maria, Dowager of Sterling."[38] The man had already been to the English villages on Long Island, touting his commission, which consisted of a document with an old, broken, indecipherable seal attached. After determining the Scotsman's demands to be illegitimate, the director and his council resolved "to send the professed governor to Holland as a prisoner with the ship *De Valckenier*, to justify his commission before their High Mightinesses."[39] As luck would have it for the Scotsman, *De Valckenier*, which left some time later, made a stop in England, where the man got off the ship and was not seen again. Van der Donck later complained that the English had been making it known that the Scotsman had been seen around Boston.[40]

Melyn and Kuyter had prepared to leave on the next ship sailing out of New Netherland. Coincidentally, it would be the very same vessel that would transport the now-disgraced Kieft back to the Dutch Republic. The *Prinses Amelia* would register 109 passengers, among them another of Kieft's adversaries, Reverend Bogardus. Along with its prominent passengers, the *Prinses* carried many important legal documents, including the actions against Kieft, Melyn, and Kuyter, as well as the paperwork, finally submitted by De Hooges for arbitration in the liability of Van der Donck's burned farm. The ship also hauled a mother lode of cargo. Besides the dyewood picked up in the Caribbean on the inbound leg of its journey, 14,000 beaver skins had been loaded in New Netherland, which alone had an estimated value of approximately 100,000 guilders.[41] A multitude of other items of intangible worth were also on board. Items such as "very exact Maps, at least a hundred different mineral samples, as well as many remonstrances and accountings of New Netherland," were not necessarily of immediate monetary value to the colony but exponentially vital to its advancement.[42] The ship even held such rarities as the pelt of an albino beaver, described later by Van der Donck as "snow white," whose "guard hairs on the back leaned a little toward the Gold."[43] The *Prinses* was a complete treasure ship, the kind of things that dreams are made of, and packed to the gills. Much of the colony's future hinged on her successful voyage.

At the helm was twenty-five-year-old Jan Claesz Bol.[44] Bol had skippered one of the ships in the contingent that arrived with Stuyvesant and had, as was customary for a ship's skipper in port, served as a councilor under Stuyvesant during his interim time in New Netherland.[45] The *Prinses* left Manhattan on or about August 16, 1647, and was making good time across the North Atlantic. However, on approach to England, with no land yet in sight, the ship made a critical, though unfortunately not unheard of, error. Attributed by some to a "drunken steersman," the ship was turned north prematurely, most likely in the mistaken belief that it had already rounded the southern tip of England.[46] Instead of sailing into the English Channel, the *Prinses* was steered into the Verkeerde Canaal, literally named "Wrong Channel," or the Bristol Channel that separates Wales from England.[47] Then, in "foule foggie stormy and tempestuous weather," the ship ran aground on a sandy shoal, and foundered.[48] Later, on the dark, moonless night, as the rising tides lifted the *Prinses* off the shoal, three strong gusts drove it crashing against the rocks off the rugged coast at Mumbles Point.[49] The ship "struck into pieces."[50] Only twenty-one of the passengers survived.[51] Gone were Kieft, the Reverend Bogardus, and Cornelis Melyn's son, along with eighty-three other souls.[52] By Melyn's account, "the ship, being beat into eight pieces, drifted the whole night in the sea until daybreak."[53] Melyn then "fell in with others who had stayed upon a part of the ship on a sand bank."[54] On an ebb tide when the sand bank became dry, they collected some planks and pieces of wood and, after fashioning sails out of shirts and other pieces of clothing, made their way in makeshift floats across the channel to the mainland. Melyn finally reached shore after reportedly floating back and forth in the sea for about eighteen hours.[55] There, he found his friend, Kuyter, who, miraculously, had also survived the wreck. Kuyter had washed ashore after clinging all night to the aft part of the ship that still had a piece of a cannon attached to it, which he had initially taken to be a dead person after he tried to talk to it and got no answer.[56] Later, the two men described having encountered "a Godless Kieft," who, "seeing death before his eyes, sighing deeply, doubtfully asked [them] both; 'Friends I have done you wrong; can you forgive me for it?'"[57]

Most of the ship's valuable cargo was lost at sea or to scavengers in the area who, from living on the unforgiving rocky coastline, knew very well the bounty that would wash up for the taking. Some of those on shore salvaged one of the ship's cannons and erected it as a memorial. In the immediate aftermath of the disaster, Melyn and Kuyter stayed on the beach trying to recover their papers, which, to them, had to have been among the most valuable cargo on the ship. By the third day, they had "fished" out to a box full.[58] The pair, now bonded more than ever, made their way back to the Dutch Republic, finally reaching their original destination a full month later.

A little bit of the heart and soul of New Netherland sank to the bottom
of the sea with the *Prinses Amelia* that fateful night. When news of the disaster finally reached the colony in January 1648, it was as much an emotional
loss as a monetary one, causing "great sadness on account of widows and or-
phans and great disparagement for the country."[59] Van der Donck would later
specifically name the loss of the *Prinses* as one of the causes of "the very poor
and low condition" of the colony, which he described as "utterly fallen."[60]
The *Prinses* had represented what seemed like their last hope. Painstakingly
drawn maps would have clarified boundaries by initiating talks to define borders. Legal documents would have settled conflicts, putting issues in front of
those who could make binding judgments. Physical specimens of the colony
would have stimulated support by illustrating New Netherland's potential
wealth. Like an SOS, the *Prinses* had carried a cry for help across the seas.
But now, all of that was lost, a flickering light snuffed out in nothing short
of a catastrophe. Their pleas would go unheard. If Van der Donck, along with
others, had hoped that the sailing of the *Prinses* meant that tides would be
changing for the better, they were back to square one. This was a turning
point.

10

Board of Nine Men

The loss of the paperwork for Van der Donck's farm in the *Prinses* tragedy meant that the dispute over liability for the fire still lingered in the courts of Rensselaerswyck. By the time the new director of Rensselaerswyck, Brandt van Slichtenhorst, arrived in March 1648, Van der Donck had requested, on several occasions, "verbally, in writing, and also by petition," the money that he claimed was coming to him in settlement of his account.[1] Van Slichtenhorst had come to a different conclusion, however, regarding the debt. Instead of ordering compensation for Van der Donck, he determined that Van der Donck owed the colony. His notice, addressed to "Adriaen van der Donck, or how you otherwise might be called by your Christian name," attached two hundred *schepels* of wheat, "and what furthermore is rightfully yours," that was still in the care of Cornelis Segersz.[2] According to Van Slichtenhorst, this judgment was made to recover costs that were owed the patroon for a black stallion and five cows that had been entrusted to Van der Donck with his farm. Indeed, in the early part of 1643, a horse belonging to Van der Donck had been crossing the ice for a wedding when the wedding party broke through the ice. The stallion, along with a mare, drowned. Van der Donck was said to have been compensated 150 guilders at the time, by the wedding guests, for the loss of the horse.[3]

Besides the issues requiring his attention in Rensselaerswyck, Van der Donck was dealing with other, more personal problems. His parents had apparently separated back home in January, splitting up their households, all their possessions, and their debts. Curiously, the separation agreement stipulated that his mother would pay his father in biannual installments. Whether this was based on the division of their property, the position of money on his mother's side of the family, or other legal reasons, is unclear. The contract even required the children to take on the obligation if their mother predeceased their father.[4] It had been seven years since Van der Donck had seen his family in Breda and they had not yet met his new wife. A trip home might not have been far from his mind.

Van der Donck was working, though, still getting around on the legal circuit as a representative in both the courts of New Amsterdam and Rensselaerswyck. In July he appeared in the court proceedings of Rensselaerswyck in an agreement to act as legal representative for Hans Vos, Court Messenger of Rensselaerswyck, to collect money owed to him in Manhattan.[5] In November he appeared in the courts of New Amsterdam as power of attorney for Jean Labatie, the French carpenter turned brewer from Rensselaerswyck with whom he had sparred, literally, in his days as *schout*.[6] It seemed that, by now, the two were at least on good enough terms for Labatie to trust Van der Donck to help in his legal matters. On the other hand, there was not much choice for legal representation in the colony. Van der Donck had been the only lawyer in Rensselaerswyck and was still only one of two lawyers in all of New Netherland along with Stuyvesant's vice director, Lubbert van Dincklagen. The following month Van der Donck was hired as legal counsel in New Amsterdam to defend the shipping merchant Thielman Willekens in litigation relating to damage to goods on his boat.[7]

During this time, Van der Donck's thoughts had not strayed from the possibility of a position of leadership in the colony. Shortly after the business of Melyn and Kuyter had been put aboard the *Prinses* with Kieft, Stuyvesant had established a nine-member board. In theory, the board would represent the opinions of the population, but in reality, the formation of the board had more to do with the fact that Stuyvesant needed help gauging and gaining the cooperation of the colonists in certain decisions affecting the colony. The advisory board would not truly have any influence beyond offering advice "when they were called on."[8] The community was first requested to nominate eighteen representatives and, from those, Stuyvesant selected a board of nine men. When reelections came up in December of 1648, Van der Donck was among those chosen for the board. His visibility within the community as well as the restraint he had exercised with Stuyvesant had paid off. He did, indeed, still seem to be in Stuyvesant's good graces. In January, Stuyvesant came to his aid with an order requiring the release of his grain held in Rensselaerswyck, on the condition that Van der Donck put up security for compensation for the horse.[9]

After the loss of the *Prinses*, the colonists had to revive their efforts to drum up badly needed support for the colony. A plan had already been in the works, before the new board was elected, to form a delegation to appeal directly to the managing West India Company or the States General governing in the Dutch Republic, for assistance in improving conditions. Stuyvesant had initially supported the idea, maintaining that his administration's hands were tied in addressing any grievances by the fact that it was bound by company orders, and so, not authorized to make changes. However, when the time came for the board to draw up a petition for the appeal, Stuyvesant assumed he would be driving the content. Realizing that this would ruin any chance that their real complaints about the West India Company administration would be heard, the board let the whole business cool down in a collective "never mind." When the board membership turned over in January, the new board, including Van der Donck, pledged to proceed, "however it went." Plans were made to convene the community in an assembly to determine their support for the issues at hand. But when the board submitted a written request to Stuyvesant, the response came in the form of a long, written annotation, which essentially boiled down to the fact that they would not be allowed to act independently. The board considered the conditions fundamentally in conflict with their mission and, therefore, "impracticable." Determining themselves, above all, "bound by oath to seek the welfare of the country," the decision was made by Van der Donck and other members of the board to, in lieu of a community meeting, speak to the colonists individually, going house to house to gather opinions. Stuyvesant immediately took this as a direct betrayal, an act of disobedience far beyond a disregard for protocol. "From this time on, the General burned with fury," Van der Donck wrote later, objecting, "and although these people had always been his good and cherished friends, and [whom] he also shortly before had regarded as the most honest, most capable, most intelligent, and most virtuous of the country, nonetheless, as soon as they did not follow the General's wishes, they were this and that, some of them boors, liars, rebels, connivers, swindlers; in a word, they were almost too corrupt to hang."[10] Van der Donck's provincial roots were showing. He had neither the political polish to pull off his two-faced approach toward Stuyvesant nor the big city savvy to realize it would eventually backfire.

To add insult to injury, Stuyvesant found out that Van der Donck, who had been designated by the board to act as secretary, had been keeping notes to create a journal for the future delegation. Incensed, Stuyvesant waited until Van der Donck was out of town, then entered the home of Machiel Jansen, another one of the Nine Men Van der Donck knew from Rensselaerswyck and where he had been staying, and personally seized the draft journal. When Stuyvesant read the notes that Van der Donck had been keeping, which he regarded as "gross slanders against their High Mightinesses," he formally accused Van der Donck of *crimen laesae majestatis* and placed him under house arrest.[11] This was the same charge of high treason that he had doled out to Cornelis Melyn two years earlier, a crime that carried the possibility of banishment from the colony, or even the prospect of a death sentence. On March 4, 1649, Stuyvesant called a meeting of his officers to decide what to do about Van der Donck and his libelous journal notes. The opinions of the council members varied. Stuyvesant's vice director, Lubbert van Dincklagen, who had also been implicated in the journal, principally took issue with Stuyvesant for placing Van der Donck under arrest without consulting him, and a committee was appointed to investigate the case. By majority vote, however, the council decided that Van der Donck should remain confined until he could be examined and answer their interrogatories. When the council called on Van der Donck to answer, "categorically," for the notes, Stuyvesant found his response to be unsatisfactory, "in contempt of the court, or dubious, or at least irresponsive to the matter."[12] Van der Donck, in what looked like an attempt defend himself by backpedaling, asserted that the notes were only a rough draft, acknowledging that "there were mistakes in it through hastiness and such," and requested the unfinished work in order to "revise it."[13] No matter how much he tried to explain it, though, Stuyvesant would not have it. "All in all," he wrote later, "we could not fix it other than it was always bad."[14] And not only did Stuyvesant not buy Van der Donck's story, he vowed to punish him as an example to others. Fortunately for Van der Donck, Stuyvesant did not have the support of his council, especially that of Vice Director Van Dincklagen, who opposed his vigilante conduct in the first place and, in the end, wanted nothing to do with the whole business. On March 15th Stuyvesant's written opinion declared that Van der Donck be ordered "to prove and demonstrate, or to revoke what he has wrongly written or spoken against the Honorable Lords States and the officers here."[15] The council voted to ban Van der Donck from attending their sessions, as well as from the meetings of the Nine Men, until he had proved the allegations he had written in his notes. It was almost like a dare.

Van der Donck had had a lot of time to sit and think while he was confined, waiting for the council to decide his fate. Everything that had happened up until now had to have been playing itself over and over again in his mind. It was wrong, he surely felt, the way the West India Company and its administrators, first Kieft, and now Stuyvesant, continually dismissed the board's obvious concerns while there was so much at stake. Stuyvesant had put the ball in his court, and backing down was no longer one of the options. He had come to love New Netherland too much to risk losing it and all that it had to offer because of the administration's lack of attention. The loss of the *Prinses* had been a call to action. In his mind, the only hope for instigating real change now would mean going over the head of the West India Company and appealing directly to the States General of the Dutch Republic. He had the support of many of the colonists. He knew the law and had the ability to function in the administrative world. Most of all, he had the willfulness to put up a fight. If anybody could do it, he could.

While all this was playing itself out in the courts of New Netherland, Melyn's recent return from the Dutch Republic ignited the fuse that lit the cannon fire. Following the drama of the shipwreck, Melyn and Kuyter had made their way to the Dutch Republic with nothing but the shirts on their backs and the few papers they had managed to drag from the sea. After all they had been through, and without Kieft to oppose them, they were more intent than ever on having their appeal heard. When they finally made it to The Hague and succeeded in submitting their petition, the committee for West India affairs was tasked with examining their reports. Based on the committee's recommendation, the States General granted a provisional appeal, finding that no offense had been committed. "On the contrary," they wrote, "it seems that the Petitioners had aimed at nothing in their writings other than the public good."[16] This action suspended Stuyvesant's sentences against them pending further investigation. While Kuyter remained in the Dutch Republic for the time being, the judgment allowed them both to return to their properties in New Netherland, to be left "free and unhindered."[17] Part of the investigation would involve hearing Stuyvesant's side of the story, of course, and in a very official sense. A judicial writ in the form of a mandamus was issued, commanding Stuyvesant or his attorneys to appear before the States General in The Hague to either defend or renounce the sentences against Melyn and Kuyter.[18] The mandamus could be served by "not only a messenger, marshal, notary, but by any other such person, public or private," of the petitioners' choosing.[19] It did not take Melyn long to decide that he would like to be present when it was served, though he may not have appreciated at the time that the rest of the community would be there to witness it.

On March 8, 1649, at a meeting in the church of more than three hundred persons of the commonalty, while Van der Donck was still in confinement and Stuyvesant was likely still stewing about how he could have let the whole idea of the delegation blow up in his face, the mandamus would be served. As Stuyvesant stood in the church watching Melyn, he slowly began to realize that he was being set up in front of the entire assembly. He finally asked Melyn if he would "now let the order be served," to which Melyn answered, "yes." On that cool spring morning it might have been possible to see the steam coming out of Stuyvesant's ears, as he reportedly grabbed the mandamus out of the server's hands such that that the seal of their High Mightinesses was left "hanging halfway to one sheet of the parchment."[20] Melyn readily gave his copy up to Stuyvesant while the original, which at least for the time being vindicated him and Kuyter, was read aloud in front of a church full of people. Watching in trepidation, they could have heard a pin drop, as the lower part of the seal fell irreverently to the floor.

On March 16, 1649, the very next day after Stuyvesant lifted Van der Donck's confinement and ordered him to substantiate the claims made in his journal notes, Van der Donck got to work. He began by putting his momentum behind Melyn's upcoming appeal, using the case as a springboard to gather evidence for his own arguments. His first action was to cast a wide net of summonses, as Melyn's representative, to the principals of Stuyvesant's administration, including his secretary and former Kieft sidekick Cornelis van Tienhoven, along with seven others. The orders demanded each of them appear in The Hague to testify in Melyn's case. Not surprisingly, they all refused on various grounds, ranging from costs that would not be covered to reasoning, simply, "this does not apply to me."[21] In April, public opinion lifted Van der Donck's cause even more as Stuyvesant became involved in a controversy over guns that he unlawfully, though purportedly on company orders, supplied to the Natives.[22]

Lastly, in a demand surely written by Van der Donck, but in Melyn's name, Stuyvesant was called on to defend himself in the case against Melyn, "if," the letter challenged, "there is yet some conscience."[23] Stuyvesant replied, by way of his own dig, in a document captioned, "Upon the irreverent protest of Cornelis Melyn, given to my Wife, as she says, by Adriaen van der Donck and A. Hardenbergh."[24] Apparently, instead of presenting the summons to Stuyvesant directly, Van der Donck had handed it to Stuyvesant's wife to pass along to her husband. Perhaps Van der Donck was operating under the mistaken assumption that he and his acquaintance with connections to Breda were still on good terms, notwithstanding his recent clashes involving her husband. But Stuyvesant's wife had obviously complained and Stuyvesant, himself, considered the gesture a personal affront that crossed a line. Besides that, he had no intention of leaving his post to appear in The Hague anyway, especially with, what he considered to be, so much unrest at hand. He would send his secretary, Van Tienhoven. The West India Company directors had chided Stuyvesant for getting involved in the first place with the problems provoked by Kieft, and they were not sympathetic that it had come to this.[25]

Van der Donck had been busy readying the documents for the delegation to the Dutch Republic. When it came time to formally choose the representatives that would go to The Hague, there was no question that he would be the choice to lead. The other two delegates would be Jacob van Couwenhoven, the son of one of the first inhabitants of New Netherland, and farmer Jan Evertsen Bout. The board of Nine Men produced a letter addressed to the "Great, Powerful, High and Mighty Sovereigns," for the purpose of introducing the delegates to the States General and to request they be given "a favorable audience."[26] The delegates also received an introduction letter from Vice Director Van Dincklagen, which gave the appearance of an earnest endorsement from the administration. "I cannot say but they intend what is right," he wrote, affirming them in another vote of confidence, as "thoroughly conversant with the situation of the country."[27] The Nine Men, including Van der Donck and the two other delegates, signed their formal complaint, the Remonstrance of the Deputies, on July 28, 1649. It was prefaced by a Petition of the Commonalty of New Netherland and detailed by the Additional Observations on the Preceding Petition, comprising, altogether, more than eighty pages of documentation. It looked as though Van Rensselaer's advice to Van der Donck about putting things in writing had sunk in.

As Stuyvesant's representative, Van Tienhoven left for the Dutch Republic sometime after August 10, 1649, the date noted on a letter he carried from Stuyvesant explaining his position against Melyn.[28] Melyn and the three delegates left two weeks later.[29] Van der Donck and Melyn were again shipmates, but this time, sailing in the opposite direction and allied more than ever under very different circumstances. Not that it was a competition, but because Van Tienhoven's ship was smaller and took a northerly route to avoid the same trouble as the *Prinses*, Van der Donck and Melyn, having left two weeks later but headed straight through the English Channel, reportedly got there first.[30]

11

The Remonstrance

Returning to the Dutch Republic must have kindled quite a contrast of emotions for Van der Donck. While it might have felt empowering to return to his old stomping grounds among the elite ranks of New World adventurers, he was not as unique a figure on this side of the Atlantic as he had become in his relatively tiny colonial outpost, and his land legs would have felt weak after the long voyage. The buzz of Amsterdam would have hit like a full sensory overload compared to the wide-open landscape he had become so accustomed to. At the same time, it must have been alternately both energizing and unnerving, after so much planning and anticipation, to be finally standing on the threshold of his long-awaited opportunity to appear before the highest level of government in the Dutch Republic.

The delegates had indeed made good time on their journey. Their letters, petitions, and remonstrance were hand delivered to the States General in The Hague on October 13, 1649, less than two months after leaving New Netherland, and only nine days after the ship arrived in the Dutch Republic.[1] The introductions they had brought from the board of Nine Men and Vice Director Van Dincklagen were accepted, along with their request that their "High Mightinesses be pleased to commit some members of your assembly" to examine their documents and to "hear the Petitioners verbally."[2] On that same day, the States General granted their request, referring the issue to their deputies for the affairs of the West India Company to inspect the documents, hear the delegates, and report back. In December, three other complaints about Stuyvesant were independently submitted to the States General and referred to the same committee for investigation. Two of these letters were from a baker and a carpenter, men without the education that would have enabled them to compose the protests submitted in their names, and decidedly aided, if not composed, by Van der Donck.[3]

Between October and January, the delegates from New Netherland made their presentations in meetings with the States General's committee on West India affairs. The Petition of the Commonalty and its detailed Additional Observations served as an introduction to the more formal Remonstrance, meticulously and dramatically setting forth the case of the "very poor and most low condition" of the colony.[4] The arguments framed the problems as the products of a progression of management mistakes, blaming the colony's misfortunes on unsuitable government by the West India Company in several enumerated examples. For instance, it charged that a lack of privileges and exemptions that continually changed to suit the administration discouraged colonists. Moreover, heavy duties and inefficient inspections encumbered the import of goods. The documents criticized Kieft's War, deemed unnecessary and unjust, as having created tremendous losses for the colonists, and listed the sinking of the *Prinses* as a loss for the entire colony. They also pointed to illegal trade, a lack of farmers to produce food, and tentative relations with the much larger population of Natives as making New Netherland an uncertain destination for settlers.

In requesting resolution, the documents stressed the overarching conviction that New Netherland needed to be better populated. "Because in case this should fail," the petition argued, "not only will it fall into the utmost ruin, once and for all, but it will also be easily incorporated by our neighbors," meaning the English. This last sentence was footnoted, possibly out of apprehension, for the sake of emphasis, or even in a premonition, with the text, "It will also even lose the name of New Netherland, and no Dutchman will have anything to say there." In asking the States General to assist in populating New Netherland, the petitioners had thought through some practical recommendations. One was that the States General sponsor ships to bring farmers to the colony, even if the farmers would initially have to be supported with clothing and farming implements, which the petition listed in detail. Another was to require all Dutch ships trading in North America to first stop in Manhattan, since many passengers would, "without a doubt, shortly come to move to New Netherland." The petition also asked for permanent privileges for the colony, including a "suitable municipal government" and exemption from duties, at least until the country could establish itself since, it asserted, "the sheep cannot very well be shorn before they have wool." The municipal government, "somewhat similar to the

FIGURE 11.1. The Assembly of the States General, The
Hague. Courtesy of the Rijksmuseum, Amsterdam.

laudable government of our Fatherland," could be adapted to circumstances
there, it argued, "without entrusting it to a party of foolhardy persons, such as
the Company throws there." Interestingly, a brief description of the political
structure of New England was included here, as an example. Last but not least,
the petition requested protection, which included the setting of boundaries
between neighboring countries to maintain peace, and "to quarter here a
company or two of soldiers" for defense. Additionally, it cautioned that the
poor condition of the forts sent the message that the Dutch were not serious
about New Netherland, and in so doing, made fools of them. This "greatly
emboldens" the neighbors, it asserted, who "often laugh at us."[5]

The Remonstrance itself was the formal legal complaint against the
West India Company and its government in New Netherland. While the
introductory documents are thought to have been a collaborative effort, it

is generally accepted and almost certain that this was Van der Donck's work. Like a formula for a self-improvement book, the Remonstrance first aimed to persuade the States General that New Netherland was something the Dutch should want. Next, it argued that there was something standing in the way of what they wanted. Lastly, once it established that there was a problem keeping them from what they wanted, it offered a solution. Opening with a narrative of the events connected with the settlement of the colony, the Remonstrance began with a short description of how the Dutch first explored New Netherland, and how that determined the Dutch claim to it. As proof that the Dutch were the first Europeans in New Netherland, Van der Donck reported that when the Natives first saw Dutch ships, they did not know whether they "came down from Heaven or whether they were Devils," and some thought that Hudson's ship was possibly a sea monster.[6] As an additional attestation, he added that the Natives "knew of no other world or people" before the arrival of the Dutch.[7] Because of "the similarity of the climate, geographical situation, and fertility, this place is rightly called New Netherland," he declared.[8] A description of the land and waterways followed, showcasing New Netherland's resources, including its most valuable feature, "a fine wide river which drops into the Ocean at each end [and] provides a very suitable passage inside along the shores," with "a great abundance of good bays and other opportunities for anchor."[9] The land in New Netherland was usable in winter and summer, Van der Donck wrote, "with less labor and tilling than in Netherland," while producing several kinds of "abundant" timber.[10] Fruits grew successfully and were "drier, sweeter and more pleasant than in Netherland."[11] The domestic animals were similar to those at home, he assured, though the milk cows were even easier to keep than the Dutch, for, "most times, or as necessity demands, one only occasionally gives them a little hay."[12] Everything seemed to be better and more fantastic in New Netherland. The squirrels could even fly.[13] He also described the birds and fish as well as the minerals, and dedicated a section to the Natives, reporting on their physical appearance, dress, culture, and languages, acknowledging that much of the success of the settlement was owed to them and the "Fountain of all Goodness."[14]

After he was finished extolling the virtues of New Netherland, Van der Donck devoted the next section to a discussion of the boundaries, the assertion of Dutch ownership, and the problem of encroachment by other countries that the colony continually had to defend. The English had intruded on Cape Cod and Rhode Island, he reported, as well as much of Long Island, which they "greatly desire," having already taken "nearly half of New Netherland."[15] Protests by the Dutch have only been "mocked at," he wrote.[16] In Kievits Hook, now Saybrook Point, Connecticut, the arms of the States General had been affixed to a tree as a sign of possession, but the English had "cast them down, and engraved a ridiculous face in their place."[17] On top of the problems of trespassing by the English, the Swedes were intruding in areas around the South River, now Delaware. All of this was just a warm-up to the true "Reasons and Causes Why and How New Netherland has thus Declined."[18]

Van der Donck asserted "in one word" (though it was actually more than one word) that the reason for New Netherland's "low and ruinous condition" was "bad government, with its adherents and supporters," and that, from the start, the West India Company had prioritized profits over the country's well-being.[19] The several pages that followed reported specific transgressions that Van der Donck contended had cost the colony in population as well as progress. He also argued that fiscal matters, such as excessive taxation and costs, misuse of public funds, and unfavorable trade laws, were as much the fault of the directors in New Netherland as of the top level of West India Company administration in the Dutch Republic. The charges included almost every government inadequacy known to man, including a fundamental disregard for infrastructure, unnecessary expenditures, and even extending to such basics as a neglect for standards in weights, measures, and currencies. As a population, the colonists felt undefended by the fort, more like a "mole-hill or a dilapidated rampart," which did not contain "a single gun carriage" nor "a piece of cannon on a proper frame."[20] As individuals, the colonists were subjected to the abuse of power and excessive harshness by the directors, Van der Donck complained, noting that this disregard extended especially unjustly to the rights of manumitted slaves. Having gained their own freedom, "nevertheless, their children remain slaves," he wrote, "contrary to all public law."[21] The list went on and on, providing examples and details on every point. "It is impossible for us to relate how everything has happened," he submitted. "Whoever did not approve and affirm was watched, and when the opportunity arose, he was remembered."[22]

Finally, Van der Donck took direct aim at the administrations of Kieft and Stuyvesant. His complaints about Kieft were somewhat abbreviated by the fact that many of the issues caused by Kieft's administration were discussed in the earlier parts on mismanaged government, and because Kieft was gone. However, a major disservice, according to Van der Donck, was Kieft's erection of the church inside the fort, a location that "surely fits as well as a fifth wheel to a wagon."[23] The church blocked the wind from the town's grain mill, he claimed, being already "quite rotten" with only two arms left, which created a shortage of bread for lack of ground grain.[24] On top of that, the location inside the fort essentially gave the West India Company ownership of the church, even though it was paid for by the commonalty, Van der Donck complained. During the wedding of Reverend Bogardus' daughter, Kieft had, reportedly, "set to work around the fourth or fifth drink" to solicit and then drive up donations from the guests.[25] Additionally, he charged, Kieft behaved as a "sovereign" or supreme ruler over his team of administrators, who would not stand up to him, extending this behavior to prosecution of his adversaries, such as Van der Donck's father-in-law.[26]

Van der Donck saved his most pointed criticism for Stuyvesant, expressing his feelings explicitly in his opening sentence. "We truly wish to be done with this administration already," he began.[27] He complained that Stuyvesant, like Kieft, had also intimidated many of his own council, so that they dared not cross him. If any of the administrators objected to one of Stuyvesant's long, lengthy, written opinions, "which is not easy to do even if he is fairly exceptional," he admitted, Stuyvesant would erupt into a rage, and "such an uproar that it is dreadful."[28] He described each of Stuyvesant's council as under his thumb in one way or another, taking exception with Vice Director Van Dincklagen, who occasionally protested as in the case of his arrest, and who had supported the delegation to the States General.

Van der Donck also related the stories of Stuyvesant's treatment of Melyn and Kuyter as part of the Eight Men, and of his own treatment as part of the board of Nine Men tasked with garnering help from the Fatherland. He questioned Stuyvesant's business dealings, citing his sale of arms to the Natives while forbidding others to do so under threat of gallows.[29] Similarly, he reported, Stuyvesant was quick to use any excuse to seize property, especially from ships entering New Netherland. This had diverted trade and raised prices, since "not a ship dares to come here" from the West Indies or Caribbean Islands for fear of confiscation, instead, stopping in Boston to unload.[30] And Stuyvesant continued to seek uncollected debts leftover from Kieft's administration, he contended, from those very people who had lost everything in the war that Kieft started. Van der Donck took the opportunity of the topic of war to, again, point out that the problems were coming from the top. The West India Company's lack of attention to the distress of Kieft's War "can clearly testify that the directors then never considered whether New Netherland sank or swam," and, at the very least, "never even examined the reason and direct cause of the war."[31] They "fall far too short," he concluded, "in the protection that they owe the country."[32]

Van der Donck had exceptionally harsh words for Secretary Van Tienhoven, who would be answering for Stuyvesant on the matters regarding his administration. He described him as "prudent, shrewd, intelligent,

sharp-witted—good gifts when used rightly." He acknowledged that
Van Tienhoven, as one of the people who had been in New Netherland
the longest, understood both the Dutch and the Natives. He found Van
Tienhoven's judgment to be lacking, however. "With the Natives, he has
even run around like a Native, with a little piece of cloth around him and
a loincloth in front, for love of the prostitutes to whom he has always been
strongly inclined." One could argue that what people do in their free time is
their own business, but apparently Van Tienhoven was not respected at work,
either. "In his words and dealings he is crafty, contrary, deceitful, and lying,
who promises everyone, and when it then comes to getting it done, no one
is home," Van der Donck wrote. The Natives, as well as many Dutch, blamed
Van Tienhoven for instigating the war, convinced that Kieft was "misled by
his false reports and lies."[33] With the responsibility for the war ascribed to Van
Tienhoven, the prevailing belief was that there would be no peace while he
was still in the country.

In the short, somewhat hasty last section of the Remonstrance, Van der
Donck offered his solution, or "In What Manner New Netherland Should Be
Redressed." If he had felt at all intimidated or that he was being presumptuous
as a young, relative commoner speaking before the High Mightinesses, it
did not show. He summarily and blatantly concluded that New Netherland
would never "flourish" under the current government but, rather, "come to
an end," without any benefit to the West India Company, suggesting that it
would better for everyone if the company would "dismiss itself from it." He
added a few other specific recommendations, such as providing the country
with stable clergy, a public school, asylums for the aged and orphaned, and
last but not least, honorable and intelligent rulers. Sagely proclaiming, "Good
population should rightly follow good government," he segued back, finally,
ending with one last push for encouraging population.[34]

Alongside the comprehensive and detailed written reports of the Petition
of the Commonalty, the Additional Observations, and the Remonstrance itself,
the delegates had also brought a show of specimens from New Netherland.
Harvest samplings as well as various animal peltries were displayed as a
demonstration of the country's bounty.[35] As a powerful, lasting visual piece
of their presentation, they also produced a map of New Netherland, likely
drawn by Augustin Herman, a cartographer and one of the Nine Men who
had signed the Remonstrance.[36] This "complete map of the country" was a
perceptible attestation of the enormity of the land in question and, at the
same time, imparted a clear sense of the proximity of neighboring countries
as a reminder of the threat encroachment.[37] The map would later be reprinted
many times over as an enduring legacy of the colony. Scholars have suggested

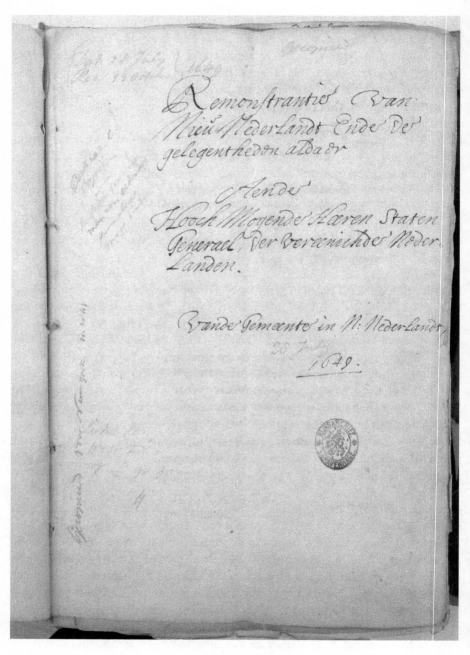

FIGURE 11.2. The Remonstrance, Notarial copy, 1649.
Nationaal Archief, The Hague.

that a hand-drawn sketch of the colony dating to the summer of 1648, only relatively recently recognized as New Amsterdam, was also brought for the presentation, used to illustrate the low condition of the colony.[38] The dating of this rough drawing coincides with the decision of the original Nine Men to send a delegation to *patria*, "over a year" before the Remonstrance was signed in August 1649, and pointing to the summer after the loss of the *Prinses* drove the colonists' hope to an all-time low.[39] The sketch of Manhattan, as viewed from the water, indeed depicted a somber view of the settlement and fort, including the two-armed windmill.[40]

Van der Donck must have felt purged of a lot of the pent-up frustration that had been mounting inside of him in the months leading up to this event. He had laid out his arguments to the best of his ability, in acute detail, "for the love of the country and of the truth."[41] Much was on the line, not just for the future of the colony, but for Van der Donck personally. If his protests were successful in ousting the current administration, he stood to gain a place in the leadership of New Netherland as one of the few patroon holders. No matter how confident he might have felt at this juncture, however, he may have been overly optimistic. The West India Company had yet to weigh in. And regardless of how much truth there may have been to his complaints, he was likely naïve to the binding history between the West India Company and the States General that had been negotiated before the company's ships first set sail in the Atlantic. While the West India Company had been patented as a merchant trading company, it had largely acted as a paramilitary arm of the Dutch Republic, intercepting Spanish, Portuguese, and English concerns in the Atlantic, for Dutch dominance, under the auspices of trade. Peace with Spain had finally been concluded two years earlier and had made the military a less pressing priority while bringing out differences in various political factions. It would remain to be seen how strong those allegiances still were and whether Van der Donck's argument would be compelling enough to break them.

12

The Response

On January 27, 1650, the two delegates, minus Van der Donck who was not at the meeting, delivered their "Abstract of the Excesses and Highly Injurious Neglect," an itemized summary of sixty-eight grievances described in the Remonstrance, to the committee of the States General, to which the West India Company was asked to respond.[1] The answer to the brief, which had been "placed in the hands of the Directors," came just four days later. Though it was signed by three members of the Amsterdam Chamber of the West India Company, the reply was obviously conceived by someone with knowledge of the history and problems of the colony, and it was in Secretary Van Tienhoven's handwriting.[2] The response addressed each of the sixty-eight points with cool and calm resolve, in contrast to the Remonstrance's dramatically styled accusations. Regarding the manipulation of exemptions, the company's response was, "the Exemptions have never been changed without the knowledge of your High Mightinesses," challenging, "show who had their sights set on their own private profit."[3] As an explanation of the circumstances surrounding Kieft's erection of the church, it countered, "The church was erected in the fort for satisfactory reasons," adding, "the church cost far over 8,000 guilders, toward which it will not be proved that the community paid eight hundred guilders."[4] At least as far as the location is concerned, De Vries mentions, in his 1655 journal, that he recommended the church be built inside the fort for security. The West India Company response continued. To the charge of Stuyvesant's harshness, the answer was, "The Directors have never heard that the Director spoke maliciously to those members who treated him respectfully."[5] And to the criticism against him, personally, Van

Tienhoven wrote, "As to the slanders against Secretary Van Tienhoven, he is prepared to answer to the petitioners if their High Mightinesses deem it necessary."[6] The responses, understandably defensive and discernibly half-hearted, were prefaced by an admonition for the "said Delegates, as they entitle themselves," for bringing up their complaints of neglect directly with the States General, "if any happened," instead of first going to the West India Company directors.[7]

Van der Donck moved quickly to counter the West India Company rebuttal. On February 7, 1650, he submitted another petition to the States General, accusing some of the company directors, for whom Van Tienhoven had spoken, of "letting themselves be swayed prematurely," or rushing to judgment, "to criminate and countermine the actions of the Remonstrants, as they are generally accustomed to doing."[8] He reiterated the charge of bad government in New Netherland as the sole cause of its predicament, citing the proof previously presented, which he considered as evident "as the sun on a clear noon-day."[9] He defended the delegates' direct appeal to the States General, reminding them that previous pleas for help to the West India Company had gone unheeded. He also took the opportunity to ask for Van Tienhoven's removal and, once again, to favor the country with "a good civil government."[10] With a motion presupposing that this was all but wrapped up, he then moved in to ask outright for a swift and favorable decision, suggesting, "the spring is at hand, and the time for preparation approaches daily, and the representatives are here at great expense."[11] The very next day, Cornelis Melyn added pressure by submitting a petition complaining of Stuyvesant's behavior during the serving of the mandamus in Manhattan and asking for expeditious resolution of his appeal.[12] Melyn's petition, in the Van der Donck style, was, of course, part of the arsenal Melyn was still building for his defense. However, it also undeniably served as another stab at Stuyvesant by Van der Donck.

Van Tienhoven and the representatives of the West India Company put together another report, not exactly backpedaling on what Van Tienhoven had written earlier but supplying some practical information, possibly in a more serious attempt to mitigate the damage that the delegates were inflicting with their accusations. The document provided a West India Company, mostly Van Tienhoven, view of the boundaries of New Netherland and a provisional plan for trade and colonization, including information about available land and the necessary supplies for settlement.[13] At about the same time, the delegates submitted their observations on the duties imposed on goods sent to New Netherland, comparing and contrasting the advantages and disadvantages of continuing, reducing, or abolishing duties under the current system.[14]

The West India Company representatives were keeping Stuyvesant abreast of the delegates' activities in the Dutch Republic and telling him how they really felt. In February, after the flurry of paperwork and demonstrations by the delegates, the directors of the Amsterdam Chamber wrote to Stuyvesant about Melyn, Van der Donck, and the others, who "seem to leave nothing untried, pretending that they suffered under too heavy a yoke."[15] Further, they informed him, "Secretary Van Tienhoven will undoubtedly give you a detailed account of how Cornelis Melyn and his companion," meaning Van der Donck, "have tried here to affront the company and you, and how we have prevented it," adding, "if we did not restrain their absurdities, they would cause us a great deal of trouble."[16]

While Van der Donck was waiting for the States General to make their move to turn New Netherland around, he was doing what more he could to take matters into his own hands by trying to drum up immigrants for New Netherland. He had his Remonstrance published as a pamphlet, under the title *Vertoogh van Nieu-Neder-Land, Wegens de Geleghentheydt, Vruchtbaerheydt, en Soberen Staet desselfs*, or, *Remonstrance of New Netherland, Concerning Its Location, Fruitfulness, and Sorry Condition*. Pamphlets, popular at the time for the dissemination of political viewpoints, were an affordable format for publications and very accessible to the literate population of the Dutch Republic. With more than a thousand printers and booksellers in Amsterdam alone, the seventeenth-century Dutch Republic dominated the European print industry with its many presses and publishers.[17] And while the *Vertoogh* was discouraging about the conditions of the country, the account nevertheless must have made New Netherland seem exotic and enticing, literally a world away. The drama the colony had experienced, told in the richness of Van der Donck's impassioned verbiage, gave New Netherland an almost instant celebrity status. Even the West India Company directors were taken aback by all the fuss it created. "Formerly New Netherland was never spoken of and now heaven and earth seem to be stirred up by it," they wrote in their communication to Stuyvesant.[18] Van der Donck also had the map he had brought engraved to serve as an accompaniment to the publication, its detailed landmarks matching the written text.[19] There was no denying the vastness of the visual representation of New Netherland on the map, something that words could not convey. The map included an inset view of New Amsterdam, taken from the delegates' original somber, hand-drawn sketch, and embellished to look successful and inviting.[20] Interestingly, another pamphlet critical of the West India Company, *Breeden-Raedt*, or *Broad Advice*, had been published a year earlier in Antwerp, Melyn's hometown. Its format differed considerably from that of *Vertoogh*, as a fictitious conversation between a group of men at sea, addressing West India Company policies in other holdings, such as Brazil, but it contained much information about Melyn's plight. The work has been largely accredited to Melyn, though some historians believe its mysterious authorship, "I.A. G.W.C.," could refer, in part, to English merchant Isaac Allerton living in New Netherland, or even a professional pamphleteer. The possibility of Van der Donck's influence has been raised, however, also justifiably discounted by some historians because of its very different style of writing.[21]

The publication of Van der Donck's *Vertoogh* attracted the interest he was hoping for, and he wasted no time in acting on it. In a March 1650 petition to the States General's committee, the delegates directed attention to the need for more passenger ships to New Netherland. The petition included an attestation by the captain of the ship, *De Valckenier*, soon to be leaving for New Netherland, that while he had agreed to transport as many people as possible, he had had to reject about thirty others seeking passage.[22] In fact, the petition read, optimistically, if there had been "six times more accommodations or ships, they would all be filled."[23] A week later, Van der Donck and the two other delegates drafted an agreement with the West India Company to charter a *fluytschip* for the purpose of conveying two hundred passengers to New Netherland, "to go to sea before the first of June."[24] One hundred of those immigrating would be farmers and farm servants and the other hundred "conversant with agriculture."[25]

FIGURE 12.1. Inset view of New Amsterdam. Courtesy of the Maritiem Museum Rotterdam.

In mid-March, with this abrupt focus on New Netherland, the States General suddenly seemed to be positioning themselves to make some decisions. Messages went out to the various West India Company chambers requesting that they send representatives to The Hague to confer "on the whole subject of New Netherland."[26] The requests sounded urgent, concluding with the terse command, "wherein fail not."[27] Momentum was on Van der Donck's side. The actions of Kieft in the war, he wrote during this period, "are damned here by the whole world."[28] "The West India Company directors try to defend Stuyvesant and Van Tienhoven," he added, but, "they themselves, except for a few, are not in much esteem but are regarded with suspicion so their actions will not mean much."[29]

On April 1, 1650, the States General dismissed the other delegates, Jacob van Couwenhoven and Jan Evertsen Bout, to return home to New Netherland, while Van der Donck stayed behind to follow through on their objectives. The delegates would be sent back along with two hundred guns for distribution among the colonists for their defense.[30] In their dismissal, the States General sent notice to Stuyvesant that required he neither "investigate nor harass these said persons . . . over matters that may have been presented here."[31] More complaints about Stuyvesant had been coming in from New Netherland. The delegates submitted two letters describing his latest offenses, "as it goes from bad to worse here," one wrote.[32] Stuyvesant had provoked the Danish crown by confiscating one of its ships, the letters reported, then

vangen huys F. de H. Generaels huys G. t'Gerecht H. de Kaeck I. Compagnies Pachuys K. Stadts Herberch

used the ship to export twenty much-needed horses to Barbados, along with a good part of the colony's winter provisions.[33]

On April 11, 1650, after months of negotiation, the committee of the States General on the affairs of New Netherland issued its findings, along with a "Provisional Order over the Government, Conservation, and Population of New Netherland." Without taking the colony completely out of the hands of the West India Company, the committee's twenty-one directives represented marked reform, passing over several points of the Remonstrance for the time being "to deal with the principal issues." It began with a condemnation and call for investigation into Kieft's War. It also addressed topics such as outlawing the sale of contraband weapons, providing for the maintenance of forts and fiscal investments, the examination of freedoms and exemptions, the structure of the administration, judicial powers of the Nine Men, and prioritizing increasing population. Most noticeably, Stuyvesant would be "summoned to come home to report," and the city of New Amsterdam would get a municipal government, similar to other cities in the Dutch Republic, which would include representation by the people.[34]

The West India Company was decidedly aggrieved. The Amsterdam chamber fired back that same day in a pointedly angry, intentionally vague response that, while not specifically in Van Tienhoven's name, seemed, again, to have had input from someone who knew New Netherland intimately. In answer to the recommendation on fiscal investments, the West India Company answered, "The intent of this article should be more clearly phrased in order to give it any consideration." As to the examination of freedoms and exemptions, it stated, "A particular proceeding has been applied to the piece about Freedoms, and could be approved by us when the copy thereof is shown." On the point of conveying passengers partially by private ships, they found it to be "impracticable and useless for the Company." And they considered the recall of Stuyvesant "entirely useless, unless some reasons to the contrary were alleged." The message was clear that the West India Company felt highly insulted that the States General's committee would rule against it, and that they should not be meddling with its business. Furthermore, it wanted nothing to do with the delegates, whose assistance in support of population was recommended by the committee, "as these people have risen up against the Company and its administrators, they are not capable of being able to contribute anything to the population and the advancement of it."[35]

On the contrary, getting the Provisional Order and winning the support of the States General over the West India Company appeared to embolden Van der Donck. While he officially praised the States General's committee for their "highly commendable zeal," in their resolution for New Netherland, he took their support one step further. He asked the committee to investigate Van Tienhoven's part in Kieft's War, using his earlier interrogatories, "not out of any particular intent I might have against Secretary Cornelis van Tienhoven," he assured them, "but that Your Noble Mightinesses could use it as a basis of investigation on the original cause of the country's ruin." He rationalized that, if Van Tienhoven would go back to New Netherland without answering for his part in the conflict, the colonists would lose faith in any hope of change and it might "completely take away the spirit of the residents there." While this may have been true, the questioning was hardly aimed at discovery, for Van der Donck's plan left no way out for Van Tienhoven. If he would answer the questions truthfully, he should be condemned, Van der Donck reasoned. But if he should "obstinately and shamelessly deny the truth," or obscure the truth with "double-meaning or indirect answers," Van der Donck would be ready to provide documentation through which Van Tienhoven would be "fully convicted of notorious falsehoods in his evasions."[36]

Van der Donck was surely thinking ahead to ensure a smooth transition into the leadership of New Netherland. Complaints coming from New Netherland accused Stuyvesant of failing to advertise the recent peace treaty with Spain, while bypassing his council in holding the "prizes," or captured ships, of West Indies plunders. He wasted no time in asking the States General to assert that the commissions of Vice Director Van Dincklagen and the board of Nine Men "remain in full force."[37] They agreed, even providing a letter to go on the ship along with the two departing delegates, ordering Stuyvesant to proclaim the peace in New Netherland and endorsing the commissions of the vice director and board of Nine Men, "until we shall have made other dispositions therein."[38] A few days later, Van der Donck penned a letter to Johannes de La Montagne, the physician councilor he had known since his days in Rensselaerswyck when they had sat together with Kieft in peace negotiations. In what seemed to be an attempt to shore up backing for his return to New Netherland, especially with those like La Montagne who might be on the fence with their political allegiance, Van der Donck assured him that he would be "included in a good position" in the new government, "which we expect shortly," and suggested he "join ranks with the complainants."[39] Although he appeared confident in his petitions for restitution of New Netherland, Van der Donck seemed to face more uncertainty than his self-assured attitude let on. "Many difficulties happened to us in the soliciting process," he acknowledged, "but we hope that the Lord God will direct everything for the better."[40]

While they stood by Stuyvesant, the West India Company directors were not pleased when they broke the news to him about Van der Donck's success, maintaining that the delegates "had known how to give their propositions such an appearance that a number of mature minds have been deceived."[41] They included a copy of the Provisional Order in their communication, warning, "You may judge by it how much trouble we have had and how dangerous it is to draw upon yourself the wrath of a community. We suppose that you have trusted too much in some of these ringleaders or become too familiar with them."[42] Stuyvesant wrote his own answer to the States General's recommendations, agreeing to abide by their decision, but also pointing out that, should there be lack of proof to condemn him, the accuser would go without reprimand. "It pains us, therefore," Stuyvesant wrote, without naming names (but mostly meaning Van der Donck), "that former pretending friends who, on their departure and setting out from this place, freely and unsolicited thanked us as their father, swearing with an oath, as well to our face as behind our back, that they had nothing either against us or against our government . . . should afterwards, when contradicting their own oath and conscience, not be obliged to answer legally for their [slanderous] and unfounded accusations."[43] The West India Company directors also expressed their disappointment to Stuyvesant in the matter of Melyn, who had won permission to return to New Netherland with protection from harassment, although, they admitted, "we must confess that the evidence, brought over by your attorney, is rather shaky."[44]

Apparently, Melyn and Van der Donck had also managed to annoy the company directors in Amsterdam when they partnered to ship goods back to New Netherland on the ship *De Nieu Nederlantse Fortuyn*. Initially, they had requested, and were granted, exemption from duties on the grounds that the goods were for agricultural purposes.[45] But when it came time for the cargo to be loaded, their agricultural goods turned out to be more than just farm implements. "By now these farmers have suddenly been transformed into merchants," the directors wrote, and demanded they pay duty.[46] Indeed, cargo in Van der Donck's name included three hundred pounds of pepper, twenty pounds of cinnamon, and ten *anckers* of brandy, better for trading than for farming.[47] Van der Donck and Melyn had apparently argued "if they were to export cattle from here, they would pay no duty on it and that they intended to invest the proceeds of the sale of these goods in cattle there, which amounted to the same (as if they had exported cattle)."[48] The directors were not amused by their reasoning but agreed to declare the agricultural goods free of duty, asking Stuyvesant to "please pay attention that the interest of the Company does not suffer beyond our good intentions, when the goods are discharged."[49] Evidently, Van der Donck and Melyn had refused even this reasonable offer.[50]

The momentum carrying the changes forward for New Netherland unexpectedly stalled over the summer. Political problems within the Dutch Republic took the States General's attention in a conflict with Prince Willem II of Orange over plans to reduce his army in favor of naval fortification.[51] The political repercussions of this administrative divide indirectly affected support for New Netherland. One of the proponents of change in New Netherland and an influential backer of the delegates was Alexander van der Capellen, who sometimes chaired the committee for West India affairs. He was also the brother of Hendrick van der Capellen, who had granted the earlier appeal for Melyn and Kuyter and had likely heard the delegates' arguments early on in Gelderland. And the Van der Capellen brothers might have also initially been instrumental in facilitating the delegates' access to the States General, in a political alignment not uncommon for maneuvering through Dutch administrative networks.[52] However, as a strong ally of Prince Willem II, Alexander van der Capellen lost his sway in the government when the prince's resistance failed, greatly diminishing any power he had to push the delegates' agenda forward.[53] In the politics of the seventeenth-century Dutch Republic, so much depended on who you knew, and your relationships within the various political factions. Moreover, many decisions were made at the committee level, such as the one sometimes chaired by Van der Capellen, before issues were even passed on to the larger administrative body of the States General.[54] It was no coincidence that Van der Donck's agenda seemed to leap forward whenever the Van der Capellens were in The Hague.[55] Van der Donck had made good use of the avenues within his reach in his own political maneuvering, employing "the three P's" that have been associated with seventeenth-century lobbying—personal connections, petitions, and pamphlets.[56]

In late summer, Van Couwenhoven and Evertsen Bout, back in New Netherland and part of the, now, "Select Men of New Amsterdam," wrote a letter to the States General in an attempt to keep the matter warm, reporting that the "distressed state of this country remains unchanged—except by [going] from bad to worse," and asking again for action.[57] However, it would be November before the States General picked up the business again, finally reading Van der Donck's full Remonstrance at their meeting and then requesting another West India Company response. Just as it had done in the earlier complaints, Van Tienhoven's answer refuted almost every charge.[58] He and the West India Company refused to budge on their position that the accusations were all false, or even hint at a compromise. Between one thing and another, the Provisional Order still hung in limbo, neither scrapped nor upheld, and along with it, the success of the delegation and Van der Donck's future.

13

The Backlash

Van der Donck's political partners in New Netherland had continued to provide him with updates on conditions in New Netherland, mostly mounting complaints against Stuyvesant, followed by renewed requests to the States General asking for approval of the Provisional Order. He was collecting the letters and declarations from New Netherland as ammunition for his case, however the reports were extremely discouraging. Stuyvesant had been acting unilaterally without consulting the Select Men, they alleged, in seizing ships for harbor duties, selling guns to the Natives, and secretly negotiating on borders with New England. He was harassing the Select Men, even to the point of taking down their pews in the church.[1] Stuyvesant and his administration were putting their own political spin on the situation, they said, confident in their positions and unafraid of any change in government. Dissent was mocked with the challenge, "Go complain to the States."[2] They had heard that the West India Company directors had told the States General that New Netherland belonged to them exclusively, and that they would support Stuyvesant "unto blood."[3] The administration also reportedly maintained it had been instructed to disregard any protections or passports issued by the States General, which would leave the returning complainants open to harassment. The States General's reluctance to confirm the proposed changes was hurting the colonists' morale. Furthermore, the letters reported that the West India Company in Amsterdam was seeking support from the Amsterdam *burgemeesters*, influential municipal leaders, in opposing the redress. It was difficult to know what was truth and what was rumor. There was even a story that Van Tienhoven would be returning with troops, causing fears of another war with the Natives.[4] To say that anxiety over a redress was high would be an understatement. By himself in The Hague, Van der Donck had to deal with this collective disquiet, in addition to any apprehension of his own that he was probably feeling. If his confidence was not shaken at this point, it would have been a wonder. He must have felt the weight of the world, or at least that of New Netherland, on his shoulders, although this might have served to strengthen his resolve. He was the only one in a position to speak for the colonists, and they were clearly counting on him. It had gone beyond his desire, and become his purpose, to stand up for himself and for the people of New Netherland. The pressure was on him to continue the fight.

In January 1651, Van der Donck renewed his push in another petition to the States General, "praying that a speedy and necessary redress may be concluded in regard to the affairs on New Netherland."[5] This time, the States General responded by ordering Van Tienhoven to finally answer the interrogatories. The West India Company had indeed secured the backing of the Amsterdam *burgemeesters* in its opposition to the proposed redress, and the States General might have felt they needed more solid evidence now that it appeared the West India Company was gearing up for a fight, or at the very least, needed a proper investigation. On the other hand, perhaps they were stalling, hoping Van der Donck would eventually give up or go home, and the whole conflict could be avoided. Van Tienhoven, for his part, was not amenable to this latest intrusion. Apparently, he had been a little distracted, busy entertaining a new fiancée and preparing to take her back with him to New Netherland. The only problem, however, was that he already had a wife and family there, awaiting his return.[6] The States General sent a more serious order summoning Van Tienhoven to appear and, by April, after still receiving no answer and amid rumors that he intended to depart, they instructed the West India Company to prevent him from leaving, pending their consent.[7] On May 5, 1651, Van Tienhoven managed to leave for New Netherland anyway, with his fiancée, without answering the interrogatories and in default of the States General's orders. It appears that the West India Company had not made much of an effort to keep Van Tienhoven off their ships. This had to have put the credibility of the West India Company directors in question as they allowed their representative to go AWOL in an adulterous escape. At the same time, the fact that they did not detain Van Tienhoven also amounted to a show of denial that they were interested in cooperating with the States General's investigation. It looked like the West India Company's passive-aggressive tactics, aimed at putting up enough hurdles to block the whole affair, might be working.

June and August documents place Van der Donck in Breda with family over the summer of 1651, as he assisted his mother in legal matters involving the transfer of his grandmother's properties.[8] His wife had joined him at some point and, if she was there by now, this may have been another impetus for him to spend time with family in the relative calm of Breda, away from the volatility of his agenda in The Hague. He continued to receive news from New Netherland throughout the fall as the situation seemed to deteriorate there. Apparently, not only had Stuyvesant ignored the Select Men's nominations for the next council, the outgoing board reported being so fearful of his reprisals that they did not even dare to meet anymore. Van Dincklagen wrote to Van der Donck in Latin, reporting, "Our great Muscovy Duke goes on as usual, with something of the wolf; the older he gets the more inclined he is to bite."[9] Augustin Herman wrote that Van Tienhoven's young runaway mistress eventually took him to court in New Netherland when she found out he was married. That same letter conveyed news that concerned Van der Donck's own livelihood, informing him, "Further, your private property is in disarray, for our enemies know how to arrange all this and to reach their objective."[10] Another letter concluded, dispiritedly, "I dare not to write anymore. I entrust matters to God."[11]

Van der Donck's purpose had not faded away. Finally, in February 1652, he summed up the events of the past two years in an unusually concise letter to the States General, beginning with the drafting of the resolutions in 1650 and describing the continuous opposition that the colonists had been met with in New Netherland. Van der Donck wanted to go home. He ended his letter with one last request that the States General formally approve the new government, so that he could leave "with the first ships this spring . . . being able to provide your High Mightinesses' good resolution, and give report of his commission to the relief and encouragement of the community there."[12] Within a week, the States General's committee, in a report by Van der Capellen, requested evidence from Van der Donck in his complaints about Stuyvesant. It also requested an explanation of boundary changes to support an assertion by Van der Donck that Stuyvesant had ceded too much prime land in negotiations with the English.[13] It looked as if the committee finally wanted to move on the changes, once and for all. Van der Donck was more than happy to turn over all the letters he had collected in the past year and a half, for exactly this purpose, as well as testimonials supporting the charges he had been making as the lone face of the protests. The States General's committee sent the Provisional Order of Government, now almost two years old, to the various West India Company chambers for their opinions, "the sooner the better."[14]

The opinions that rolled in from the various chambers were not helpful in offering a united path to a solution. Some agreed with the changes, while others deferred to other chambers, and one simply took the opportunity to expose rivalries within the organization. All of them were careful, however, to stake a claim for their own share in whatever happened with New Netherland. Not surprisingly, the most vocal opinion came from the Amsterdam Chamber, as the directors there expressed, perhaps feigning, surprise at seeing the draft provisions brought up again. As far as they were concerned, they had already given their opinion when the issue first came up almost two years earlier and had conferred on the matter on various occasions since then. By now, they assumed that the States General had dismissed the matter as "the unfounded complaints of the Delegates and ill-affected Committee of some malcontents in New Netherland," and they had considered it "disposed of."[15] In April, however, "to stop the mouth of all the world," the West India Company directors gave approval for Stuyvesant to establish "a bench of justice formed as much as possible after the common laws of this city," entailing a municipal government that would include representation from the citizens.[16] While the idea for a bench of justice appears to have been proposed earlier by Stuyvesant and his council, it has been argued that this interaction prompted the West India Company decision for the approval.[17] Granted, a precedent for small benches of justice had already been established in New Netherland, mostly on Long Island. Additionally, Stuyvesant's self-appointed council, the one he had chosen himself after ignoring the previous board's nominations, would roll into the new government positions, minimizing conflict.[18] Contextually, however, the directive for "one *schout*, two *burgemeesters*, and five *schepens*" follows a discussion of what the West India Company considered its civility toward the New Netherland complainants, eventually conceding, "nevertheless, in order to stop the mouth of all the world."[19] In other words, it was Van der Donck's persistence that paid off. The citizens of New Amsterdam would finally get a voice in their own government.

The West India Company's attempt to circumvent the renewed attention on the issues of New Netherland did not convince the States General to drop the matter. By now, Van der Donck's report on the boundary changes had been reviewed, as well as the multiple letters he had submitted, detailing complaints from the colonists. The shenanigans of Stuyvesant's spokesman, Van Tienhoven, had left a lingering bad taste, and the boundary questions had caused yet additional misgivings. Perhaps they finally wanted to hear from Stuyvesant personally. On April 27, 1652, the States General resolved to recall Stuyvesant to The Hague, to report on the circumstances, "the true and actual condition of the country," and on the boundaries between the

English and the Dutch.[20] The letter recalling Stuyvesant would be sent to New Netherland in the hands of Adriaen van der Donck, to be delivered personally to the director.

Van der Donck must have felt elated as he was finally able to begin preparations to return home. He secured a distinctive status from the States General for his property at Colendonck, giving him the right to determine the heirs to his estate, whether family or others.[21] He contracted with servants willing to go abroad to work on his property. Apparently, his enthusiasm for New Netherland had been contagious. A few months earlier, his mother, Agatha van Bergen, had begun making serious preparations to immigrate with her son to New Netherland and sold the meadow property near Breda she had inherited from her grandfather. In early May, she sold her other property, De Tolhuys, in Breda.[22] Van der Donck's father, Cornelis, had already decided to go to New Netherland previously, in the summer of 1650, after the issuance of the draft Provisional Order. At the time, he gave a power of attorney to his son "to manage his affairs during his voyage and absence," though he appears in the records of New Netherland only much later.[23] On May 4, 1652, Agatha van Bergen, Anna van der Donck, Adriaen van der Donck, and Mary Doughty officially signed out of the Markendaalse Kerk, or the Kleine Kerk, in Breda.[24] All the plans he had worked so hard for seemed to be finally coming together. On May 13, 1652, with his goods and people already embarked, waiting on the ship in Texel, Van der Donck applied for dismissal with the clause *de non offendendo*, protection from harassment, and to be reinstated as the President of the Commonalty.[25] This time, however, the politically powerful Lords of Holland, representatives of the most dominant province in the Dutch Republic, and largely funded by the city of Amsterdam, asked to weigh in on the request. The States General deferred. It would cast a very long shadow onto Van der Donck's newfound moment in the sun.

Van der Donck's preparations had given him only a glimpse of the work ahead. As he had helped ready his family for the trip, along with the sorely needed workers he had recruited to restore his neglected estate, his mind was surely filled with imaginings. He would have been fantasizing, not just about being back home in New Netherland, but also about the changes in the new government. As he finalized his last pieces of business in the Dutch Republic, he knew that, like his first voyage, the documents tucked into his coat pocket would be his ticket to an auspicious new life. What he did not yet know, however, was that as soon as the West India Company directors received notice of the seemingly sudden recall of Stuyvesant, they had set to work to reverse it.

With the ships in Texel poised to depart for New Netherland, the directors had penned a hurried letter to Stuyvesant apprising him of the situation.
They made it clear that they would argue the recall on the grounds that it
was done without their knowledge and, therefore, "contrary to the Charter,"
which stated that matters of this sort should be referred to their assembly.[26] They ordered him to await their further instructions before returning.
"We hope and trust in the meantime," they wrote, "to educate their High
Mightinesses, who have been poorly informed, and to bring about that the
said resolution is dismissed."[27] More critically, they also sent Jacob Pergens
of the West India Company's Amsterdam chamber to The Hague to lobby
support for their argument. The morning of May 16, 1652, a small force
of representatives from the States of Holland, along with *burgemeesters* from
Amsterdam, managed to campaign successfully against the States General's
decision, on the basis that it required their approval.[28] In the middle of their
communication to Stuyvesant, evidently, the West India Company directors
received, "cito," or promptly, notice that the States General had agreed to revoke the recall.[29] Later, the Amsterdam Chamber of the West India Company
offered its humble thanks to the States General, assuring them that their resolution prevented "the disorders and confusion" that the recall "would have
likely generated and escalated in New Netherland."[30]

Just three days after he thought that his business with the States General
had been neatly wrapped up and that he would be on his way back to New
Netherland as President of the Commonalty, Van der Donck was ordered to
surrender the recall letter.[31] Seemingly overnight, it looked like he would
go back empty handed, with no immediate relief in sight from Stuyvesant,
and little to show for the two and a half years he had spent away from
home, working to improve the conditions in the colony. At that moment,
he probably felt things could not get any worse. Except that they could.
As he readied to make his way home with all his belongings, his family,
friends, and new employees, he was informed that the directors of the West
India Company Amsterdam Chamber had forbidden their skippers to let
him aboard their ships.

While the actions initiated by Pergens were arguably a primary cause in
overturning the recall of Stuyvesant, some historians have put forth a different event that, while possibly secondary, certainly has broad implications.[32] At
the same time that Van der Donck was being labeled a risk, the stability in
New Netherland was being threatened by a different but real event, which,
on the surface, did not seem to have anything to do with him. However, it
would be hard to ignore that the very day that Van der Donck presented his
petition for dismissal, the States General was in secret deliberations regarding

a treaty with England. A particular sticking point was the limit on trade that the English held up in their territories abroad. The States General had warned that the ambassadors "shall be careful," in their negotiations, urging them to use "all imaginable reasons and arguments" on the issue of trade access that the English would not concede.[33] The situation was tense. The thought of a possible war with England, whose territories flanked the Dutch colony, might have been on the minds of the States General as they faced the West India Company's formidable maneuvering over Stuyvesant's recall. Though they had come to the aid of the West India Company in its past financial troubles, they had also become dependent on the West India Company's fleet of warships to provide the lion's share of the republic's defense. They might have considered it a bad time for both a new government in New Netherland and a test of the West India Company's allegiance.

On May 24, 1652, Van der Donck presented an appeal to the States General's assembly. "Wholly disheartened and cast down," his heartfelt words reflected his state of disbelief at this cruel twist, as his whole world was crashing down around him. His petition described his position for the past two and a half years in his commission as delegate, having been affirmed by the States General by the Provisional Order, while continuously disavowed by the West India Company. He had been ready to leave, he explained, "with his wife, mother, sister, brother, servants, maids, and had packed and shipped all his implements and goods to that end, intending to depart from day to day." Only once he was tying up his affairs in Amsterdam had he heard he had been denied passage, in his words, "very strangely and unexpectedly, at the last moment when it came time to board." Thinking that it must be some kind of misunderstanding, he called on the help of "distinguished friends," in Amsterdam, who attempted to facilitate matters with the directors there.[34] Initially, it appeared as though the issue would be resolved, however, shortly thereafter, when the directors learned of the glitch in his dismissal, they turned argumentative. They first "altogether once and for all" rejected the legitimacy of his delegation, calling the men "a scrappy and mutinous lot," and Van der Donck, himself, "one of the most notorious leaders thereof, presenting himself as Delegate of the Commonalty." For this, they "were not inclined, but even did not want him to leave," and what was more, they considered the recall of Stuyvesant Van der Donck's "ordained work." Moreover, they would not take any action without orders from the Amsterdam *burgemeesters*, in whose hands the matter now rested. The directors reiterated their stance that the delegates had "very wrongly" applied to the States General with their protests, and that the States General–issued letters of dismissal or safeguard were "of no value." On the contrary, they said, those with such

letters would be "persecuted above others." Van der Donck's pleas for consent were met with disregard, he reported, even while he "openly and clearly
showed that his ruin was sufficiently connected to it, and also proposed and
offered everything that could in any way be required, to the Directors' satis-
faction," so that he could leave with his friends and family, "encouraged by
him to immigrate."[35]

Van der Donck unquestionably felt he was being condemned, "without
any debate or any knowledge of his opponents," and "without any form of
procedure," in nothing short of "a civil banishment." He placed himself at
the mercy of the States General in the role of a public servant, describing
himself as a "Delegate of the Commonalty of New Netherland" and even
bringing up his pedigree as "a free native of this country, whose mother's
father, through the capture of the city of Breda with the *turfschip* . . . was a
participant in the acquired freedom." It was the only argument he had left.
He summed up his petition in a practical move aimed at getting to the heart
of the matter, asking the States General to either approve or annul his commission as delegate, and to declare whether the delegates, once and for all,
had or had not "improperly applied to your High Mightinesses." In his own
defense, he reminded them of the opposition the colonists had met with in
their complaints against the administration in New Netherland. It was a risky
ultimatum. But if the States General denied him at this point, he would at
least, he concluded, have the opportunity to change his course of action in
time to prevent "complete ruin."[36] The last thing he wanted was to be left
without any way out.

Van der Donck's request certainly sounded earnestly urgent. However,
rather than trying to expeditiously right the wrong of this unduly hard-
hearted punishment, the States General referred the appeal to the West India
Company for information, as if they were unwilling, anymore, to cross the
company's directors. And, not only did the States General refer the matter to
the West India Company for report, they asked for input from its "respec-
tive Chambers."[37] The States of Holland, who had been involved in revok-
ing Stuyvesant's recall, also requested a copy of the petition. The Amsterdam
Chamber took its time sending its response, finally submitting it almost a
full month later, even though the request had specifically called for a speedy
answer.[38] The States General then forwarded the response to its committee for the affairs of the West India Company for handling, along with the
answer from the Dordrecht Chamber, which could not "perceive" why Van
der Donck would be forbidden to leave with his "entire family," nor how his
application to the States General was made improperly, "inasmuch as your
High Mightinesses, in ratifying the Charter, have retained the chief authority

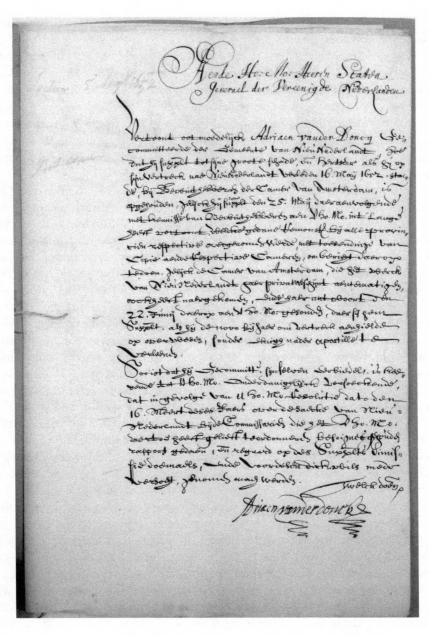

FIGURE 13.1. Petition of Adriaen van der Donck asking the States General for action on his request for dismissal, August 5, 1652. Nationaal Archief, The Hague.

to yourselves."[39] The ship carrying Van der Donck's family, hired hands, and belongings was long gone.

Van der Donck's attempts to return became caught up in a baffling game of "tag–you're it." When he again requested permission to leave of the West India Company in Amsterdam, it referred him back to the States General, to whom it had sent its June response. He then followed up with the States General in August, asking for dismissal based on their findings. Frustratingly, they referred his request to their committee for the affairs of the West India Company. The runaround he was getting created a vicious circle that paralyzed any progress.

In all fairness to the States General, they had a lot on their plates. The trepidations over hostilities with England had become a reality when, after a bloody naval skirmish near Dover at the end of May, the English declared war on the Dutch in July. Not only was Van der Donck's predicament lost amid the States General's secret meetings and new priorities surrounding the war, political apprehensions had cast his case in an even worse light. One of the States General's secret resolutions instructed Stuyvesant to "take good care and keep a watchful eye," employing only those "whose fidelity and affection to this State can be fully relied on."[40] As someone who might challenge the government during this critical period, Van der Donck would never fit this profile, and, his wife happened to be English. And whereas the complaints about New Netherland had made the colony somewhat of a burden in the past, it was suddenly gaining clout as a strategic location for the Dutch in the war. In another secret memoir, New Netherland was identified as "the only place" from which to attack the English in various locations, especially in the Caribbean.[41] In early September, news of an imminent invasion of New Netherland by the English was reported, making Stuyvesant's stalwart command even more crucial. He was ordered to fortify New Amsterdam and built a wall of palisades that came to be known as Wall Street.[42] Van der Donck had to have been getting tired of waiting and watching, with the winter travel season approaching and no plans in sight, for someone else to decide his fate. At the same time, cutting to the bone of his frustration was the hopeless realization that he had hit a dead end in his bargaining, at least in this current volatile climate. Inaction, however, was not in Van der Donck's repertoire. He needed to find a way to move forward, but with a different strategy. In the months ahead, his next steps would center on two tracks aimed, indirectly, at taking some control of his situation. One would involve a publication, and the other, a degree.

14

A Description of New Netherland

Between his feelings of frustration and insecurity about his future, at some point during this unexpected and unwanted downtime, Van der Donck decided to do what he could to help himself. Sitting alone by candlelight on long cold nights broken by short, gray days, he again, picked up his pen, this time to channel his energy into writing about his beloved New Netherland, now farther away than ever. There is no question that his writing was meant to aid his cause to encourage immigration and bolster the colony. However, at the same time, it seemed to serve as an outlet for his homesickness, sustaining him by keeping the dreams of his distant country alive. It is unknown exactly when he decided to write his book on New Netherland. However, in his "Introduction of the Author," he explained why.

> Both those who make their living writing about exotic and wondrous histories, or [of] unknown lands, usually have smooth, pleasant, and sweet-flowing words at their service and disposal, in order to make what they describe (that otherwise, in itself, would not be so very exceptional) all the more appealing to the reader. I have never been inclined to disparage these abilities, but maintain, on the contrary, that such praiseworthy opportunities generally do more to elevate the reader's interest in the subject matter when the subject [itself] would even be capable, being presented stripped and without flair. Through this insight alone I have deemed it advisable to restrain my pen until now; though I must confess, it is with difficulty that I have been able to overcome scarcely this much on my own, always hoping that some more clever, Loving spirit would

be revealed who would have been so moved by New Netherland that it had been unnecessary for me to take on this effort. But now, having anticipated and waited long enough, and seeing that nothing notable appears to give the curious enthusiasts sufficient knowledge and information about this country, and to convey the circumstances of it; and moreover being driven by such friends that I would not want to disappoint (although our own lack of ability seems to absolutely advise us against it), such is, nevertheless, the inner longing for New Netherland so powerful in us that she bursts loose this and other similar restraints, and gives voice to us of things that I, myself, have seen and experienced, and therefore know to be true, yet am not skilled enough to describe in a worthy manner; however, while this place has been left open to us up to now, we shall hope that the cherished reader, taking our humble work at its best, will see more by the subject itself, than by the ordinary and unrefined words with which we are presenting it.[1]

Van der Donck's humble and insightful introduction presents an opportunity to observe, in his own, almost poetic words, the strength of his feelings for New Netherland, a self-proclaimed "inner longing . . . so powerful" his words could not do it justice. Though the book that followed aimed to highlight the resources and possibilities in New Netherland in an effort to draw potential immigrants, Van der Donck's admiration for New Netherland also shined through the text as more than just a practical guide. His words read like the yearning for a faraway love. As in the Remonstrance, some parts of which seem to have been used for his book, Van der Donck painted New Netherland in a positive and welcoming light, utilitarian, yet at the same time, extraordinary. Divided into four main chapters, the book began, "New Netherland, so named by the Dutch for reasons that we hereafter shall relate, is a very beautiful, pleasant, healthy, and delightful country, where people of all means can earn a better and more ample living or more easily make their way through the world, than in the Netherlands or any other region of the world known to me."[2]

The book's first section, as in the Remonstrance, introduced a physical description of the country as well as the Dutch rights to it. It offered a sense of security, while presenting the land as functional, yet beautiful. For instance, Van der Donck's depiction of the South River (now the Delaware River) characterized it as "expansive and wide, clear and deep . . . suitable everywhere to moor and to anchor," yet somehow it defied description, he implied, noting, "we willingly confess to being unable or unfit to describe it to its worthy or rightful situation."[3] Whole forests of pine trees abounded, "heavy enough for ships' masts," he wrote, yet he described a surreal scene when those dying trees fell and fire set in, "spectacular, when one sails on the rivers at night, and that then the fire is in the forest on both sides of the river."[4] Detailed subsections on the soil, vineyards, agriculture, and crops were demonstrative of the opportunity and the availability of land and, at the same time, planted the idea that New Netherland was capable of supporting its colonists. Both wild and domestic animals such as cattle and deer, as well as birds such as wild turkey and geese, provided a plentiful food source. Seasonally, dense flocks of birds would "hang like clouds in the sky," and at times, so many swans covered the bays and riverbanks that the water would appear white.[5] Though he described troublesome blackbirds that could damage the corn crops he also mentioned a "very unusual little bird, over which some argue whether it is a bird or a West Indian Bee." It was so delicate, he related, that "some people spray them with water and dry them between two pieces of paper in the sun to present to one friend or another."[6] Fish were readily available in the rivers as well as further out to sea. Providing some mixed reviews made the story credible. The mulberries, for example, were "better than this country's," however, the persimmons, "not as good."[7] He presented information on the country's poisons, including rattlesnakes (though there were not many).[8] Nevertheless, his descriptions highlighted the country's vast variety of bountiful natural resources, including minerals and dyes, as well as the seasons and the air, "as dry, pure, and healthy as one could wish for."[9]

The second section, on the Natives, endeavored to dispel any fears, especially in light of stories of unpredictable Native encounters in New Netherland that had surely made their way back to the Dutch Republic. Van der Donck portrayed the indigenous peoples as both familiar and exotic. "It is true," he wrote, "at first sight they appear rather strange to our people . . . but for those who deal with them somewhat often, it is soon over," noting with tempting appeal, "and it seems that their women have an alluring gracefulness about them."[10] His comprehensive account covered Native appearance, settlements, food, dress, customs, languages, wars and weapons, and even such constructs as political structure. He praised their ability to treat illnesses "so easily that they would shame many an Italian physician," farm methods yielding "so much corn and beans that we trade from them with full yachts and sloops," and skills as hunters "adept at catching all sorts of game in various ways."[11] This positive framing of Native practices hinted at an interaction that, rather than hinder life for the colonists, could instead enhance it. To be fair, however, Van der Donck also reported aspects of Native culture that would be considered negative. His character descriptions were uncomplimentary, labeling the Natives "simple and ignorant" (though teachable under the Dutch), "careless . . . vindictive and stubborn."[12] He considered their administration of justice and punishment decidedly lacking, as well as their "glimmer" of government.[13] More publicly debated, he believed the Natives' conversion to Christianity would remain out of reach until proper instruction could be provided. Van der Donck's chapter on the Natives was authoritatively packaged, though it appears as if some information in this section was extracted from other New World accounts.[14] Nevertheless, his effort to provide such a thorough exposition of the Natives exemplifies his willingness to see this group as more human than conventional thinking allowed. At the same time, the prevailing seventeenth-century Eurocentric attitude was evident as he also hinted at this section as a tribute documentary. In what now seems shockingly matter-of-fact, he offered, as the reason for the chapter, "that so when the Christians will have multiplied there, and the Natives melted away, that [we] do not grieve, with one and all, their ways and manners escaping the memory."[15] He did not realize when he wrote this that he was underestimating his own vulnerability.

Van der Donck chose to dedicate his third chapter to the beavers, as "the principal foundation and the means wherefore or whereby this fine country was first occupied."[16] Besides being a commodity for its fur, the beaver had other practical uses, he suggested, such as providing hats and coats, acting as a potential food source, and providing cures for ailments, in various forms. In dissections he performed himself that he likely learned in the anatomy theater at Leiden, he described looking for glands containing castoreum, thought to have medicinal properties.[17] While aiming to provide a factual representation, his writing in this section also seemed to reflect a genuine admiration for the industrious, self-sufficient animal, as well as its "lively and cheerful" nature.[18] Though this chapter was not as expansive as the previous two, choosing to dedicate his third chapter to the beavers, in a sense, positioned the beaver on the level of the land and the people in importance. As an omnipresent feature, the beaver was of fundamental importance to the colony, not just monetarily, but also as the basis of its business and social interactions. In light of the experiential role that nature played in the seventeenth-century understanding of the world, Van der Donck's portrayal of the beaver as an adept, interactive component of the colony and its livelihood may have unconsciously served to depict it as a natural symbol of opportunity in New Netherland, and a link between the land and the people.[19]

The last section of Van der Donck's book strived to answered questions of potential immigrants by offering a fictional conversation, in a format common for the day, between a Patriot and a New Netherlander. In the mock discussion, the Patriot expressed concerns about life in New Netherland and the New Netherlander answered with conversational but thorough counsel. Most of the questions related to the reliability of the country's security and future, and the opportunities to earn a living in trade. Not surprisingly, the answers pointed to bright prospects for settlers. "In conclusion," the New Netherlander advised, "a territory like New Netherland, so suited to commerce as we have heard here, and one which, on its own, produces superior goods and essentials, also has enough to spare, and shares with others, should that not (if it is guided and steered in that direction) in time, go well? Judge for yourself."[20]

On May 2, 1653, Van der Donck submitted a copy of "a certain little book," *Beschryvinge van Nieuw-Nederlant*, or, *A Description of New Netherland*, to the Amsterdam Chamber of the West India Company and requested a letter of recommendation for a copyright from the States General.[21] On the one hand, he probably knew that the States General would not approve it without it being sanctioned by the West India Company and was just saving some time by presenting it there first. However, if the West India Company would interpret this as a gesture toward reconciliation, it could benefit Van der Donck by reopening negotiations while allowing him to save face. Perhaps his experiences had taught him something about how to maneuver in the corporate world, though the biggest lesson might have been not to underestimate your opponents. And it was a hard lesson, at that. The West India Company, possibly in the interest of promoting population in New Netherland, recommended the book to the States General without hesitation. The States General granted him a fifteen-year copyright.[22]

On May 5, 1653, a few days after he submitted his book for the copyright, Van der Donck took prerequisite exams for a law degree at Leiden University, reenrolling officially on May 7th.[23] This time, he gave his age as thirty-three and an address in Leiden, around the corner from the university.[24] He had a sponsor for his exam, law professor Daniel Colonius, and might have been using the library to prepare.[25] The Hague would have been an easy commute from Leiden, using public transportation by *trekschuit*, a horse-drawn barge on the canal.[26] On May 10, 1653, Van der Donck was finally awarded his *Supremus in jure*, which gave him the credentials to appear in the highest courts as Doctor of both Civil and Canon Law.[27] Following university tradition, the auditorium walls would have been decked with tapestries. With the entire faculty in official dress, the graduates, wearing black robes, would have appeared individually at the foot of the pulpit to receive their honors. There, the graduates were awarded a velvet cap as a symbol of "immunity," exemptions from burden, and a gold ring signifying "scholarly nobility."[28] Besides the right to be officially recognized in the highest courts of the Dutch Republic, the degree would certainly aid any aspirations Van der Donck might have for a life in public office.

Van der Donck had been, without a doubt, keeping up with things in New Netherland from across the ocean. The installation of the new city government, to which the West India Company had agreed the previous April, had taken place in February, coinciding with the customary date for elections in Amsterdam.[29] This action formally extended a municipal charter to the city of New Amsterdam. Van der Donck had heard from his wife that most of the people he had sent over to work on his farm had refused to honor their contracts for one reason or another and had abandoned their commitments.[30] There had been no English invasion on New Netherland; however, the relationship between the Dutch and the English had become extremely strained. A rumor that Stuyvesant was planning to hire Natives to attack the English spiraled out of control with the publication, in London, of an inflammatory pamphlet recalling a 1623 Dutch attack on English and other merchants on the island of Amboyna.[31] The pamphlet, which the West India Company referred to as "the most shameless and lying libel which the devil in hell could not have produced," accused the Dutch of a plot to murder colonists in New England.[32] Truth be told, it is not as if the idea of allying with the Natives had never crossed the minds of the Dutch. In a letter the previous year, with the war with England having just begun, the West India Company advised Stuyvesant that in the case of New Netherland suffering any affront from New England, "then we consider it proper and necessary, that you should make use of the Indians, who as we learn, do not like the English."[33]

The English had been collecting testimonies about the rumored plan from the English colonists living in New Netherland. In May, Mary Doughty, "Miss Vandunk," had given a statement with her father in Flushing, relating a story she had been told by "a very trusty Indian" upriver. The fiscal, one of the administrative officers, had come from Fort Orange, he told her, calling the Natives in the early dawn by beating on his drum. When they had all gathered, the fiscal told them "the English would cut them off; and therefore would have them cut off the English." As payment, they would receive, "of him and the Governor, a shiploading of guns, powder and shot, and trading cloth." The Natives did not agree to the plan, believing it was the fiscal's "roguery," in trying to set them up against the English, and burned the agreement he had left with them so that there would be no evidence. Additionally, Mary Doughty reported, "shee could say much in the case but that shee dares not for fear; and knows she could produce many witnesses that would testify the plot to the Dutch Governor and fiscal's face if she

FIGURE 14.1. Graduation ceremony at Leiden University,
ca. 1650. Courtesy of the Rijksmuseum, Amsterdam.

might bee secured." One of her workers also testified that she had related the same story to him a few weeks earlier, adding that Mary Doughty "can speake very good Indian," and that "many Indians testify the same namely that the Dutch Governor and the fiscal had hired them to cut off the English and kill all they could." She had told the worker she would have written this to New England "but she durst not."[34]

This kind of unsettling news from his wife must have made Van der Donck more anxious than ever to get home. However, if he had any ambitions of going back and getting involved in the politics there, he was forced to rethink them, since apparently, it was the very issue that represented a major roadblock to his return. In the end, Van der Donck traded any political ambitions he might have had for the ability to sail home. On May 26, 1653, he presented a petition to the West India Company, "humbly" requesting passport to New Netherland, "offering to resign the commission previously given him as President of the community," further promising to "accept no office whatever it may be, but rather to live in private peacefully and quietly as a common inhabitant, submitting to the orders and commands of the Company or those enacted by its director."[35] Whether he conceded this on his own, or whether it was demanded of him as a condition of his passport, this had to have been tough to swallow. Having surrendered to this, Van der Donck did, at least, ask for some assistance in restoring his life there. Besides the problems with his servants abandoning their contracts, the six guns he had sent with them had been seized, and squatters were threatening his farmland.[36] The West India Company directors forwarded his petitions to Stuyvesant with the recommendation to investigate his reports and, if the stories checked out, to facilitate putting the matters in order.[37]

Looking toward the future, Van der Donck requested two more things of the West India Company. First, he requested that he be allowed to practice as a lawyer in New Netherland, and second, he asked for permission to examine documents and papers from the colony in order to write a history of the colony for his *Description*. Referring to him in their letter to Stuyvesant as Meester Van der Donck, the title he had earned with his law degree, the company directors consented to his working as a lawyer, "to offer his advice etc. to everyone who so desires it." However, as to his appearing in court, they advised, "we are unable to see, according to our judgment, that for now such would be of service there," adding that they did not know whether there would be anyone in New Netherland with the necessary qualifications to oppose him. With this opinion, they did not outright forbid Van der Donck to appear in the courts, but they left it to Stuyvesant to "do in this matter what is considered best for [the country] and its inhabitants." They took a similar stance on his request for access to the colony's documents, delegating the business to Stuyvesant. They warned Stuyvesant, however, that "as this matter is not without difficulty and requires consideration, we also want to recommend that your honors take care herein that the Company's own weapons are not turned upon itself, and that it is not drawn into new troubles and difficulties in the process."[38]

At the end of July 1653, Van der Donck was finally going home. It had been almost four years, to the month, since he left New Netherland in August 1649 for what he thought would be a short stay, and he had spent the past year in exile. In the colony's political circles, he would be returning as a hero to some and as a villain to others, however the establishment of the municipal government had taken some pressure off the conflicts that had been so urgent when he had left. In the bigger picture, the colony had gone about its business without him. Any plans to make up for lost time would have to begin with restoring his own land that had been neglected almost to the point of loss. The past couple of months had kept him busy contracting, again, with new workers to staff his farm and property, hiring a tile maker, barrel maker, gardener, and carpenters.[39] Mostly, he was looking forward to going home, back to a life at his beloved Colendonck.

15

Return to New Netherland

It would be tempting to imagine Van der Donck, after all he had been through, sitting back in a rocking chair on a crisp fall day after his arrival, gazing out from his porch over the vastness of his land, the Hudson in view. But this would not fit the Van der Donck we have come to know. There would have been plenty to do when he got back to Colendonck, managing the work on the property, settling in all the workers he had brought back with him and tracking down the ones who had abandoned their earlier posts. Then, there would be the sowing of the farm's crops, if the season still allowed. There would have been family reunions and visits with friends. His mother would be living in a house on Pearl Street on the edge of Manhattan, facing the water.[1] His friend, Cornelis Melyn, was back on Staten Island after facing more harassment from Stuyvesant, who had accused him of illegal trading after a harrowing return voyage forced the ship into New England, then seized his ship and goods, and confiscated his property in Manhattan.[2]

In the heart of New Amsterdam, with the directorship no longer under threat and the new council in place, administrative affairs were running relatively smoothly. Stuyvesant made it clear, however, that he had far from forgiven Van der Donck. In fact, if anything, it seemed as if he was looking for a reason to indict him again. Van der Donck had appeared in the courts of New Amsterdam on December 1, 1653, soon after his return to New Netherland, applying for protection of his rights as a burgher, a citizen under the municipal government.[3] This timing may have had to do with a December remonstrance that the predominantly English villages on Long Island had prepared for Stuyvesant, seeking the privileges and protections now afforded New

Amsterdam under the municipal charter.[4] Not only did Stuyvesant reject the English remonstrance on several points, he immediately associated it with Van der Donck. He complained about Van der Donck in a January letter to the West India Company directors, who answered, "We do not know whether you have sufficient reasons to be so suspicious of Adriaen van der Donck, as all the charges against him are based upon nothing but suspicions and presumptions, however we shall not take his part, and only say that as we have heretofore recommended him to you on condition of his good behavior, we intend also that he be reprimanded and punished, if contrary to his promise he should misdemean himself."[5] Historians have noted similarities in the English remonstrance to other writings by Van der Donck, suggesting that he may have actually had some input in the complaint, originally written in English and then translated into Dutch for submission.[6] However, in their advice to Stuyvesant, the directors also advocated a voice of reason, adding, "On the other side we hope that your suspicions of him are to be imputed more to the unfavorable conjecture of the times, than to his presence there."[7]

Following a notice providing surety for the rent due on his mother's house in early 1654, the next appearance of Van der Donck in government documents came almost a year later. His name appeared in a January 1655 petition by a worker requesting to leave in order to "enter the Company's service," though the court upheld Van der Donck's contract.[8] In June of that year, his name appeared again in court records when a different worker sued him for back pay.[9] The fact that Van der Donck does not appear in the court records as a lawyer during this period makes it fairly apparent that Stuyvesant had not approved his request to work in that capacity. Not surprisingly, it also looks as though Stuyvesant denied him access to the colony's records, since, even after delaying publication of his book, it contained no history of the colony beyond a cursory introduction.

A Description of New Netherland, "by Adriaen van der Donck, Doctor of both Laws," was published that same year in Amsterdam.[10] Van der Donck's original choice of publisher, Joost Hartgers, who had earlier compiled and published *Description of Virginia, New Netherland, and New England, etc.*, had died in 1653, and this might have been the reason that Van der Donck's book was not published until 1655.[11] Its eventual publisher, Evert Nieuwenhof, successful in his own right and well established in Amsterdam, dedicated the book to the *burgemeesters* of that city, and to the directors of the Amsterdam Chamber of the West India Company. The city of Amsterdam had partnered with the West India Company to begin its own campaign to populate New Netherland in the area around the South River that would become New Amstel, now New Castle, Delaware. The publication rights to the book had been transferred to the West India Company in February.[12] The book's dedications tasked them, as a driving force for populating the colony, with holding New Netherland in the high regard that it deserved, so that "those who might otherwise not know of that good and healthy air and the potentials of New Netherland, can now be stimulated to go there."[13] The approximately 100-page book included a small, half-page print of Hartgers' view of New Netherland that had appeared in Hartgers' earlier publication and depicted a harmonious scene of Dutch vessels and Native canoes sharing the waters, presumably in trade, surrounding a quaint and fortressed Manhattan. Van der Donck's book was unusual as a resource about the New World from an eyewitness author who was also qualified as a writer, yet it was formatted to be affordable and easily accessible to the broad audience of the literate Dutch Republic.[14] The war with England had ended in 1654 and the West India Company had lost its colony in Brazil. The timing of the book, singing the praises of New Netherland, coincided with a renewed focus on the colony. The book sold out in its first year.

In the same period that Van der Donck was enjoying the success of his popular publication, the only known portrait of him, or thought to be him, was painted. The portrait was originally attributed to New Netherland tailor Jacobus Strycker and passed down through generations of the artist's family. It showed a man in typical mid-seventeenth-century Dutch attire, wearing a doublet and collar, the small black cap of a scholar, and a cloak over his right shoulder accented with a large, brass, wire fastener.[15] An inscription on the back reads, "Jonkeer Adrian Van der Donck, Given to Altje by her father, Jacobus Gerritsen Stricker, Who drew it with his own hand."[16] Unfortunately, uncertainties surrounding the artist, the later inscription, as well as the handling of the painting, have called the provenance of the portrait into question and it cannot be verified.[17] Though the expression on the subject's face shows no trace of the passion indelibly infused into Van der Donck's persona, the sympathetic authority it portrays nevertheless makes it a believable depiction.

On August 26, 1655, Van der Donck's father, Cornelis, appeared in the records of New Netherland when Stuyvesant issued him a land patent for fifty *morgens* of land, roughly one hundred acres, "on the North side of Manhattan Island," near his son's property.[18] It looks as though Stuyvesant's dislike of Van der Donck did not extend to his father. Perhaps in the relative quiet of the period since the war, while each of them tended to their own business, tensions were finally beginning to ease. On the other hand, the land Stuyvesant granted may have been the meadowland in the southern portion of Van der Donck's original land grant bordering the Spuyten Duyvil Kill near present-day Kingsbridge, which was the subject of Van der Donck's earlier request for intervention, and this was Stuyvesant's way of compromising.[19] Either way,

BESCHRYVINGE
Van
NIEUVV-NEDERLANT,
(Ghelijck het tegenwoordigh in Staet is)

Begrijpende de Nature, Aert, gelegentheyt en vrucht-
baerheyt van het selve Lant ; mitsgaders de proffijtelijcke ende gewenste toevallen, die aldaer tot onderhout der Menschen, (soo
uyt haer selven als van buyten ingebracht) gevonden worden.

ALS MEDE
De maniere en onghemeyne eygenschappen
vande Wilden ofte Naturellen vanden Lande.
Ende
Een bysonder verhael vanden wonderlijcken Aert
ende het Weesen der BEVERS,

DAER NOCH BY GEVOEGHT IS
Een Discours over de gelegentheyt van Nieuw Nederlandt,
tusschen een Nederlandts Patriot, ende een
Nieuw Nederlander.

Beschreven door
ADRIAEN vander DONCK,
Beyder Rechten Doctoor, die teghenwoor-
digh noch in Nieuw Nederlant is.

t'AEMSTELDAM,

By Evert Nieuwenhof, Boeck-verkooper / woonende op 't
Ruslandt in 't Schrijf-boeck / Anno 1655.

FIGURE 15.1. *Beschryvinge van Nieuw-Nederlant, 1655.*
Courtesy of the New York State Library.

FIGURE 15.2. t' Fort niew Amsterdam op de Manhatans.
Courtesy of the New York Public Library.

Cornelis van der Donck must have been elated to officially join his son in his New Netherland venture. His timing, however, could not have been worse. Within a few weeks of lifting his glass with his son in a toast to their new future, he would be looking at quite a different picture, and not a good one.

In the early dawn of September 15, 1655, the city of New Amsterdam was stunned by an unexpected multitribal Native attack. The assault happened while Stuyvesant was away, surely no coincidence, after taking his military to confront the Swedes who had been living on the South River

FIGURE 15.3. Portrait of a man thought to be Adriaen van der Donck. Courtesy of the National Gallery of Art.

and claiming it as New Sweden. According to reports, at least five hundred Natives in sixty-four canoes landed on the shores of the southern tip of Manhattan and across the river to the east, forcibly entering homes before most of the people had even risen for the day. Large crowds of armed Natives ran through the streets, in a chaotic riot, "breaking locks and doors, hitting and kicking people, searching houses."[20] The townsfolk managed to push the unruly bands back to shore where they had landed, while the burgher contingent reacted by securing the fort as much as possible. The council then invited the chiefs of the various tribes into the fort for questioning and negotiated an agreement that the Natives would retreat to Nut Island (now Governor's Island) before sunset.[21] However, instead of drawing back as had been agreed, toward evening the Natives were joined by even greater numbers, about two hundred strong, and were still on the shore when night fell. At about nine o'clock that evening, one of them shot an arrow, wounding former fiscal Hendrick van Dyck who was standing at the garden gate of his home facing the water, and another man was threatened with a hatchet.[22] At this point "a cry was raised, 'Murder, murder, the Indians are killing the Dutch.'"[23] In the panic and confusion that ensued, the burghers keeping watch at the fort scrambled over the walls and through the gates and engaged in a skirmish with the Natives, still standing on the shore. Two Dutchmen and three Natives were killed. In a developing frenzy, the group of Natives crossed the river to Pavonia and started on a rampage, burning houses through the night, murdering colonists, and killing cattle.

The next day, the council sent an emergency postil to Stuyvesant, which finally reached him a week later with preliminary reports of a "great murder of 100 people in nine hours" and "earnestly" requesting his return, "as quickly as possible with your accompanying troops."[24] "On this island they do nothing but burn and blaze," the missive read, describing an overpowering number of nine hundred Natives on the island.[25] By then the attack had moved north on Manhattan, ravaging the Kuyter *bouwerie* in what is now Harlem and then crossing the rivers to the Van der Donck and Bronck farms. Within a few days, the marauding band had "cleared Staten Island of people and houses" in a similar assault.[26] There, a group of people had taken shelter in the house of Cornelis Melyn, who had been urgently released in the calamity from yet another round of imprisonment by Stuyvesant. The group huddled in fear inside the house, until it was finally set on fire and, "the cinders began to fall down."[27] Breaking through the Natives, they then managed to escape to another house close to shore; however, seeing no other option, they finally surrendered as hostages. By then, fifteen or sixteen people had already been shot and killed there, including Melyn's twenty-two-year-old son, his son-in-law, and two nephews. Like a cat with nine lives, Melyn had escaped another brush with death. Afterward, he reported being forced to raise a ransom for himself and his family, under threat of being burned alive in a fire that had, as he described, "already been prepared and was burning."[28] One contingent returning from the Dutch expedition to New Sweden sailed past a burned-out Staten Island to find a man dead in a canoe and buried him. The man had been out on a "pleasure excursion" when the ship he was on was attacked. Both the man and the ship's captain had been murdered, and his wife and sister taken captive.[29]

Little is known about the attacks that occurred north of Manhattan, but signs trickling into the records in the following months indicate that the Van der Donck estate had, indeed, also been targeted in the assault. It has long been known that the house was looted in the attack and that hostages were taken from his property. Tragically, and without warning, it appears that this dark moment in New Netherland history also most likely took the life of Adriaen van der Donck. As early as January 10, 1656, court records reference him, for the first time, as deceased, and his wife, as a widow.[30] That same month, Stuyvesant also loosely linked him to the event in a report referencing talks on the incident between a New Englander and a Native, who "had been a good friend of Van der Donck and had taken care of his cows for some time."[31] As the details of his death remain shrouded in mystery, the strongest indication of what may have happened to him has gone unnoticed until now, as new information has recently come to light. The records of an orphan court, established in New Amsterdam following the events of September to administer aid to the wives and children left without support, contains an elucidating entry. The November 1655 Minutes of the Orphanmasters of New Amsterdam names three young men, Jan Mewes, Evert Jansen, and Jan Gerritsen, "living at Verdoncx," as having perished, "during the late disaster."[32] This critical evidence pointing to the loss of life at Colendonck during the offensive had been overlooked, probably due to seventeenth-century spelling variations. These three men were the carpenters Van der Donck had brought under contract to his farm from the Dutch Republic, two years earlier.[33] All three men from the same village in the Dutch Republic shared not only a place of origin and work responsibilities, but also a house on Van der Donck's property. If the men were killed and the women and children kidnapped for ransom, which had happened in earlier Native incidents, this evidence makes it more plausible than ever that Van der Donck's death occurred in the attack at Colendonck. It is sadly ironic, however, that Van der Donck, who had always shown an appreciation for the Natives far beyond that of most of his contemporaries, would, in the end, die by Native hands. Many of the Natives involved in the multitribal attack appeared to have been from outside the area and would not have known him as a friend. In a broader sense, Van der Donck had foreshadowed this finality in his earlier Remonstrance, when he prophesied, "We are also beholden to the Natives in the highest, who not only yielded this rich and fertile country, and for a trifle in property ceded it to us. . . . It is now our great shame, and fortunate would we be, had we duly acknowledged this good deed, and in return for what the Natives have shared with us, had endeavored to share with them the eternal good, for as much as is in us. It is to be feared that on the last day they will rise up against us for this injustice."[34] He was not immune to the volatility of the world he chose to live in.

The final numbers that Stuyvesant reported in October were, within three days, fifty colonists killed; more than one hundred, mostly women and children, captured and held for ransom; twenty-eight *bouweries* in addition to twelve to fifteen thousand *schepels* of grain burned; and five to six hundred cattle killed or taken.[35] In what he described as "such an unfortunate and unexpected accident as New Netherland never witnessed," many more had lost all of their possessions, with "nothing left to procure food and clothing for themselves and their families."[36] Hostage negotiations continued for months. The attack, later inaccurately labeled the Peach War, was deemed revenge for an earlier incident when Hendrick van Dyck killed a squaw taking peaches from his garden. The fact that Van Dyck seemed to be targeted in the arrow attack lends some support to this. However, another report suggested that the Natives had claimed to be looking for "Northern Indians," or those "on the east end of Long Island," in the raid, and this explanation could account for their initial focus on the house of Isaac Allerton, who often traded with New England.[37] Still others believed the attack was an attempt by the Swedish-allied Natives to revenge Stuyvesant's confrontation with New Sweden.[38] Though there had been no resistance in New Sweden and the action in Manhattan did not begin violently, the offense could have, at least, been intended as a diversion.[39]

Later, the West India Company investigation blamed Hendrick Van Dyck for laying "the first foundation" of the massacre by the brutal murder of the squaw and questioned why he had not been held accountable for the killing.[40] They especially pointed to Van Tienhoven, who, allegedly drunk, had urged the citizens on to the second, profoundly more lethal event, charging that "with clouded brains, filled with liquor, he was a prime cause of this dreadful massacre."[41] The colonists called for revenge against Van Tienhoven, at the same time complaining that Stuyvesant had defended him, in part, by subsequently neglecting to investigate his role in the fighting. The West India

Company directors in Amsterdam ultimately dismissed Van Tienhoven from service, expressing their astonishment that Stuyvesant would "shield" him in such a way.[42] Ever unpopular and under investigation for fraud in other mounting discrepancies, Van Tienhoven seems to have faked his own death a year later. He absconded, leaving his very pregnant wife behind, and his hat and cane, floating in the river.[43] Much of what Van der Donck had said about him had turned out to be true, accusing him of being the mastermind behind Kieft's War, "a Villain, Murderer and a traitor," and now this.[44] In short, Van Tienhoven was probably the most deceptive, behind-the-scenes manipulator in the colony, with a hand in almost all its miseries. Looking back, he might have also been Van der Donck's biggest nemesis, and a far greater threat than Stuyvesant had ever been.

No fanfare marked Van der Donck's death, and no document, known to date, records his name among those slain in the September event. Whether this was a manifestation of Stuyvesant's feelings about Van der Donck or whether it simply reflects a lack, or even a loss, of records, may never be known. The loss of all "Christian lives" was rued in the subsequent communications with the States General and the West India Company. Regardless, it seems as though news of Van der Donck's death should have at least been noted, and that they would have wanted to know. Just when it seemed as if, at any moment, Adriaen van der Donck was perched to launch into an encore performance, instead, his life ground suddenly to a halt, with what seemed like much unfinished business.

16

The Aftermath

Van der Donck's Colendonck property was abandoned in the attack.[1] However, during the period that followed, a few accounts surfaced that offer clues as to what happened that September. On January 10, 1656, Catalyntie Verbeek appeared in the courts of New Amsterdam in an effort to recover two bibles belonging to her that had been stolen from Van der Donck's house at the time of the raid, and which the Natives had later given to a girl in captivity.[2] The girl had carried them around with her for some time, and her mother had traded four packs of cards for them. Her father was in court, where the books were being held, to try to get them back for his daughter. Verbeek had brought with her a declaration from Mary Doughty that the books were indeed hers, taken by the Natives out of the Van der Doncks' home. The court ruled that the books, bibles containing Verbeek's handwritten notes, should be returned to her. The three workers that had been killed on Van der Donck's property left behind a chest with some clothing, which the report of the Orphanmasters acknowledged "might be spoiled."[3] Their chest was scheduled to be opened and inventoried, in order to sell the contents for the benefit of the young men's heirs.

Another story surfaced, much later, of four sisters who had reportedly been taken hostage from Van der Donck's property in the incident.[4] At the time of their release, Ytie Hendricks and two of her sisters were taken in by guardians in the village of Beverwyck, near Rensselaerswyck.[5] Another sister, Albrechie Hendricks, having been held much longer, ended up in New Haven, in New England. That the girls had been orphaned in the event raises the question of whether there had been even more murders on Van der Donck's land. When

Ytie got married in 1667, she petitioned for Albrechie's release, hoping for a reunion with the sister she had not seen in thirteen years.[6]

In October 1656, carpenter Abram Jacobsen reported, along with "Schout Silla," to the Court of New Amsterdam that an account book of "old Verdoncks" was at his house.[7] "Whereas his property and account book were delivered to them by said Verdonck," the entry read, they had requested "that the book be examined, [so] that they might obtain what is theirs."[8] This story suggests that Cornelis van der Donck was alive after the attack and subsequently left New Netherland. It was also not the only time the word "old" was used in connection with Cornelis Van der Donck, and it could have been used to differentiate him from his son. In a much later 1664 report to the West India Company directors, Stuyvesant referred to the land north of Manhattan as "the lands of Jonas Bronck, and the lands of old Van der Donck's children and partners that was divided into several farms and plantations."[9] This statement has been the source of questions about whether Adriaen van der Donck and Mary Doughty had children, but it almost certainly refers to the children of Cornelis van der Donck. There is no evidence in church records, court documents, or other communications, that Adriaen van der Donck had any children.

The name of Van der Donck's mother, Agatha van Bergen, appears just above that of her daughter-in-law, Anna van der Donck, in the later years of membership lists for the Reformed Dutch Church of New Amsterdam. Records of the brother who, according to Van der Donck, accompanied the family to New Netherland in 1652 have been difficult to identify with any certainty. Court records in New Netherland naming Gysbert van der Donck mostly pertain to Anna's son. At least one early court entry from the fall after the family arrived in New Netherland is a complaint by Gysbert van der Donck that a servant has run away.[10] The following spring, a legal complaint was filed against Gysbert, for the loss of farm laborer Gulyam Jansen's property, "through the neglect of the defendant's father, then his master."[11] The suit does not specifically name the father, but a 1650 record in Breda listing Adriaen van der Donck authorizes a Ghysbrecht van der Donck to pick up tools and goods belonging to Gulyam Jansen from his previous employer. It is possible that Ghysbrecht, a Van der Donck family name, is the father of Gysbert, the husband of Anna, and the brother of Adriaen van der Donck. The fact that Gysbert appears to have stepped up in his father's place for the suit, however, points to the likelihood that the father was no longer there by the spring of 1653. Neither of the men is noted in later records, raising the question of whether at least the younger Gysbert might have also been a victim of the September attacks.

Mary Doughty moved to Northampton County, Virginia, sometime before August 1656, where her father had recently been elected minister.[12] She supported herself there as a medical practitioner, being paid in tobacco at least once in the case of a delivery and, on occasion, in cattle.[13] Her own cattle mark, "a flower de luce on the right ear and a slitt in the left," was registered in 1659.[14] It is interesting to think, and very possible, that Mary Doughty had been inspired to learn medicinal practices from the Beguines of Breda. The Beguines and their fragrant medicinal gardens, close to the Van der Donck family home where she most likely stayed while her husband was in working in The Hague, would have offered a welcome way to pass the time. Or, perhaps her calling was influenced by the trauma she experienced at Colendonck, and the helplessness she must have felt as a witness to the violence there that changed her life forever.

Even from the grave, Van der Donck continued to support New Netherland. The second edition of his book, *A Description of New Netherland*, which had already been in the works, was published in 1656, one year after the first. This version did not include the idealistic scene of Dutch vessels and Native canoes but had something even better. "Cleared of many print errors," the second edition was enhanced with a sweeping full map of the country, including the inset view of the city of New Amsterdam at the bottom.[15] Moreover, it included a pamphlet of "Conditions" as an appendix, a guide by the Amsterdam *burgemeesters* to the policies for colonization under the West India Company.[16] The pamphlet addition was an astute pairing. Piggybacked to the book as a vehicle for disseminating information, it transformed the publication into a complete handbook for immigration. Anything and everything a potential immigrant would want to know could be found in this latest edition of Van der Donck's book, both the wonders of the country as well as attractive new incentives for settlers, not found under earlier West India Company programs. The book had become an authoritative resource on New Netherland, and one that was referenced in later publications on colonization, *'t Verheer-lickte Nederland*, a pamphlet published in 1659, and *Kort Verhael van Nieuw-Nederlants gelegentheit*, published in 1662.[17]

In late 1660 or early 1661, Mary and her father both relocated to Maryland, where she continued her medical practice. There, she practiced more than midwifery, as evidenced by one patient's bill that charged for "a purge . . . a dose of sweating," and "two portions for the fever."[18] Another patient had been treated with "something in a pot, and something in a paper," from which she dosed "a portion of that upon the point of a knife."[19] Working as a healer was not for the faint-hearted. Mary Doughty's name showed up in suits for payment after curing a man's "very dangerous legg" that was almost "past cure," and the man's friend believed she had "saved his life."[20] Another patient was not nearly as happy with her services, accusing Mary Doughty of poisoning her and then, later, dying from her illness.[21] After the estate administrator refused payment, Mary sued him for defamation.[22] By this time, Mary's brother Enoch had also moved to Maryland and testified on her behalf.[23] She had learned a thing or two about asserting herself in court.

New Netherland remained a part of Mary Doughty's past. She remarried an Englishman, Hugh O'Neale of Patuxent, Maryland, on September 26, 1661, though she continued to use the name Van der Donck, "Alias O'Neale," in pending court cases.[24] She and O'Neale settled in Maryland and had four children. The question has been raised as to whether their first three children, Daniell, Charles, and Joy, were O'Neale's children with Mary Doughty or whether O'Neale had brought them into the marriage. This is most likely based on documents naming the three children as Hugh O'Neale's, though this could be chalked up to legal conventions at the time.[25] There is no reason to believe the children were not Mary Doughty's. The fourth child, Wenifrett, appeared for the first time, later, in a 1669 document wherein her father deeded her "a brown cow called Cherry with a starr on her foreheade and a flowre de luce on both ears."[26] This child, born later, would certainly be theirs together.

New Netherland had prospered in the years after Mary Doughty left, in no small part due to its stability under the municipal government and through increased immigration, both a result of Van der Donck's hard work. It had become the principal point of trade between North America and Europe, and accordingly, had never been out from under the covetous eye of the English. With the colony's success came England's renewed interest in the prime territory that stood, literally, between its two North American enclaves, and domination of the eastern seaboard. Most of New Netherland's commercial success was concentrated in New Amsterdam, yet, despite Stuyvesant's requests, the city had never been adequately secured by the debt-ridden West India Company. The surrounding areas were left even less protected. The English on Long Island had been continuously encroaching in these regions, supported by the New England colonies' repeated motions toward engulfing the entire Dutch territory.

At the end of August 1664, the threat of an invasion became a stark reality when four English frigates appeared before New Amsterdam. The English issued proclamations for distribution among the inhabitants and the villages of Long Island, promising generous conditions under voluntary submission, "without opposition," and alternatively, the "miseries of war."[27] Stuyvesant, having just returned from Fort Orange, was working to ascertain the threat and the colony's potential for defense.[28] A few days later, an English contingent, carrying a white flag, came ashore to meet with Stuyvesant, politely saying that they had come "in the King's name, to present all the equitable conditions to the inhabitants, and, upon non-acceptance of these, to excuse themselves for any harm otherwise to follow."[29] They carried a sealed letter from their commander, Richard Nicolls, basically bearing the same message, which amounted to a demand for the surrender of the city, or else it would be attacked.

Stuyvesant read the letter to his council in the presence of two *burgemeesters*, who asked to communicate it further. Stuyvesant refused their request and, just to make sure the message did not get out, promptly tore the letter to pieces. He had tried this stalling tactic before. He was not about to put any decision at risk by inviting a popular vote in the heat of the moment. But the word was already out. The city's inhabitants had been aware of the English threat for several days and wanted some part in deciding their fate. People gathered around the city hall, demanding to see the letter and arguing that they could not defend the place for more than a few days, being outnumbered, and with no relief in sight. Fearing a mutiny and hoping to appease the crowd, Stuyvesant had the letter pieced together, copied, and delivered to the *burgemeesters*.[30]

The cards were stacked against Stuyvesant. Provisions in the colony had become low. A large store had recently been sent to Curaçao, leaving only enough to last, possibly, eight days. Moreover, many of the English living in the peripheral areas of the colony, such as Long Island, were uniting with the English and cutting off all supplies by water and by land. Stuyvesant later cited a lack of fit gunpowder, using the words of his gunner as evidence. "If I begin firing in the morning," he had reportedly voiced, "I will be done by noon."[31] In addition to a scarcity of munitions, the English soldiers far outnumbered the approximately 150 Dutch soldiers. The Dutch soldiers were willing to fight; however, any chance at successfully defending the city would have necessitated rallying armed burghers and farmers to the battle. The city leaders expressed their opinion to Stuyvesant, dimming his hopes even more: "Let the Honorable Company be so little concerned with the protection of the country and its inhabitants that they, in such urgent need, have not wanted to send one ship of war to its aid nor even a letter of advice upon which we might depend, and what assistance we could expect; we are not in the least empowered, and, consequently, not obliged to defend the city, or to put our lives, property, wives and children in peril without hope of support or relief, and after two or three days resistance, to lose everything."[32] Fifteen

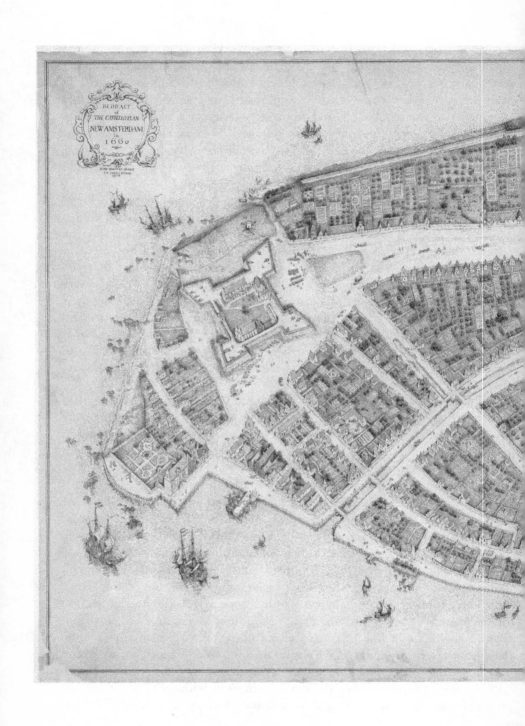

REDRACT
of
THE CASTELLO PLAN
NEW AMSTERDAM
in
1660

FIGURE 16.1.
Redraft map of the
Castello Plan of
New Amsterdam,
1660. Courtesy
of the New York
Public Library
Digital Collections.

years after Van der Donck presented his Remonstrance to the States General in the Dutch Republic, to protest the West India Company's lack of attention to the colony and to appeal for support, the people had not forgotten.

On September 5, 1664, in an impassioned Remonstrance of the People of New Netherland, the colonists implored Stuyvesant "not to reject the conditions of such a generous adversary." They urged, "On all sides we are surrounded and confined by our enemies," while "Your Honor's reported fortress cannot save the least bit of our country, property, and, what is more important to us, our wives and children, from total ruin."[33] If Stuyvesant had had the backing of the people, he might have had a fighting chance against the English, but with his limited forces and insufficient gunpowder, it would have been a complete annihilation. With the fate of the colonists on his head, who had threatened "before God and the world . . . to summon the vengeance of Heaven for all the innocent blood that would be spilled through your Honor's obstinacy," he reluctantly arranged a meeting with local merchants and the English contingent to hash out the conditions of a transfer.[34] A few days later, New Netherland was surrendered to the English crown in the name of the Duke of York, without a single shot being fired, as the story goes. The colony's West India Company rule had failed New Netherland. Van der Donck had predicted this, too. It was a bittersweet revenge.

In 1666 Mary Doughty returned to her former home, seeking to reestablish a claim, under the English, to her property at Colendonck, as well as the land in Maspeth, or Newtown, Long Island, that her father had deeded to her on marriage to Van der Donck. In August of that year, a former New Netherland council member, now administrator for the English, wrote to Stuyvesant that Mary Doughty would "again take possession of Nipperha[em]," adding that she was "also claiming land in Mespadt," and that she had been asking about some ironwork that Stuyvesant had had removed.[35] In September she and Hugh O'Neale appeared before the courts in New York to lay claim to "a certain parcel of land . . . called ye Youncker's Land."[36] They brought with them seven or eight Natives to testify to the location and former purchase of the land, who acknowledged that they had received payment for it. Shortly after receiving the English patent, the couple sold it to Mary Doughty's brother, Elias, possibly to sell it for them, since he was still living there.[37] Returning for this property must have transported Mary Doughty back to the life she had had together with Van der Donck. The property had been rightly hers, whether she had been keeping it in order to keep his legacy alive or had just not gotten around to dealing with it. Nevertheless, the rights Van der Donck had secured for his property when he was still in the Dutch Republic indicate that he had intended for Colendonck to go to his heirs, and he would have wanted her to have it. Over the next few years, Elias Doughty sold and parceled out the land, though not without creating a bit of a legal mess in a dispute with farmers there. They had been using the southern portion of the property's prime meadowlands, which had, as far as they could tell, been left abandoned.[38]

Despite their efforts, it appears the O'Neales did not manage to get the Newtown property back. Van der Donck had taken on a tenant a few years after he obtained the patent, but Stuyvesant had issued a new patent to the tenant while he was detained in the Dutch Republic. The property had changed hands again since then and the new occupant had lived there for quite some time. Hugh O'Neale filed suit in an attempt to reclaim the land, but the case was decided against him. Two years later, however, as Elias Doughty transferred the Colendonck property to new owners, the court certified that its judgment on Newtown in no way affected the earlier ruling on Colendonck preserving the rights of "ye patent belonging to Youncker van der Donck, who ought to have his full proportion of land."[39]

17

Legacy

The city of Yonkers today marks part of Van der Donck's seventeenth-century land grant, where the Saw Mill River Parkway runs alongside the waterway where Van der Donck's saw mill once stood. Oddly, rather than fading away, Van der Donck's seventeenth-century world seems to be coming back to life. The Saw Mill River had been cemented over in downtown Yonkers in the early 1900s for storm control, but a recent campaign to "daylight" the river restored it to its natural historic grace and aquatic habitat as it drains into the Hudson. The downtown plaza along the river was renamed Van der Donck Park in 2012. Even Van der Donck's playful beavers, once hunted to extinction, have finally returned to the Bronx River after two hundred years, heartily welcomed by the community in an acknowledgment of their significance to the lasting New York landscape. Standing in Van Cortlandt Park in the Bronx, on a clear crisp day with blue skies overhead, it is not difficult to imagine the majesty of the natural surroundings of Colendonck in a time warp—Rensselaerswyck to the North, New Amsterdam to the south, and the lifeblood of the colony, the Hudson River, within view. The Van Cortlandt Manor Parade Ground now covers the earth, several layers deep, where Van der Donck once farmed on ancient corn grounds. A 1910 excavation for a sewer pipe in the area exposed the foundation of a seventeenth-century house.[1] In 1990, an archaeological study was carried out near the site, where a 1667 map showed a house labeled "Van Duncks." The dig revealed fragments of blue and white porcelain, clam and oyster shells, pipe stems, bricks, and glass.[2]

Remnants of Adriaen van der Donck's life in the seventeenth century are also still visible in Breda. A statue of his grandfather, Adriaen van Bergen, stands in the square tucked behind the City Hall. In the moat next to the turreted entrance to the Castle of Breda, a replica peat boat floats. It has been redesigned into a bar and named "Spinola," in a mock tribute to the city's Spanish adversary. The castle's two turrets now house chapels, one Catholic and one Protestant, in a nod to the city's mixed religious past. The city's marketplaces, such as the Havermarkt where Van der Donck's grandfather lived, are still known by the same names and still attract busy crowds to the shops that line them. The Grote Kerk stands as regally now as before, as a towering beacon marking the city center. In the courtyard of the Begijnhof, fragrant heirloom herbs, once again, grace the many planting beds. Surrounding the gardens, the rectangular building is checkered by its long rows of intermittent doors identifying individual residences, still rented only to single women.

In the city of New York, things have changed at a slightly faster pace. Or have they? Using the New York Public Library Map Warper tool to overlay the 1660 Castello Plan map of New Amsterdam onto a current street map of New York, the old lines are surprisingly evident, defying the typical street grid of Manhattan. Broadway, Beaver Street, Stone Street, Pearl Street—they are all still there today. In the financial district, yellow bricks on Pearl Street outline the site of the New Amsterdam city tavern, which became the Stadt Huis, or City Hall, in 1653. Business inside the fort would have taken place in about the location of today's National Museum of the American Indian. The fort was on the tip of Manhattan, before modern landfill, and along with the houses on Greenwich and Pearl, it was waterfront property. Wall Street to the north, now an icon of financial institutions, is still named for the wall that Stuyvesant erected in the same location to protect the city from the English, if they had only come by land.

Though the English renamed many of the geographic locations in New Netherland, much of the Dutch linguistic influence persevered, largely due to the map Van der Donck had printed to accompany his *Vertoogh* publication of the Remonstrance. Van der Donck knew, as well as many in the seventeenth-century world, that propaganda in maps was powerful. Knowing the lay of a land was equivalent to possessing it and part of the reason why, in the age of exploration, maps were highly guarded secrets, with thefts sometimes even punishable by death. Dutch names assigned by earlier explorers and printed on Van der Donck's map made a statement that those places were Dutch territory. Though it did not stop other countries from doing the same thing, Dutch mapmakers enjoyed a formidable reputation and their products were widely referenced. When Van der Donck's map was engraved by Jan Jansson and then published, it was one of the most up-to-date and well-regarded maps of colonial North America. Distribution of this map acted to seal the names in the collective memory, in an imprint of the country that long outlasted New Netherland. Names such as Rood Eylandt, meaning Red Island, and 't Lange Eylandt stuck as Rhode Island and Long Island, as well as Staten Eylandt, named for the States General. Breukelen survived as Brooklyn, Vlissingen as Flushing, and Conynen Eylandt, whose Dutch name probably indicates that it was overrun with rabbits, became Coney Island. The map was corrected and revised by cartographer Claes Janszoon Visscher shortly after its initial printing, to add the inset view of New Amsterdam by Johannes Blaeu, which Blaeu had also distributed as a stand-alone "cutting."[3] Thirty-one iterations later, this series of maps, known as the Jansson-Visscher series, makes the map the most definitive representation of the area for its time.[4]

Van der Donck's textual accounts of New Netherland, perhaps his most tangible legacy, have also lasted, while other evidence and documents have not, amid reconstructions, fire and water damage, reorganizations, and various changes over time. Beyond other Dutch influences, his writings stand apart, transcending later myths and Anglocentric attitudes, as testimony to a dynamic Dutch presence in the history of New York and early America. Van der Donck's Remonstrance survives as a detailed recording of the history of New Netherland, apart from his *Description*, documenting the most turbulent years of the colony and Kieft's administration. It lays the groundwork for understanding the battle that pitted the colonists against the West India Company, involving the States General and, eventually, provincial and city leaders in the Dutch Republic, in a four-year clash for control of the colony. And perhaps it offers clues to the fate of the colony, different from other West India Company holdings, in portraying the depth of the hopes and dreams of those who dared venture to this remote settlement under uncertain conditions in search of a brighter future.

A Description of New Netherland provides an expansive contribution to our knowledge, not only of the seventeenth-century colony, but also of its surroundings. The account serves, today, as a work of extraordinary environmental and anthropologic value, documenting the land, animals, plants, and the indigenous peoples of the area, before large-scale European immigration. Because it was written in Dutch, Van der Donck's book received little attention until it was translated into English in the mid-1800s. Sometime after its first English-language publication, it became apparent that faulty translation in some parts misinterpreted Dutch grammar, making the book unreliable as an accurate historical source.[5] Moreover, in the 1970s, a large section on the Natives was rediscovered in the Dutch archives and translated for the first

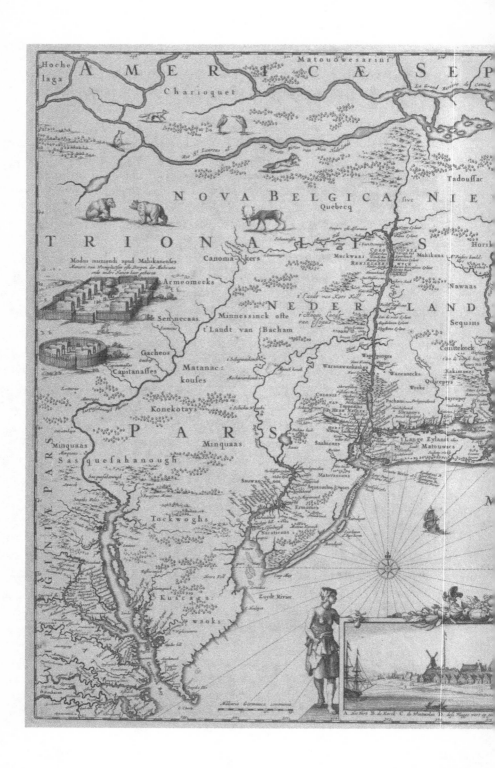

Hoche
laga

Charioquet

AMERICÆ SEP

Matouowesarini

La Grand Rivière de Cana

Rio St. Laurens S.   De Groote Rivier van Hou Alelolant

Tadoussac

NOVA BELGICA sive NIE

Quebecq

TRIONALIS

Canoma-kers

Hori

Modus muniendi apud Mahikanenses   Macwaas   Mahikans   Nawaas Sandh
Maniere van Versterckinge die Bergen der Mahicans   COLO
ende andere Nacien haer gehoren   RENSLAERS

Armeomecks   WYCK

Sennecaas   t'Zand van Kars Kill   NEDER   LAND

Minnessinck ofte   Sequins

t'Landt van Bacham

Gacheos   Wappingos   Contekock

Matanac.   Waranawankongs   Wanrancks   Jakimes:
kouses   Wickc   Quireprs

Konekotays   Pachami   Sinanoys

PARS   Saahicans   Lange Eylant alias
Matouwacs
Minquaas   Minquaas
Matovancons
Sasquesahanough
Sauwan

Ermanem

Tockwoghs   Naraticons

Minuas Germanica communia

A. het Fort B. de Kerk C. de Windmolen D. dese Wuggs wort op

Kuscara:
wicks   Zuydt Rivier

FIGURE 17.1. Map known as the Jansson–Visscher map of New Netherland, 1651–1656. Courtesy of the New York Public Library Digital Collections.

time, having been left out of the previous publications.[6] The latest translation, published in 2008, provides an up to date and accurate context for this
veritable treasure trove of information.[7]

Each of these publications by Van der Donck played a part in increasing
the population of New Netherland in the period after their distribution. The
map provided a sense of a boundless Dutch territory, there for the taking
for prospective adventurers, with the name "Nieuw Nederlandt" spread out
over a vast, open domain. The Dutch names added a sense of permanence
and a welcoming touch, like a home away from home, yet in a literal New
World. The drama of the *Vertoogh*, as the printed Remonstrance, planted New
Netherland, for the first time, in the consciousness of the Dutch Republic's
general population. Publication of *A Description of New Netherland* could be
seen as one of Van der Donck's purest victories in terms of his oft-stated
desire to populate the colony. Though his love for the country made New
Netherland an easy sell for him, the book, as a tool to encourage immigration with its accessible account of an unparalleled landscape, seems to have
set a machine in motion. Between 1653 and 1660, settlers flocked to New
Netherland in a more than fourfold increase in population, from approximately two thousand settlers in 1653 to as much as nine thousand by 1660.[8]

While the increase in population strengthened the colony's presence and
supported its economic growth, the installation of the municipal government
worked to stabilize tensions with its recognized, reliable, and more predictable
structure. The new organization widened administrative decision-making to
include the colonists, one of Van der Donck's most prominent goals, giving
them a hand in regulating economy, trade, and public works. The new city
government also included broader judicial functions, which meant that problems could be settled locally and more efficiently, without delay, and without
the additional layer of complexity involving mediators in *patria*.[9] The healthy
trade that resulted became a force in the colony's growth and prosperity in
these later years of the administration, persisting well after the Dutch flag no
longer flew above Fort Amsterdam.

It is truly unfortunate that Van der Donck did not live to see the long-
term effects of these changes that he helped bring about. In large measure,
it was the success of New Amsterdam that made it so attractive to England
as the North American center of trade. It has been argued that the fac-
tors put in place by Van der Donck influenced New York's evolution as a
confluence of trade, finance, democracy, and immigrant stories and, if ex-
trapolated over time, set it on a trajectory for the world center it is today.[10]
While these successes surely grew from early influences, they belong to
the larger story of the colony and the history of New York. Taken from

another, more personal perspective, much of Van der Donck's efforts were unsuccessful. He returned to New Netherland, defeated from his attempt at ousting the West India Company and playing a key role in a new leadership. As punishment, he had to concede any ability to hold political office, as well as a large part of his capacity to work as a lawyer, all while remaining suspect in the eyes of the colony's administration, only to lose his life a relatively short time later. It is difficult not to wonder how the story of the colony might have turned out differently had he lived longer. The two years after his return to New Netherland may have found him tending to the much-needed domestic matters of his Colendonck property but potentially also biding his time, waiting for the right moment, or right place, to get involved again. He was not one to give up. Any chance he had was cut short by his premature death, long before his beloved New Netherland fell, indefensibly, to a very determined England.

Yet, do these failures negate Van der Donck's place in history? If there would be any reparation for Van der Donck, it has lain dormant until this century as his efforts come to light long after his death and he is acknowledged for his contributions to early American history. Not only does Van der Donck deserve recognition for his role in the development of the municipality that eventually became New York, there is no denying that he is also part of the larger American story, despite the fact that much of his political battle took place on European ground. In this early example of a democratic process, the right of the people to come together for a say in their government and their right to bring grievances to the highest level of government, his cause began and ended on American soil, for what became American territory and now belongs to the broader landscape of the American narrative. This new land had become Van der Donck's home, his identity firmly rooted in the surroundings of the North American continent, forever changed, and looking toward the future. Respected historian Thomas O'Donnell later described him as "a confirmed American" with a "great purpose," to share his unique vision of America, while calling his book "one of America's oldest literary treasures."[11] A 1919 antiquarian catalogue provides a similar attestation of Van der Donck's place in American history in its commentary on an original, Dutch-language, "very fine copy of the extremely rare first edition of [Van der] Donck's *Description of New Netherland*," describing it as possessing "an interest beyond its rarity."[12] "So important is this work," it read, that one prominent bibliographer had been quoted as saying, "What the 1st Folio is to an English collector, a Van der Donck is to an American."[13] An original 1655 copy at the New York State Library is kept locked in the vault.

Van der Donck had a clear vision for New Netherland that was both served and hindered by his headstrong nature. While his strong will and tenacity lifted his cause, his methods may have made him as many enemies as friends. Nevertheless, his knowledge of the law, his capacity to lead, and his extraordinary gift for writing set him apart from his seventeenth-century peers. But over and above his most discernible achievements—the documentary writings, the populating of the country, and the stability under the municipal government, what stands out the most for Adriaen van der Donck is the fight for New Netherland, itself. As a true visionary who recognized the boundless potential of the country, his purpose gained momentum that carried him beyond his personal motivations and became an objective to save the colony at all costs. What he stood to gain paled in comparison to what he stood to lose. Ultimately, he worked tirelessly and passionately to lead change for the people of New Netherland and for the love of the country he had learned to call home. It is this monumental effort to stand up and persevere in his convictions, at great personal risk, that rouses our attention, and the reason we are still talking about him more than 350 years after his death. Adriaen van der Donck did not die in vain. There is a something about his fight for New Netherland, in the incredible determination he showed in seeking to right the wrongs in something truly worth fighting for, that buoys and inspires today. It is a spirit that resonates with us as human beings, in an intangible, soul-touching way that makes his life worth examining and holds, justly and rightly, his place in history.

Notes

ABBREVIATIONS

VRBM   *Van Rensselaer Bowier Manuscripts*
DRCHNY   *Documents Relative to the Colonial History of the State of New York*
NL-HaNA   Nationaal Archief, The Hague, the Netherlands
NYHM   New York Historical Manuscripts
NYSA   New York State Archives

PREFACE

1. Ada Louise van Gastel, "Adriaen van der Donck als woordvoerder van de Nieuw-Nederlandse Bevolking," in *Jaarboek Centraal Bureau voor Genealogie* (Den Haag: Centraal Bureau voor Genealogie, 1996); Jaap Jacobs, "Migration, Population, and Government," in *Four Centuries of Dutch-American Relations: 1609–2009*, ed. Hans Krabbendam, Cornelis A. van Minnen, and Giles Scott-Smith (Albany: State University of New York Press, 2009).

2. Adriaen van der Donck, *A Description of the New Netherlands*, ed. Thomas O'Donnell, trans. Jeremiah Johnson (Syracuse: Syracuse University Press, 1968), xii.

3. The print known as "Hartgers' View" was produced in 1625 and first appeared in Joost Hartgers, *Beschrijvinge van Virginia, Nieuw Nederlandt, Nieuw Engelandt, en d'Eylanden Bermudes, Berbados, en S. Christoffel* (Amsterdam: Joost Hartgers, 1651). It was also featured in the first edition of Adriaen van der Donck, *Beschryvinge van Nieuw-Nederlant* (Amsterdam: Evert Nieuwenhof, 1655). See Joep de Koning, "From Van der Donck to Visscher," *Mercator's World* 5, no. 4 (July/August 2000): 8.

CHAPTER 1

1. Jan van Oudheusden, *Geschiedenis van Brabant: van het hertogdom tot heden* (Zwolle: Waanders, 2004), 388.

2. Peat is made of decomposing plant matter found in boggy areas that was dried and used as a common fuel source.

3. Govert G. Hoeven, *Geschiedenis der Vesting Breda* (Breda: Broese, 1868), 67.

4. Fish market, livestock market, timber market, and oat market.

5. William J. Hoffman, "An Armory of American Families of Dutch Descent: Van der Donck-Van Bergen," *New York Genealogical and Biographical Record* 67 (New York: New York Genealogical and Biographical Society, 1936), 342. Rampant, in the context of heraldry, typically refers to an animal in profile, facing the left side, standing on its hind foot, forefeet and tail raised.

6. The letters "z" or "dr" at the end of names such as Gysbrechtsz and Adriaensdr, noted with or without a period at the end, were abbreviations for *zoon* (son of) and *dochter* (daughter of).

7. Hoffman, "Van der Donck-Van Bergen," 232, 342.

8. Ibid., 231.

9. Van der Donck's exact date of birth is uncertain. These dates are popularly derived from ages recorded on enrollment records at Leiden University, which were often inaccurate. His first enrollment in 1638 listed him as twenty, and his second enrollment in 1653, as thirty-three. A 1650 legal document from the archives in Amsterdam recorded his age as thirty-two (Stadsarchief Amsterdam, Notarial Archive 5075, Jacob de Winter, inventory 2278 IV, 61–62, November 9, 1650). For the purposes of this book, a birth year of 1618 is generally assumed. Birth records were not kept in the early 1600s and baptismal records for the Protestant churches in Breda, except for the Walloon Church, begin in 1637. This year coincides with the recapture of Breda by the Protestant Dutch Republic after Catholic rule from 1625 to 1637, suggesting that the Protestant records might have been lost or destroyed during the Catholic period. There are earlier records for Catholic churches in Breda.

10. Recently available records from the Staadsarchief Breda indicate that Johanna van der Donck, previously thought to be a sister, is a cousin. The name Ghysbrecht van der Donck appears together in a 1650 document with Adriaen van der Donck in Breda when he is authorized to pick up items belonging to worker Gulyam Jansen. Stadsarchief Breda, J.P. Beeris, Procuratiën, attestatiën enz., 1644–1650, inventarisnummer 0132, blad 46r. Ghysbrecht may also be the brother who supposedly journeyed to New Netherland in 1652, and the father of Gysbert van der Donck, whom Jansen later sued in New Netherland in the father's absence.

11. L. de Jonge and A. Huijsmans, *Breda, de Korte Boschstraat, Archeologische begeleiding* (Breda: Erfgoedrapport, 2013).

12. Hoeven, *Geschiedenis der Vesting Breda*, 101–112.

13. Ibid., 115.

14. Ibid., 131–133.

15. Ibid., 119–120

16. "Oosterhoutse Tijdmachine, 1621," www.tijdmachineoosterhout.nl (accessed March 29, 2017). Barony is an old word meaning the estates of a baron, or the land surrounding a particular area, in this case, incorporating several villages in the area surrounding Breda.

17. Stadsarchief Breda, *Vestbrieven 1599–1600*, inv. nr. 499, 106v.

18. Willem Otterspeer, *The Bastion of Liberty: Leiden University Today and Yesterday*, trans. Beverly Jackson (Amsterdam: Leiden University Press, 2008), 74–78.

19. Stadsarchief Breda, *Vestbrieven 1638–1639*, inv. nr. 531, 110r.

20. Balthasar van Donck, "Bewindvoerder van de Veenhuizen venen 1652, juli," Stadhouderlijk Archief: Het Archief in Treosar, Correspondenten, abk-7, Inventaris 1.2.3.09.2.

21. *Volumen Inscriptionum 1631–1645*, Universiteit Leiden Special Collections, v. 205.

CHAPTER 2

1. *Volumen Inscriptionum*, v. 205.

2. Otterspeer, *The Bastion of Liberty*, 29–31.

3. J. J. Woltjer, *De Leidse Universiteit in Verleden en Heden* (Leiden: Universitaire Pers, 1965), 4.

4. Otterspeer, *The Bastion of Liberty*, 84.

5. Lunsingh Scheurleer, Theodoor Herman, and G. H. M. Posthumus Meyjes, eds., *Leiden University in the Seventeenth Century: An Exchange of Learning* (Leiden: Brill, 1975), 5.

6. Otterspeer, *The Bastion of Liberty*, 73–74; Scheurleer, Herman, and Meyjes, *Leiden University*, 32.

7. Kiliaen van Rensselaer to Johannes de Laet, February 4, 1641. Kiliaen van Rensselaer, *Brievenboek van Kiliaen van Rensselaer*, Het Scheepvaartmuseum, Amsterdam, Inv. HS–2179, f. 142a. Henceforth cited as *Brievenboek*. For a previously published English translation of the full document, see A. J. F. van Laer, trans. and ed., *Van Rensselaer Bowier Manuscripts, Being the Letters of Kiliaen van Rensselaer, 1630–1643, and Other Documents Relating to the Colony of Rensselaerswyck* (Albany: University of the State of New York, 1908), 534. Henceforth cited as *VRBM*.

8. Woltjer, *De Leidse Universiteit*, 31.

9. Ibid.

10. Willem Otterspeer, *Groepsportret met Dame: Het bolwerk van de vrijheid* (Amsterdam: Bakker, 2000), 361.

11. J. M. Smits, *The Making of European Private Law: Toward a Ius Commune Europaeum as a Mixed Legal System* (Antwerp: Intersentia, 2002), 156–159.

12. Otterspeer, *The Bastion of Liberty*, 10.

13. Ibid., 71.

14. Ibid.

15. Rembrandt van Rijn, *The Anatomy Lesson of Dr. Nicolaes Tulp*, 1632, oil on canvas, Mauritshuis, The Hague.

16. Woltjer, *De Leidse Universiteit*, 23.

17. Otterspeer, *The Bastion of Liberty*, 100.

18. Ibid., 101.

19. Ibid., 98.

20. Otterspeer, *Groepsportret*, 226.

21. Otterspeer, *The Bastion of Liberty*, 93.

22. Otterspeer, *Groepsportret*, 272–273.

23. *Volumen Inscriptionum 1631–1645*, Leiden Universiteit Special Collections, v. 205.

24. Otterspeer, *The Bastion of Liberty*, 41.

25. Ibid., 38.

26. Ibid.

27. Ibid, 84.

28. Ibid., 81–84.

29. Universiteit Leiden Special Collections, Archieven van Senaat en Faculteiten, 1575–1877 (ASF 22-252); Curator Leiden University archives, email message to author, July 2016.

30. Otterspeer, *Groepsportret*, 239–241.

31. *VRBM*, 527–547.

32. Otterspeer, *Groepsportret*, 222–223.

33. Otterspeer, *The Bastion of Liberty*, 15.

34. Ibid., 95.

35. The Walloons were French-speaking people from an area in the Southern Low Countries located in what is now contained mostly in the southern portion of Belgium.

CHAPTER 3

1. Janny Venema, *Kiliaen van Rensselaer (1586–1643): Designing a New World* (Hilversum: Verloren, 2010), 268.

2. Kiliaen van Rensselaer to Toussaint Muyssart, January 25, 1641. *Brievenboek*, f. 137. For an earlier translation in a published document, see *VRBM*, 524.

3. Thomas E. Burke, *Mohawk Frontier: The Dutch Community of Schenectady, New York, 1661–1710* (Ithaca: Cornell University Press, 1991), 3.

4. Harmen Meyndertsz. van den Bogaert, *A Journey into Mohawk and Oneida Country, 1634–1635: The Journal of Harmen Meyndertsz van den Bogaert*, trans. and ed. Charles T. Gehring and William Starna (Syracuse: Syracuse University Press, 1988), xvi.

5. Willem Frijhoff, *Fulfilling God's Mission: The Two Worlds of Dominie Everardus Bogardus, 1607–1647*, trans. Myra J. Heerspink Scholz (Boston: Brill, 2007), 382; Venema, *Kiliaen van Rensselaer*, 216–224.

6. Kiliaen van Rensselaer to Toussaint Muyssart, January 25, 1641. *Brievenboek*, f. 137. For an earlier translation in a published document, see *VRBM*, 524.

7. Venema, *Kiliaen van Rensselaer*, 255.

8. Kiliaen van Rensselaer to Toussaint Muyssart, January 31, 1641. *Brievenboek*, f. 138b. For an earlier translation in a published document, see *VRBM*, 527.

9. Ibid.

10. *VRBM*, 527n. Louys Saulmon appears in the records of the Stadsarchief Breda, *Vestbrieven, 1618–1622.*

11. Kiliaen van Rensselaer to Toussaint Muyssart, January 31, 1641. *Brievenboek*, f. 138b. For an earlier translation in a published document, see *VRBM*, 527.

12. Kiliaen van Rensselaer to Toussaint Muyssart, February 5, 1641. *Brievenboek*, f. 142. For an earlier translation in a published document, see *VRBM*, 536.

13. Kiliaen van Rensselaer to Louys Saulmon, February 21, 1641. *Brievenboek*, f. 142b. For an earlier translation in a published document, see *VRBM*, 543.

14. Kiliaen van Rensselaer to Adriaen van der Donck, May 4, 1641. *Brievenboek*, f. 144. For an earlier translation in a published document, see *VRBM*, 547.

15. Ibid.

16. Ibid.

17. *VRBM*, 809.

18. Instructions and Commission for Adriaen van der Donck, May 13/14, 1641. Ibid., 703. Van Laer notes that the full instructions are not included in the *Van Rensselaer Bouwier Manuscripts*.

19. Ibid.

20. Ibid.

21. Instructions to Rutger Hendricksz van Soest, July 20, 1632. *Brievenboek*, f. 17. For an earlier translation in a published document, see *VRBM*, 208.

22. Ibid.

23. Ibid.

24. Ibid., f. 17–17b. For an earlier translation in a published document, see *VRBM*, 209.

25. Ibid., f. 17b. For an earlier translation in a published document, see *VRBM*, 209.

26. Kiliaen van Rensselaer to Adriaen van der Donck, March 9, 1643. *Brievenboek*, f. 161. For an earlier translation in a published document, see *VRBM*, 636.

27. "Een versilverde degen met een draegbant," in Memoranda from Kiliaen van Rensselaer to Wouter van Twiller, July 20, 1632. *Brievenboek*, f. 14b. For an earlier translation in a published document, see *VRBM*, 204–205.

28. Kiliaen van Rensselaer to Willem Kieft, May 14, 1641. *Brievenboek*, f. 144b. For an earlier translation in a published document, see *VRBM*, 549.

CHAPTER 4

1. A. J. F. van Laer, trans., *Register of the Provincial Secretary, 1638–1642* (Baltimore: Genealogical Publishing Co., 1974), 341. Hereafter, cited as *NYHM*, volume 1.

2. Charlotte Wilcoxen, "Ships and Work Boats of New Netherland, 1609–1674," in *A Beautiful and Fruitful Place: Selected Rensselaerswijck Seminar Papers*, ed. Nancy Zeller and Charles T. Gehring (Albany: New Netherland Publishing, 1991), 66.

3. Wilcoxen, "Ships and Work Boats of New Netherland," 58.

4. Robert Parthesius, *Dutch Ships in Tropical Waters: The Development of the Dutch East India Company (VOC) Shipping Network in Asia 1595–1660* (Amsterdam: Amsterdam University Press, 2010), 12.

5. Wilcoxen, "Ships and Work Boats of New Netherland," 57.

6. Charter Party of *Den Eyckenboom*, January 25, 1659. NYSA_A1883-78_V17_044, Digital Collections, New York State Archives. Hereafter, cited as NYSA.

7. Cornelis Melyn, "Melyn Papers, 1640–1699," Collections of the New York Historical Society for the Year 1913 (New York: New York Historical Society and Jacob Melyn, 1914), 110.

8. *NYHM*, 1: 341. The term "last" was used as a measure of cargo space but could refer to either volume (about 125 cubic feet) or weight (about 4,000 pounds). For more on "the ambiguity of the last," see Parthesius, *Dutch Ships in Tropical Waters*, 17.

9. Ibid., 346–349.

10. Melyn, "Melyn Papers," 109–110.

11. For biographical information on Cornelis Melyn, see Paul G. Burton, "The Antwerp Ancestry of Cornelis Melyn," in *New York Genealogical and Biographical Record* 67 (New York: New York Genealogical and Biographical Society, 1936), 167–164, 246–255, and Paul G. Burton, "Cornelis Melyn, Patroon of Staten Island and Some of His Descendants," in *New York Genealogical and Biographical Record* 68 (New York: New York Genealogical and Biographical Society, 1937), 3–17, 132.

12. *VRBM*, 419.

13. Melyn, "Melyn Papers," 109; *VRBM*, 548.

14. *VRBM*, 548.

15. Willem Frijhoff, "Director Willem Kieft and His Dutch Relatives," in *Revisiting New Netherland: Perspectives on Early Dutch America*, ed. Joyce D. Goodfriend (Leiden: Brill, 2005), 176–177. For a comprehensive review of Kieft's background, see Frijhoff's full essay.

16. Kiliaen van Rensselaer to Willem Kieft, May 14, 1641. *Brievenboek*, f. 144b. For an earlier translation in a published document, see *VRBM*, 549.

17. Kiliaen van Rensselaer to Arent van Curler, May 14, 1641. *Brievenboek*, f. 145. For an earlier translation in a published document, see *VRBM*, 549.

18. Donna Merwick, *Possessing Albany, 1630–1710: The Dutch and English Experiences* (Cambridge: Cambridge University Press, 1990), 54–55.

19. Kiliaen van Rensselaer to Arent van Curler. May 13, 1639. *Brievenboek*, f. 111. For an earlier translation in a published document, see *VRBM*, 438–439.

20. Kiliaen van Rensselaer to Arent van Curler, May 14, 1641. *Brievenboek*, f. 145. For an earlier translation in a published document, see *VRBM*, 550.

Chapter 5

1. Venema, *Kiliaen van Rensselaer*, 246.

2. Ibid., 255.

3. Dirk Mouw, trans., *The Memorandum Book of Anthony de Hooges* (Albany: The New Netherland Institute, 2012), xii.

4. Ibid., xii.

5. Ibid., v–vi.

6. *VRBM*, 580–603.

7. Kiliaen van Rensselaer to Anthony de Hooges, June 8, 1642. *Brievenboek*, f. 157. For an earlier translation in a published document, see *VRBM*, 620.

8. Kiliaen van Rensselaer to Arent van Curler, July 18, 1641. *Brievenboek*, f. 149. For an earlier translation in a published document, see *VRBM*, 564.

9. Venema, *Kiliaen van Rensselaer*, 262.

10. Kiliaen van Rensselaer to Arent van Curler, July 18, 1641. *Brievenboek*, f. 147b. For an earlier translation in a published document, see *VRBM*, 559.

11. Ibid.

12. *VRBM*, 560, 44n.

13. Kiliaen van Rensselaer to Arent van Curler, July 18, 1641. *Brievenboek*, f. 147b.

14. Ibid.

15. Kiliaen van Rensselaer to Adriaen van der Donck, July 23, 1641. *Brievenboek*, f. 151b. For an earlier translation in a published document, see *VRBM*, 571.

16. *VRBM*, 555.

17. Kiliaen van Rensselaer to Cornelis van der Donck, June 18, 1641. *Brievenboek*, f. 146b. For an earlier translation in a published document, see *VRBM*, 555.

18. *Welgeboren* means "of noble birth." *VRBM*, 555.

19. Kiliaen van Rensselaer to Cornelis van der Donck, August 1, 1641. *Brievenboek*, f. 152. For an earlier translation in a published document, see *VRBM*, 573.

20. Kiliaen van Rensselaer to Cornelis van der Donck, September 21, 1641. *Brievenboek*, f. 152. For an earlier translation in a published document, see *VRBM*, 575.

21. Probably Claes Jansen from Waalwijk (who Van Laer says appears in Van der Donck's account books, *VRBM*, 827), and Paulus Jansen from Geertruidenberg, both from North Brabant. See Kiliaen van Rensselaer to Cornelis van der Donck, May 14, 1642. *Brievenboek*, f. 156b, f. 168. For an earlier translation in a published document, see *VRBM*, 608–610.

22. Kiliaen van Rensselaer to Cornelis van der Donck, December 10, 1641. *Brievenboek* f. 154b. For an earlier translation in a published document, see *VRBM*, 603.

23. Historian Thomas O'Donnell suggests that Van Rensselaer dictated this ordinance to De Hooges as his secretary, during an earlier interview with Van der Donck, and that Van der Donck carried the document with him to New Netherland. See Van der Donck, *A Description of the New Netherlands*, xvii–xviii.

24. Ordinance of the Colony of Rensselaerswyck Regulating Trade, August 12, 1641. *VRBM*, 573–574.

25. Ordinance of the Colony of Rensselaerswyck, October 10, 1642; October 18, 1642; and date unknown. *VRBM*, 626–628.

26. Ibid., 626–627.

27. Memorandum from Kiliaen van Rensselaer to Johannes Megapolensis, June 3, 1642. *Brievenboek*, f. 169b. For an earlier translation in a published document, see *VRBM*, 614.

28. A. J. F. van Laer, trans., *Council Minutes, 1638–1649* (Baltimore: Genealogical Publishing Co., 1974), 170. Hereafter cited as *NYHM*, volume 4.

29. Kiliaen van Rensselaer to Willem Kieft, June 8, 1642. *Brievenboek*, f. 157b. For an earlier translation in a published document, see *VRBM*, 621.

30. Memorandum from Kiliaen van Rensselaer to Johannes Megapolensis, June 3, 1642. *Brievenboek*, f. 171. For an earlier translation in a published document, see *VRBM*, 618.

31. Ibid., f. 170. For an earlier translation in a published document, see *VRBM*, 616.

CHAPTER 6

1. "Ick neme seer qualyck." *Brievenboek*, 170b. For an earlier translation in a published document, see *VRBM*, 617.

2. Ibid.

3. Kiliaen van Rensselaer to Adriaen van der Donck, March 9, 1643. *Brievenboek*, f. 158b. For an earlier translation in a published document, see *VRBM*, 630.

4. Ibid., f. 159. For an earlier translation in a published document, see *VRBM*, 631.

5. Ibid.

6. Ibid.

7. Ibid.

8. "ue eygen nett te roocken." Ibid. For an earlier translation in a published document, see *VRBM*, 631–632.

9. Ibid., 159b. For an earlier translation in a published document, see *VRBM*, 632.

10. Ibid.

11. Ibid.

12. Ibid., f. 160. For an earlier translation in a published document, see *VRBM*, 633.

13. Ibid., f. 161. For an earlier translation in a published document, see *VRBM*, 636.

14. Ibid., f. 161b. For an earlier translation in a published document, see *VRBM*, 637.

15. Ibid., f. 171b. For an earlier translation in a published document, see *VRBM*, 642.

16. Ibid.

17. Kiliaen van Rensselaer to Arent Van Curler, March 16, 1643. *Brievenboek*, f. 181. For an earlier translation in a published document, see *VRBM*, 666.

18. Kiliaen van Rensselaer to Johannes Megapolensis, March 13, 1643. *Brievenboek*, f. 174b. For an earlier translation in a published document, see *VRBM*, 649.

19. Ibid.

20. Kiliaen van Rensselaer to Adriaen van der Donck, March 9, 1643. *Brievenboek*, f. 172–172b. For an earlier translation in a published document, see *VRBM*, 644.

21. Ibid., f. 172b.

22. Ibid.

23. The original manuscript is badly damaged by fire and under restricted access. Arent van Curler to Kiliaen van Rensselaer, June 16, 1643. "Arent van Curler & the Flatts," Digital Exhibition, New Netherland Institute. https://www.newnetherlandinstitute.org (accessed January 19, 2017), 1.

24. Ibid., 3.

25. Ibid., 4.

26. My translation of "seer eygenbatich ende tot sich treckende." Ibid., 6n21.

27. Ibid., 6–7.

28. Dutch colonial council minutes, 12-14 November, 1642. NYSA_A1809-78_V04_p148, Digital Collections, NYSA. For an earlier translation in a published document, see *NYHM*, 4: 173.

29. Arent van Curler to Kiliaen van Rensselaer, June 16, 1643. "Arent van Curler & the Flatts," 8.

30. *VRBM*, 666.

31. Arent van Curler to Kiliaen van Rensselaer, June 16, 1643. "Arent van Curler & the Flatts," 8. Van Rensselaer had instructed Van Curler, on several occasions, not to accept credit for payment. See *VRBM*, 455, 511, 550.

32. Ibid.

33. Ibid., 9.

34. A "knock on the head" is taken from a Native expression that usually carried the meaning of a tomahawk to the head.

35. Ibid., 9.

36. *VRBM*, 686.

37. E. B. O'Callaghan, *The History of New Netherland* (New York: D. Appleton and Co., 1848), I: 338. The original document in the archives of the New York State Library is partially burned and some text is lost. A seal on the back partially obscures text on the back. New York State Library Historical Document Inventory (GDM)NY-06-0072.

38. Ibid., 339.

39. A *bouwerie* is a farm. Ibid.

40. Venema, *Kiliaen van Rensselaer*, 283–284.

41. Ibid., 266.

42. A. J. F. van Laer, trans., *Minutes of the Court of Rensselaerswyck, 1648–1652* (Albany: University of the State of New York, 1922), 16–17. *VRBM*, 717n.

43. *VRBM*, 777.

44. *VRBM*, 680, 832.

45. Discharge of Isbrant Clasen and Harmen Arentsen, April 6, 1644. NYSA_A0270-78_V2_108a, Digital Collections, NYSA. For an earlier translation in a published document, see A. J. F. van Laer, trans., *Register of the Provincial Secretary, 1642–1647* (Baltimore: Genealogical Publishing Co., 1974), 217. Hereafter cited as *NYHM*, volume 2.

46. Declaration of Nicolaes Coorn, October 23, 1645. NYSA_A0270-78_V2_147e, Digital Collections, NYSA. For an earlier translation in a published document, see *NYHM*, 2: 316.

47. Testimony Regarding Permission Granted to Nicolaes Coorn, May 5, 1646. NYSL_sc7079_dehooghes-memo-book_A37, Digital Collections, NYSA. For an earlier translation in a published document, see Mouw, *Memorandum Book*, 44.

Chapter 7

1. Adriaen van der Donck, *A Description of New Netherland*, ed. Charles T. Gehring and William A. Starna, trans. Diederik Willem Goedhuys (Lincoln: University of Nebraska Press, 2010), 164.

2. A *schepel* is equal to 0.764 bushel. O'Callaghan, *The History of New Netherland*, I: 472.

3. *NYHM*, 4: 221–277.

4. *Geschreuw* can also be interpreted as a shout or scream. David Pietersz. de Vries, *Korte Historiael ende Journaels Aenteyckeninge van Verscheyden Voyagiens in de Vier Deelen des Wereldts-Ronde, also Europa, Africa, ende Amerika Gedaen* ('s Gravenhage: M. Nijhoff, 1911), 264. De Vries likely borrowed part of this story from the earlier publication, *Breeden-Raedt*.

5. Pavonia is present-day Hudson County in New Jersey. Ibid.

6. I. A. and G. W. C., *Breeden-Raedt aende Vereenichde Nederlandsche Provintien* (Antwerp: Francoys van Duynen, 1649), 18.

7. Letter of the Eight Men, October 24, 1643. Nationaal Archief, Den Haag, Staten-Generaal, nummer toegang 1.01.02, inventarisnummer 12564.25. For an earlier translation in a published document, see E. B. O'Callaghan and Berthold Fernow, trans., *Documents Relative to the Colonial History of the State of New York* (Albany: Weed, Parsons and Company, 1856–1887), I: 190. Hereafter, cited as *DRCHNY*.

8. Ibid. For an earlier translation in a published document, see *DRCHNY*, I: 191.

9. Ibid. For an earlier translation in a published document, see *DRCHNY*, I: 190.

10. Ibid.

11. Memorial of the Eight Men at the Manhattans to the States General, November 3, 1643. *DRCHNY*, I: 140.

12. Letter of the Eight Men to the Amsterdam Chamber of the West India Company, October 28, 1644. NL-HaNA, Staten-Generaal, 1.01.02, inv. nummer 12564.25. For an earlier translation in a published document, see *DRCHNY*, I: 209–213. Russell Shorto implies that Van der Donck's involvement in the writing of the colony's complaints began with this secret letter, while Willem Frijhoff argues that the letter was mainly influenced by Domine Bogardus. See Russell Shorto, *The Island at the Center of the World: The Epic Story of Dutch Manhattan and the Forgotten Colony That Shaped America* (New York: Vintage Books, 2005), 142–143, and Frijhoff, *Fulfilling God's Mission*, 497–499. I would argue that the style of writing aligning with Van der Donck's other writings begins later, with the interrogatories in defense of Melyn and Kuyter, and not with this October 28, 1644, secret letter of the Eight Men. Interrogatories in NL-HaNA, Staten-Generaal, 1.01.02, inv. nummer 12564.25. For an earlier translation in a published document, see *DRCHNY*, I: 196–201.

13. Ex-Director Kieft to Stuyvesant, June 18, 1647. NL-HaNA, Staten-Generaal, 1.01.02, inv. nummer 12564.25. For an earlier translation in a published document, see *DRCHNY*, I: 203.

14. Report of the Board, December 15, 1644. NL-HaNA, Staten-Generaal, 1.01.02, inv. nummer 12564.30A. For an earlier translation in a published document, see *DRCHNY*, I: 151–153.

15. Frijhoff, *Fulfilling God's Mission*, 482.

16. Van der Donck, *Beschryvinge van Nieuw-Nederlant*, 29. For the most recent published English translation of Van der Donck's book, see Van der Donck, *A Description of New Netherland*.

17. *Sewant* was shell beads, sometimes known as wampum, made by the Natives, typically from whelk and quahog shells and used as a form of currency. Petition of Adriaen van der Donck concerning land granted him at Saegkil in 1645, May 26, 1653. NYSA_A1810-78_VII_80a, Digital Collections, NYSA. For an earlier translation in a published document, see Charles Gehring, trans. and ed., *Correspondence, 1647–1653* (Syracuse: Syracuse University Press, 2000), 204..

18. Van der Donck, *Beschryvinge*, 74–75.

19. Ibid., 28–29; Ada Louise van Gastel, "Adriaen van Der Donck, New Netherland and America: A Thesis in English" (PhD diss., The Pennsylvania State University, 1985), 256.

20. Dutch colonial council minutes, 30 August–4 September 1645. NYSA_A1809-78_V04_p232-234, Digital Collections, NYSA. For an earlier translation in a published document, see *NYHM*, 4: 278.

21. Ibid.

22. Dutch colonial council minutes, 30 August–4 September 1645. NYSA_A1809-78_V04_p233-234, Digital Collections, NYSA. For an earlier translation in a published document, see *NYHM*, 4: 280.

23. The original land grant is not among the extant documents. See O'Callaghan, *The History of New Netherland*, I: 383.

24. Charter of Freedoms and Exemptions, June 7, 1629. *VRBM*, 136–152.

Chapter 8

1. Various genealogies report Mary Doughty's birthdate as 1625–1626. An article by Ethan Allen Doty reports a birthdate of 1628. See Ethan Allen Doty, "The Doughty Family of Long Island," in the *New York Genealogical and Biographical Record*, 43 (New York: New York Genealogical and Biographical Society, 1912), 312–324.

2. Henry A. Parker, "The Reverend Francis Doughty," in *Transactions, 1904–1906*, vol. X of Publications of the Colonial Society of Massachusetts (Boston: The Colonial Society of Massachusetts, 1907), 262.

3. John Bruce, ed., *Calendar of State Papers, Domestic Series, of the Reign of Charles I. 1635–1636* (London: Longmans, Green, Reader, and Dyer, 1866), 505.

4. Thomas Lechford, *Plain Dealing: or, News from England*, ed. J. Hammond Trumbull (Boston: J.K. Wiggin and W.P. Lunt, 1867), 91.

5. Ibid.

6. Adriaen van der Donck, *Vertoogh van Nieu-Neder-land, Wegens de Gelegenheydt, Vruchbaerheydt, en Soberen Staet desselfs* ('s Gravenhage: Michiel Stael, 1650), 35.

7. *Latrina* is Latin for lavatory. Letter of Revs. Megapolensis and Drisius to the Classis of Amsterdam, October 25, 1657. Franklin J. Jameson, *Narratives of New Netherland, 1609–1664* (New York: C. Scribner's Sons, 1909), 400.

8. Patent of Francis Doughty and Associates. NYSA_A1880-78_VGG_0049, Digital Collections, NYSA. For an earlier translation in a published document, see Charles Gehring, trans. and ed., *Land Papers, 1630–1664* (Baltimore: Genealogical Publishing Co., 1980), 15.

9. Parker, "The Reverend Francis Doughty," 269–270.

10. Dutch colonial council minutes, 10 June 1645. NYSA_A1809-78_V04_p224, Digital Collections, NYSA. For an earlier translation in a published document, see *NYHM*, 4: 266–267.

11. Samuel Smith Purple, *Index to the Marriage Records from 1639–1801 of the Reformed Dutch Church in New Amsterdam and New York* (New York: Priv. print., 1890), 13.

12. O'Callaghan, *The History of New Netherland*, I: 472.

13. In *The History of New Netherland*, O'Callaghan records the date of the fire as January 17th, but De Hooges writes January 18th. Memorandum of De Hooges' Dispute with Adriaen van der Donck, February–March 1646. NYSL_sc7079_dehooghes-memo-book_A20-A24, Digital Collections, NYSA. For an earlier translation in a published document, see Mouw, *Memorandum Book*, 27.

14. Van Gastel, "Adriaen van Der Donck, New Netherland and America," 82.

15. Memorandum of De Hooges' Dispute with Adriaen van der Donck, February–March 1646. NYSL_sc7079_dehooghes-memo-book_A20-A24, Digital Collections, NYSA. For an earlier translation in a published document, see Mouw, *Memorandum Book*, 26.

16. Ibid.

17. Van Rensselaer, *Brievenboek*, f. 163. For an earlier translation in a published document, see *VRBM*, 433.

18. Memorandum of De Hooges' Dispute with Adriaen van der Donck, February–March 1646. NYSL_sc7079_dehooghes-memo-book_A20-A24, Digital Collections, NYSA. For an earlier translation in a published document, see Mouw, *Memorandum Book*, 27.

19. Ibid.

20. A *tonne* is the same as a barrel. Ibid.

21. Mouw, *Memorandum Book*, 27.

22. Memorandum of De Hooges' Dispute with Adriaen van der Donck, February–March 1646. NYSL_sc7079_dehooghes-memo-book_A20-A24, Digital Collections, NYSA. For an earlier translation in a published document, see Mouw, *Memorandum Book*, 28.

23. Ibid.

24. Ibid., 25; Henry T. Riley, *A Dictionary of Latin and Greek Quotations, Proverbs, Maxims and Mottos* (London: Bell, 1909), 224.

25. Ibid., 29.

26. "Master Harmani" refers to Harman Meyndertsz van den Bogaert. "All for show," Ibid.

27. Ibid.

28. "God weet het." Ibid.

29. Fragment of a Contract by Which Cornelis Segersz van Voorhout Assumed the Remaining Three Years of the Lease of Adriaen van der Donck's Farm, April 1646. Ibid., 34.

30. Fragment of a Contract between Adriaen van der Donck and Cornelis Segersz van Voorhout, April 1646. Ibid., 46.

31. Agreement between De Hooges and Van der Donck to Submit to Arbitration. Ibid., 36.

32. Ibid.

33. Ibid.

CHAPTER 9

1. Documents in Antony de Hooges' *Memorandum Book* place Van der Donck in Rensselaerswyck through May 1646.

2. Though the name Colendonck has been assumed to mean "Colony of Donck," this name could have had its basis in geographical forms, or could have been play on words. The Dutch word *col* has been used to refer to a mountain pass, while *donk*, or the earlier form *donc* described a marsh, especially an area of hill and marsh. *Donk* appears commonly in the names of places in North Brabant, such as Arendonk, Raamsdonk, and Soerendonk. See M. Gysseling, *Toponymisch Woordenboek van België, Nederland, Luxemburg, Noord-Frankrijk en West-Duitsland* (Brussel: Belgisch Interuniversitair Centrum voor Nederlandistiek, 1960). Patent Empowering Adriaen van der Donck to Dispose of His Colonie by Will, April 26, 1652. *DRCHNY*, I: 470.

3. Hoffman, "Van der Donck-van Bergen," 238.

4. *NYHM*, 4: 294.

5. Copy of Abraham Clock's Bill for Carpentry, May 1646. NYSL_sc7079_dehooghes-memo-book_A35, Digital Collections, NYSA. For an earlier translation in a published document, see Mouw, *Memorandum Book*, 43.

6. Work done by landscape ecologist Eric Sanderson on the Mannahatta and Welikia Projects tells us that this waterway was once a much smaller and winding course than today's bridged Spuyten Duyvil Creek. Older texts that have translated the Lenape name Shorakapok to mean "wading place" also suggest that the Harlem River was once crossable at low tide. Additionally, Stuyvesant describes this land as being separated by "a very narrow kill, . . . fordable . . . when the water is low." See Extract from a Letter of Stuyvesant to the Directors, June 10, 1664. *DRCHNY*, XIIII: 550. For more on this fascinating topographical reconstruction of Manhattan, see Eric W. Sanderson, *Mannahatta: A Natural History of New York City* (New York: Abrams, 2009).

7. *NYHM*, 4: 318.

8. Frijhoff, *Fulfilling God's Mission*, 508.

9. Answer to the Remonstrance by Cornelis van Tienhoven, November 29, 1650. NL-HaNA, Staten-Generaal, 1.01.02, inv. nummer 12564.30A. For an earlier translation in a published document, see *DRCHNY*, I: 426; James Riker, *The Annals of Newtown in Queens County, New York* (New York: D. Fanshaw, 1852), 22–24.

10. Van der Donck, *Vertoogh*, 35.

11. Frijhoff, *Fulfilling God's Mission*, 359.

12. Van der Donck, *Vertoogh*, 35.

13. Shorto, *Island at the Center of the World*, 146–148.

14. The Huguenots were French Protestants who, in many cases, had fled religious persecution. Shorto, *Island at the Center of the World*, 153.

15. Stadsarchief Breda, *Dopen Wals-gereformeerd kerk, 1607–1810*, Collectie DTB Breda inv. nr. 89, 5.

16. Shorto, *Island at the Center of the World*, 154n.

17. West India Company to the States General, July 13, 1646. *DRCHNY*, I: 175.

18. Commission of Peter Stuyvesant, July 29, 1646. *DRCHNY*, I: 178.

19. Simon Groenveld, "New Light on a Drowned Princess—Information from London," *de Halve Maen* 74 (Summer 2001): 24–25.

20. Ibid., 25.

21. Van der Donck, *Vertoogh*, 40.

22. Ibid.

23. I. A. and G. W. C., *Breeden-Raedt*, 28.

24. Van der Donck, *Vertoogh*, 29.

25. Contract of Cornelis Segersen, June 14, 1647. NYSA_A0270-78_V2_157c, Digital Collections, NYSA. For an earlier translation in a published document, see *NHYM*, 2: 407.

26. Extraordinary Session, May 31, 1649. NYSL_sc7079-b13-f32_p32r-f33_p33v_ncn, Digital Collections, NYSA. For an earlier translation in a published document, see Van Laer, *Minutes of the Court of Rensselaerswyck, 1648–1652*, 78–79.

27. For a discussion by Shorto on Van der Donck's use of the term "American" to refer to Native Americans, see Shorto, *Island at the Center of the World*, 143. Interrogatories to be proposed to Van Dyck and Van Tienhoven (undated). NL-HaNA, Staten-Generaal, 1.01.02, inv. nummer 12564.25. For an earlier translation in a published document, see *DRCHNY*, I: 196, 200.

28. Shorto, *Island at the Center of the World*, 172.

29. Dutch colonial council minutes, 31 May–14 June 1647. NYSA_A1809-78_V04_ p289-292, Digital Collections, NYSA. For an earlier translation in a published document, see *NYHM*, 4: 370.

30. Ex-Director Kieft to Stuyvesant, June 18, 1647. NL-HaNA, Staten-Generaal, 1.01.02, inv. nummer 12564.25. For an earlier translation in a published document, see *DRCHNY*, I: 204.

31. Kuyter and Melyn to Stuyvesant, June 22, 1647. NL-HaNA, Staten-Generaal, 1.01.02, inv. nummer 12564.25. For an earlier translation in a published document, see *DRCHNY*, I: 205.

32. Ibid., 205–209.

33. For more on the argument originally suggested by Willem Frijhoff and expanded upon by Russell Shorto, on documents thought to have been written by Adriaen van der Donck, see Willem Frijhoff, *Wegen van Evert Willemz.: Een Hollands Weesking Op Zoek Naar Zichzelf, 1607–1647* (Nijmegen: SUN, 1995), 736–737; Frijhoff, *Fulfilling God's Mission*, 498; and Shorto, *Island at the Center of the World*, 143.

34. *NYHM*, 4: 417.

35. Sentence in Melyn Report of the Board, December 15, 1644. July 25, 1647. NL-HaNA, Staten-Generaal, 1.01.02, inv. nummer 12564.25. For an earlier translation in a published document, see *DRCHNY*, I: 349–350.

36. Judgment on Jochem Pietersen Kuyter, July 25, 1647. NL-HaNA, Staten-Generaal, 1.01.02, inv. nummer 12564.25. For an earlier translation in a published document, see *DRCHNY*, I: 213–214.

37. Dutch colonial council minutes, 28 September 1647. NYSA_A1809-78_V04_ p337, Digital Collections, NYSA. For an earlier translation in a published document, see *NYHM*, 4: 444.

38. Van der Donck, *Vertoogh*, 14.

39. *Geprenderende*, is used as in the French *prétendant*, or one who claims or professes (to be) something. Dutch colonial council minutes, 28 September 1647. NYSA_A1809-78_V04_p338, Digital Collections, NYSA. For an earlier translation in a published document, see *NYHM*, 4: 445.

40. Van der Donck, *Vertoogh*, 14.

41. Groenveld, "New Light on a Drowned Princess," 25.

42. Additional Observations, July 26, 1649. NL-HaNA, Staten-Generaal, 1.01.02, inv. nummer 12564.30A. For an earlier translation in a published document, see *DRCHNY*, I: 262.

43. Van der Donck, *Beschryvinge*, 89.

44. Groenveld, "New Light on a Drowned Princess," 25n12.

45. *NYHM*, 4: 418.

46. Frijhoff, *Fulfilling God's Mission*, 552.

47. Verkeerde Canaal was the Dutch name for the Bristol Channel. I. A. and G. W. C., *Breeden-Raedt*, 31.

48. Groenveld, "New Light on a Drowned Princess," 25.

49. Frijhoff, *Fulfilling God's Mission*, 552.

50. Melyn, *Breeden-Raedt*, 31.

51. Charles Gehring, "Wringing Information from a Drowned Princess," in *A Beautiful and Fruitful Place, Selected Rensselaerswyck Papers, Vol. 2*, ed. Elizabeth P. Funk and Martha D. Shattuck (Albany: State University of New York Press, 2011), 133.

52. Two passengers had died previously.

53. I. A. and G. W. C., *Breeden-Raedt*, 31.

54. Ibid. 32.

55. Melyn, *Melyn Papers*, 110.

56. I. A. and G. W. C., *Breeden-Raedt*, 32.

57. Ibid., 31.

58. Ibid., 32.

59. Govert Loockermans to Gillis Verbrugge, May 27, 1648. Govert Loockermans Correspondence and Papers, Stuyvesant-Rutherford Papers, Transcribed by Janny Venema from Microfilm A-FM-200-C. New Netherland Institute web publication.

60. Additional Observations, July 26, 1649. NL-HaNA, Staten-Generaal, 1.01.02, inv. nummer 12564.30A. For an earlier translation in a published document, see *DRCHNY*, I: 262.

Chapter 10

1. Extraordinary Session, May 31, 1649. NYSL_sc7079-b13-f32_p32r-f33_p33v_ncn, Digital Collections, NYSA. For an earlier translation in a published document, see Van Laer, *Minutes of the Court of Rensselaerswyck*, 79.

2. Summons to Adriaen van der Donck, February 1649. NYSL_sc7079-b13-f23_p23v_ncn, Digital Collections, NYSA. For an earlier translation in a published document, see Van Laer, *Minutes of the Court of Rensselaerswyck*, 61.

3. Van Laer, *Minutes of the Court of Rensselaerswyck*, 67–68.

4. Stadsarchief Breda, *Vestbrieven 1647–1650*, inv. nr. 534, 122v.

5. Van Laer, *Minutes of the Court of Rensselaerswyck*, 32.

6. Ibid. *VRBM*, 813.

7. A. J. F. Van Laer, *Register of the Provincial Secretary, 1648–1660* (Baltimore: Genealogical Publishing Co., 1974), 76.

8. Dutch colonial council minutes, 25 July–20 September 1647. NYSA_A1809-78_V04_p324-331, Digital Collections, NYSA. For an earlier translation in a published document, see *NYHM*, 4: 430.

9. Van Laer, *Minutes of the Court of Rensselaerswyck*, 60.

10. Van der Donck, *Vertoogh*, 46.

11. Van der Donck, *Vertoogh*, 46–47.

12. Dutch colonial council minutes, 15-23 March 1649. NYSA_A1809-78_V04_p429-430, Digital Collections, NYSA. For an earlier translation in a published document, see *NYHM*, 4: 586.

13. Van der Donck, *Vertoogh*, 47.

14. Ibid.

15. Dutch colonial council minutes, 15-23 March 1649. NYSA_A1809-78_V04_p429-430, Digital Collections, NYSA. For an earlier translation in a published document, see *NYHM*, 4: 587.

16. Mandamus in the case of appeal of Cuyter and Melyn, April 28, 1648. NL-HaNA, Staten-Generaal, 1.01.02, inv. nummer 12564.25. For an earlier translation in a published document, see *DRCHNY*, I: 249–251.

17. *Vrij ende Liber.* States General to Director Stuyvesant, April 28, 1648. NL-HaNA, Staten-Generaal, 1.01.02, inv. nummer 12564.25. For an earlier translation in a published document, see *DRCHNY*, I: 249.

18. Mandamus in the case of appeal of Cuyter and Melyn, April 28, 1648. NL-HaNA, Staten-Generaal, 1.01.02, inv. nummer 12564.25. For an earlier translation in a published document, see *DRCHNY*, I: 249–251.

19. States General Safeguard to Cuyter and Melyn, May 6, 1648. NL-HaNA, Staten-Generaal, 1.01.02, inv. nummer 12564.25. For an earlier translation in a published document, see *DRCHNY*, I: 252.

20. I. A. and G. W. C., *Breeden-Raedt*, 35.

21. Untitled responses to summonses by Cornelis Melyn, March–May 1649. NL-HaNA, Staten-Generaal, 1.01.02, inv. nummer 12564.25. For an earlier translation in a published document, see *DRCHNY*, I: 355–357.

22. *NYHM*, 4: 595–598.

23. Protest to Director Stuyvesant, July 29, 1649. NL-HaNA, Staten-Generaal, 1.01.02, inv. nummer 12564.25. For an earlier translation in a published document, see *DRCHNY*, I: 353.

24. Stuyvesant to Melyn's "Irreverent Protest," August 1, 1649. NL-HaNA, Staten-Generaal, 1.01.02, inv. nummer 12564.25. For an earlier translation in a published document, see *DRCHNY*, I: 354.

25. The records in this volume are badly damaged. Letter from the Directors at Amsterdam to Petrus Stuyvesant, January 27, 1649. Gehring, *Correspondence 1647–1653*, 65–66.

26. Nine Men to States General, July 26, 1649. NL-HaNA, Staten-Generaal, 1.01.02, inv. nummer 12564.30A. For an earlier translation in a published document, see *DRCHNY*, I: 258.

27. Vice Director Dincklagen to the State General, August 12, 1649. *DRCHNY*, I: 319.

28. Stuyvesant to States General, August 10, 1649. NL-HaNA, Staten-Generaal, 1.01.02, inv. nummer 12564.30A. For an earlier translation in a published document, see *DRCHNY*, I: 321–324.

29. I. A. and G. W. C., *Breeden-Raedt*, 38.

30. Ibid.

CHAPTER 12

1. Van der Donck, *Vertoogh*, 49.

2. Delegates to States General, October 13, 1649. NL-HaNA, Staten-Generaal, 1.01.02, inv. nummer 12564.30A. For an earlier translation in a published document, see *DRCHNY*, I: 259.

3. *DRCHNY*, I: 326–330.

4. Petition of the Commonalty, July 26, 1649. *DRCHNY*, I: 259. Additional Observations, July 26, 1649. NL-HaNA, Staten-Generaal, 1.01.02, inv. nummer 12564.30A.

For an earlier translation in a published document, see *DRCHNY*, I: 262–270. The Additional Observations were likely the result of a collaboration of the merchant signers of the Remonstrance. For more on the merchants of New Netherland, see Dennis J. Maika, "Commerce and Community: Manhattan Merchants in the Seventeenth Century," PhD diss., New York University, 1995.

    5. Additional Observations, July 26, 1649. NL-HaNA, Staten-Generaal, 1.01.02, inv. nummer 12564.30A. For an earlier translation in a published document, see *DRCHNY*, I: 262–270.

    6. Van der Donck, *Vertoogh*, 3.

    7. Ibid.

    8. Ibid.

    9. Ibid., 4.

    10. Ibid., 4–5.

    11. Ibid., 5

    12. Ibid., 6.

    13. Ibid.

    14. Ibid., 23.

    15. Ibid., 14, 17.

    16. Ibid., 15.

    17. Ibid., 16.

    18. Ibid., 25.

    19. "dat het is de quade regering met haer ghevolch en aenhangh/om met een woord te noemen/en daer is geen andere dat daer beter op past." Ibid.

    20. Ibid., 33.

    21. Ibid., 32.

    22. Ibid.

    23. Ibid., 29.

    24. Ibid.

    25. Ibid.

    26. Ibid., 28.

    27. Ibid., 37.

    28. Ibid., 37.

    29. Ibid., 42.

    30. Ibid., 43.

    31. Ibid., 44.

    32. Ibid.

    33. Ibid., 39.

    34. Ibid., 48.

    35. Petition of the Delegates, February 7, 1650. NL-HaNA, Staten-Generaal, 1.01.02, inv. nummer 12564.25. For an earlier translation in a published document, see *DRCHNY*, I: 346.

    36. Shorto, *Island at the Center of the World*, 217.

    37. Petition of the Delegates, February 7, 1650. NL-HaNA, Staten-Generaal, 1.01.02, inv. nummer 12564.25. For an earlier translation in a published document, see *DRCHNY*, I: 346.

38. De Koning, "From Van der Donck to Visscher," 6; Shorto, *Island at the Center of the World*, 217.

39. Van der Donck, *Vertoogh*, 45.

40. De Koning, "From Van der Donck to Visscher," 3.

41. Van der Donck, *Vertoogh*, 47.

Chapter 12

1. Abstract of the Excesses, January 27, 1650. NL-HaNA, Staten-Generaal, 1.01.02, inv. nummer 12564.30A. For an earlier translation in a published document, see *DRCHNY*, I: 332.

2. Answer of the West India Company, Jan. 31, 1650. NL-HaNA, Staten-Generaal, 1.01.02, inv. nummer 12564.30A. For an earlier translation in a published document, see *DRCHNY*, I: lx., 338–346.

3. Ibid.

4. Ibid. In his journal, David Pietersz. de Vries indicates that he recommended the church be built inside the fort "to guard against any surprise by Indians." David Peterson de Vries, *Voyages from Holland to America, A.D. 1632–1644*, trans. Henry C. Murphy (New York: Kraus Reprint, 1853), 149.

5. Ibid.

6. Ibid.

7. Ibid.

8. Petition of the Delegates, Feb 7, 1650. NL-HaNA, Staten-Generaal, 1.01.02, inv. nummer 12564.25. For an earlier translation in a published document, see *DRCHNY*, I: 346–347.

9. Ibid.

10. Ibid.

11. Ibid.

12. Petition of Cornelis Melyn, Feb. 8, 1650. NL-HaNA, Staten-Generaal, 1.01.02, inv. nummer 12564.25. For an earlier translation in a published document, see *DRCHNY*, I: 348–349.

13. Considerations on the Boundaries, February 22, 1650. NL-HaNA, Staten-Generaal, 1.01.02, inv. nummer 12564.30A. For an earlier translation in a published document, see *DRCHNY*, I: 359–371.

14. Observations on Duties Levied on Goods, March 7, 1649. *DRCHNY*, I: 372.

15. Letter from the Directors at Amsterdam to Petrus Stuyvesant, January 28, 1649. Gehring, *Correspondence, 1647–1653*, 82.

16. Ibid., 83–84.

17. Femke Deen, David Onnekink, and Michel Reinders, eds., *Pamphlets and Politics in the Dutch Republic* (Leiden: Brill, 2011), 4–16.

18. Letter from the Directors at Amsterdam to Petrus Stuyvesant, January 28, 1649. Gehring, *Correspondence, 1647–1653*, 84.

19. De Koning, "From Van der Donck to Visscher," 5.

20. Ibid., 9.

21. Van Gastel, "Adriaen van der Donck, New Netherland and America," 300–305.

22. Testimony of the Skipper of *De Valckenier*, March 12, 1650 NL-HaNA, Staten-Generaal, 1.01.02, inv. nummer 12564.30A. For an earlier translation in a published document, see in *DRCHNY*, I: 377.

23. Petition of the Delegates. March 12, 1650 NL-HaNA, Staten-Generaal, 1.01.02, inv. nummer 12564.30A. For an earlier translation in a published document, see *DRCHNY*, I: 376.

24. Draft Contract to Convey Emigrants, March 19, 1650. *DRCHNY*, I: 379.

25. Ibid.

26. States General to WIC, March 12, 1650. *DRCHNY*, I: 378.

27. Ibid., 379.

28. Jaap Jacobs, "A Hitherto Unknown Letter of Adriaen van der Donck," *de Halve Maen* 71 (Spring 1998): 6.

29. Ibid., 6.

30. States General to Director of New Netherland, April 1, 1650. NL-HaNA, Staten-Generaal, 1.01.02, inv. nummer 12564.36. For an earlier translation in a published document, see *DRCHNY*, I: 382–383.

31. Ibid.

32. Janneken Melyn to Cornelis Melyn, Dec. 17, 1649. NL-HaNA, Staten-Generaal, 1.01.02, inv. nummer 12564.30A. For an earlier translation in a published document, see *DRCHNY*, I: 386.

33. Delegates of New Netherland to States General, April 11, 1650. NL-HaNA, Staten-Generaal, 1.01.02, inv. nummer 12564.30A. For an earlier translation in a published document, see *DRCHNY*, I: 385–387.

34. April 11, 1650, Draft Provisional Order. NL-HaNA, Staten-Generaal, 1.01.02, inv. nummer 12564.30A. For an earlier translation in a published document, see *DRCHNY*, I: 390.

35. Observations of the Amsterdam Chamber, April 11, 1650. NL-HaNA, Staten-Generaal, 1.01.02, inv. nummer 12564.30A. For an earlier translation in a published document, see *DRCHNY*, I: 391–395.

36. Van der Donck to States General, April 11, 1650. NL-HaNA, Staten-Generaal, 1.01.02, inv. nummer 12564.30A. For an earlier translation in a published document, see *DRCHNY*, I: 395–396.

37. Delegates to the States General, April 12, 1650. *DRCHNY*, I: 398.

38. States General to Stuyvesant, April 7, 1650. *DRCHNY*, I: 400.

39. Jacobs, "A Hitherto Unknown Letter of Adriaen van der Donck," 6.

40. Ibid.

41. Letter from the Directors at Amsterdam to Petrus Stuyvesant, April 20, 1650. Gehring, *Correspondence, 1647–1653*, 87.

42. Ibid., 88.

43. Stuyvesant to the States General, August 17, 1650. *DRCHNY*, I: 419.

44. Letter from the Directors at Amsterdam to Petrus Stuyvesant, April 20, 1650. Gehring, *Correspondence, 1647–1653*, 88. Resolution of the States General, June 30, 1650. *DRCHNY*, I: 407–408.

45. Ibid., 88, 91.

46. Ibid., 91.

47. An *ancker* was equal to about ten gallons. A notarized copy of this manifest appears in the records of February 19, 1652, with a petition for restitution for confiscated goods, but the manifest was actually made for the ship's voyage in August 1650. Copy of the Manifest of *De Nieu Nederlantse Fortuyn*. August 9, 1650. NYSA_A1810-78_VII_52, Digital Collections, NYSA. For an earlier translation in a published document, see Gehring, *Correspondence, 1647–1653*, 142.

48. Ibid., 92.

49. Ibid.

50. Ibid., 92, 95.

51. Jacobs, "A Hitherto Unknown Letter of Adriaen van der Donck," 4.

52. Ibid., 4. For an illuminating example of political maneuvering in the seventeenth-century Dutch Republic, see Joris van den Tol, "Hendrick Haecxs: Amateuristisch Lobbyen door de WIC in de Republiek van 1647," in *Politieke Belangenbehartiging in De Vroegmoderne Nederlanden: De Rol Van Lobby, Petities, En Officiële Delegaties in De Politieke Besluitvorming*, ed. Elisabeth Geevers and Griet Vermeesch (Maastricht: Shaker Publishing, 2014).

53. Jaap Jacobs, *The Colony of New Netherland: A Dutch Settlement in Seventeenth-Century America* (Ithaca: Cornell University Press, 2009), 85.

54. Groenveld, "De Institutionele en Politieke Context," in *Tresorier tot Thesaurier-Generaal*, ed. J. T. de Smidt and R. M. Sprenger (Hilversum: Verloren, 1996), 64–65.

55. Many thanks to Jaap Jacobs for his email communications to discuss the various political factions in the Dutch Republic and their influence on the delegates' issues.

56. "The three P's," by Joris van den Tol, Leiden University. For more on lobbying in the seventeenth-century Dutch Republic, see his forthcoming PhD dissertation, "Lobbying in Company: Mechanisms of Political Decision-Making and Economic Interests in the History of Dutch Brazil, 1621–1656."

57. Select Men to the States General, Sept. 13, 1650. *DRCHNY*, I: 421.

58. WIC Response to Remonstrance, Nov. 29, 1650. NL-HaNA, Staten-Generaal, 1.01.02, inv. nummer 12564.30A. For an earlier translation in a published document, see *DRCHNY*, I: 422–432.

Chapter 13

1. *DRCHNY*, I: 438–459.

2. Extract of letter from Augustin Herman, September 10, 1650. NL-HaNA, Staten-Generaal, 1.01.02, inv. nummer 12564.36. For an earlier translation in a published document, see *DRCHNY*, I: 444.

3. Extract of Declaration of Joachem Pieters Cuyter, Nov.–Dec. 1650. NL-HaNA, Staten-Generaal, 1.01.02, inv. nummer 12564.36. For an earlier translation in a published document, see *DRCHNY*, I: 450.

4. Extract of a Letter from Jacob van Couwenhoven and Dirck van Schelluyne, October 6, 1650. *DRCHNY*, I: 446–447.

5. Resolution of the States General, Jan. 14, 1651. *DRCHNY*, I: 433.

6. Memorial of Adriaen van der Donck, February 10, 1652. NL-HaNA,

Staten-Generaal, 1.01.02, inv. nummer 12564.36. For an earlier translation in a published document, see *DRCHNY*, I: 439.

7. Resolution of the States General, April 21, 1651. *DRCHNY*, I: 435.

8. Stadsarchief Breda, *Vestbrieven, 1651–1655*, inv. nr. 535, 51r, 51v, 63r.

9. Letter from Van Dincklagen (in Latin), September 19, 1651. NL-HaNA, Staten-Generaal, 1.01.02, inv. nummer 12564.36. For an earlier translation in a published document, see *DRCHNY*, I: 453.

10. Letter from Augustin Herman, September 20, 1651. NL-HaNA, Staten-Generaal, 1.01.02, inv. nummer 12564.36. For an earlier translation in a published document, see *DRCHNY*, I: 453.

11. Letter from Dirck van Schelluyne, October 18, 1651. NL-HaNA, Staten-Generaal, 1.01.02, inv. nummer 12564.36. For an earlier translation in a published document, see *DRCHNY*, I: 452.

12. Memorial of Adriaen van der Donck, February 10, 1652. NL-HaNA, Staten-Generaal, 1.01.02, inv. nummer 12564.36. For an earlier translation in a published document, see *DRCHNY*, I: 440.

13. Memoir on the Boundaries, February 16, 1562. NL-HaNA, Staten-Generaal, 1.01.02, inv. nummer 12564.36. For an earlier translation in a published document, see *DRCHNY*, I: 456–459.

14. Extracts of Letters, Journals, Resolutions, Feb 16, 1652. NL-HaNA, Staten-Generaal, 1.01.02, inv. nummer 12564.36. For an earlier translation in a published document, see in *DRCHNY*, I: 444.

15. Amsterdam Chamber to States General, February 23, 1652. *DRCHNY*, I: 462.

16. "Nochtans, om alle de wereld den mont te stoppen." Letter from the Directors in Amsterdam to Petrus Stuyvesant, April 4, 1652. NYSA_A1810-78_VII_53, f 114, Digital Collections, NYSA. For an earlier translation in a published document, see Gehring, *Correspondence, 1647–1653*, 149.

17. Jacobs, "To Favor This New and Growing City of New Amsterdam," *de Halve Maen* 76 (Winter 2003): 64–65.

18. Jacobs, *The Colony of New Netherland*, 86–88.

19. "Letter from the Directors in Amsterdam to Petrus Stuyvesant, April 4, 1652. NYSA_A1810-78_VII_53, f 114, Digital Collections, NYSA. For an earlier translation in a published document, see in Gehring, *Correspondence, 1647–1653*, 149.

20. Resolution of the States General, April 27, 1652. Gehring, *Correspondence, 1647–1653*, 173; States General to Director Stuyvesant, April 27, 1652. *DRCHNY*, I: 472.

21. Patent empowering Adriaen van der Donck, April 26, 1652. *DRCHNY*, I: 470.

22. Stadsarchief Breda, *Vestbrieven 1651-1655*, inv. nr. 535, 109v.

23. Ibid. Stadsarchief Amsterdam, Notarial Archive 5075, Jacob de Winter, inventory 2278.

24. Stadsarchief Breda, *Vertrokken Lidmaten Breda, 1642–1679*, inv. nr. 88, 20r. Email communication, Stadsarchief Breda to author, August 2014.

25. Memorial of Adriaen van der Donck, May 13, 1652. NL-HaNA, Staten-Generaal, 1.01.02, inv. nummer 12564.36. For an earlier translation in a published document, see *DRCHNY*, I: 473.

26. Letter from the Directors to Petrus Stuyvesant, April 17, 1652. NYSA_ A1810-78_V11_59, Digital Collections, NYSA; Gehring, *Correspondence, 1647– 1653*, 166.

27. Ibid.

28. Jacobs, *The Colony of New Netherland*, 85. Thank you, again, to Jaap Jacobs for expanding my understanding of the roles of the various players in this politically complex event.

29. This letter, dated April 17, 1652, must have been written May 17, 1652, since it discusses events of April 27, 1652, and was written just as the recall of Stuyvesant was overturned on May 16, 1652. Letter from the Directors to Petrus Stuyvesant, April 17, 1652. NYSA_A1810-78_V11_59, Digital Collections, NYSA. For an earlier translation in a published document, see Gehring, *Correspondence, 1647–1653*, 166–167.

30. Amsterdam Chamber to the States General, May 27, 1652. NL-HaNA, Staten-Generaal, 1.01.02, inv. nummer 12564.36. For an earlier translation in a published document, see *DRCHNY*, I: 479.

31. Resolution of the States General, May 16, 1652. *DRCHNY*, I: 475.

32. Jaap Jacobs has argued that the events initiated by Pergens overturned the States General's decision, while Van Gastel and Shorto have argued that the impending war with England prompted the reversal. See Jacobs, *The Colony of New Netherland*, 85; Van Gastel, "Adriaen van der Donck, New Netherland and America," 210; Shorto, *Island at the Center of the World*, 245–249.

33. Secret Resolution on the Negotiation with England, May 13, 1652. *DRCHNY*, I: 475, 486.

34. Ibid., 477. Possibly Van der Capellen.

35. Petition of Adriaen van der Donck, May 24, 1652. NL-HaNA, Staten-Generaal, 1.01.02, inv. nummer 12564.36. For an earlier translation in a published document, see *DRCHNY*, I: 476–477.

36. Petition of Adriaen van der Donck, May 24, 1652. NL-HaNA, Staten-Generaal, 1.01.02, inv. nummer 12564.36. For an earlier translation in a published document, see *DRCHNY*, I: 476–477.

37. Resolution of the States General, May 24, 1652. *DRCHNY*, I: 478.

38. Resolution of the States General on a Letter from the Amsterdam Chamber, June 22, 1652. *DRCHNY*, I: 480.

39. Chamber at Dort to the States General, June 24, 1652. *DRCHNY*, I: 480–481. See NL-HaNA, Staten-Generaal, 1.01.02, inv. nummer 12564.36.

40. Secret Resolution of the States General, July 22, 1652. *DRCHNY*, I: 482.

41. Secret Memoir of the West India Company, July 30, 1652. *DRCHNY*, I: 483–484.

42. Resolution of the States General, September 3, 1652. *DRCHNY*, I: 487–488. For more on plans for the palisaded wall, along with a very small sketch, see Court Minutes of New Amsterdam, March 17, 1653. RNA_v1_bk2, n27, NYC Municipal Records Online, Books and Manuscripts. For an earlier translation in a published document, see Berthold Fernow, ed., *The Records of New Amsterdam, 1653–1674* (New York: Knickerbocker Press, 1897), I: 72.

CHAPTER 14

1. This introduction appeared in the first edition of Van der Donck's book and is the first English-language publication of his "Inleiding van de Auteur" in its entirety. Van der Donck, *Beschryvinge*, 9.

2. Ibid., 1.

3. Ibid., 7.

4. Ibid., 17.

5. Ibid., 40, 42.

6. Ibid., 41.

7. Ibid., 18.

8. Ibid., 45.

9. Ibid., 46.

10. Ibid., 53.

11. Ibid., 69, 70, 71.

12. Ibid., 68.

13. Ibid., 73, 75.

14. For example, those written by Megapolensis, Champlain, and Van den Bogaert. Ibid., 164n15, 165n20, 166n27, 167n34, n37.

15. Ibid., 52.

16. Ibid., 82.

17. Castoreum is produced in the scent glands of beavers and was believed to have medicinal properties. Ibid. 88–89, 169–170n11.

18. Ibid., 88.

19. Julie van den Hout, "The Omnipotent Beaver in Van der Donck's *A Description of New Netherland*." UC Berkeley: UC Berkeley Library. http://escholarship.org/uc/item/870174nb.

20. Van der Donck, *Beschryvinge*, 100.

21. Chamber at Amsterdam to the States General, May 2, 1653. *DRCHNY*, I: 530.

22. Resolution of the States General, May 24, 1653. *DRCHNY*, I: 533.

23. *Actorum Juridica Facultatis Vol. 1.* May 5, 1563, Universiteit Leiden Special Collections, Leiden. For enrollment, see *Volumen Inscriptionum-Album Studiosorum, Academiae Leydensis, 1645–1662*, Universiteit Leiden Special Collections, Leiden, f. 359.

24. Ibid. Record of Judith Hercules, Archief Erfgoed Leiden.

25. *Acta Senatus* (Leiden: De Rieu, 1875), 70. Historians have interpreted the degree date recorded as April 10, 1653, one month prior to the date recorded in the *Actorum Juridica Facultatis* as an interim or master's level degree. In fact, the April date has been discovered to be the result of a clerical error, where May was transcribed as April in the draft of the *Acta Senatus* and then printed. May 10, 1653, is the correct date of Van der Donck's degree. Thank you to Leiden University curator Dr. J. M. van Duijn for helping to verify this by locating the source of the discrepancy. Email communication to author, September 2015.

26. Jan de Vries, *Barges and Capitalism: Passenger Transportation in the Dutch Economy, 1632–1839* (Utrecht: HES Publishers, 1981), 14–50.

27. *Actorum Juridica Facultatis*, May 10, 1653, Universiteit Leiden Special Collections, Leiden.

28. Otterspeer, *Groepsportret*, 239–242.

29. Jacobs, *The Colony of New Netherland*, 93; Shorto, *Island at the Center of the World*, 258.

30. Petition of Adriaen van der Donck, May 26, 1653. NYSA_A1810-78_VII_80b, Digital Collections, NYSA. For an earlier translation in a published document, see Gehring, *Correspondence, 1647–1653*, 205–206.

31. The pamphlet was titled, *The Second Part of the Tragedy of Amboyna: Or a True Relation of a Most Bloody, Treacherous, and Cruel Design of the Dutch in the New Netherlands in America. For the total Ruining and Murthering of the English Colonies in New-England.* Shorto, *Island at the Center of the World*, 260–261.

32. Letter from the Directors at Amsterdam to Petrus Stuyvesant, November 4, 1653. Gehring, *Correspondence, 1647–1653*, 229–230.

33. Letter from the Directors at Amsterdam to Petrus Stuyvesant, August 6, 1652. Gehring, *Correspondence, 1647–1653*, 184.

34. David Pulsifer, ed., *Records of the Colony of New Plymouth, in New England, Volume 2* (Boston: Press of W. White, 1856), 45–46.

35. Petition of Adriaen van der Donck, May 26, 1653. Gehring, *Correspondence, 1647–1653*, 203.

36. Petition of Adriaen van der Donck Concerning Land Granted Him at Saegkil in 1645 and Petition of Adriaen van der Donck Concerning Obligations of His Servants, May 26, 1653. Ibid., 204–206.

37. Letter from the Directors at Amsterdam to Petrus Stuyvesant, June 6, 1653. Ibid., 215–216.

38. Letter from the Directors at Amsterdam to Petrus Stuyvesant, July 24, 1653. Ibid., 220–221.

39. Hendrick Cornelisz. Broeck, Jan Mewes, Evert Janz., Jan Gerritsen, Hendrick Claesz., Gommert Paulusz., Arent Martsz., Jan Hoffman, and Joris van Vorst. Stadsarchief Amsterdam, Notarial Archive 5075, Jacob de Winter, inventory 2280.

CHAPTER 15

1. I. N. Phelps Stokes et al., *The Iconography of Manhattan Island, 1498–1909* (New York: R. H. Dodd, 1915) 2: 327–328.

2. Melyn, *Melyn Papers*, 111–112. Petition of Geraert van der Voorde, Isaac Melyn and Others. February 19, 1652. Gehring, *Correspondence 1647–1653*, 139.

3. Court Minutes of New Amsterdam, December 1, 153, RNA_VI_bk2, n95. NYC Municipal Archives Online, Books and Manuscripts. For an earlier translation in a published document, see Fernow, *Records of New Amsterdam*, I: 134.

4. See Shorto, *Island at the Center of the World*, 262–264, for an expanded explanation about the English Remonstrance.

5. Letter from the Directors in Amsterdam to Director General and Council, May 18, 1654. Charles Gehring, trans. and ed., *Correspondence, 1654–1658* (Syracuse: Syracuse University Press, 2003), 11.

6. *DRCHNY*, I: 553.

7. Letter from the Directors in Amsterdam to Director General and Council, May 18, 1654. Gehring, *Correspondence, 1654–1658*, 11.

8. Order Rejecting a Petition of Joris van Vorst, January 19, 1655. NYSA_A1809-78_V06_0002a. Digital Collections, NYSA. For an earlier translation in a published document, see Charles Gehring, trans. and ed., *Council Minutes, 1655–1656* (Syracuse: Syracuse University Press, 1995), 4.

9. Court Minutes of New Amsterdam, June 21, 1655. RNA_vi_bk3, n87, NYC Municipal Archives Online, Books and Manuscripts. For an earlier translation in a published document, see Fernow, *Records of New Amsterdam*, I: 323.

10. Van der Donck, *Beschryvinge*, title page.

11. Van Gastel, "Adriaen van Der Donck, New Netherland and America," 317; M. M. Kleerkooper, *De Boekhandel te Amsterdam Voornamelijk in de 17e Eeuw* ('s Gravenhage: M. Nijhoff, 1914), 525.

12. F. Blom and H. Looijesteijn, "Ordinary People in the New World: The City of Amsterdam, Colonial Policy, and Initiatives from Below, 1656–1664," in *In Praise of Ordinary People*, ed. M. Jacob and H. Secretan (New York: Palgrave Macmillan, 2013), 205.

13. F. R. E. Blom, "Picturing New Netherland and New York," in *The Dutch Trading Companies as Knowledge Networks*, ed. S. Huigen, J. de Jong, et al. (Leiden: Brill, 2010), 104.

14. Ibid., 106.

15. Thank you to Elizabeth McFadden of UC Berkeley and Jos Koldeweij of Radboud Universiteit for their insights and expertise on the subject's clothing and clasp. *Portrait of a Man*, National Gallery of Art, Washington, DC. Andrew Mellon Collection.

16. Charles Harris, "Jacobus Gerritsen Strycker (c. 1619–1687) an Artist of New Amsterdam," *The New York Historical Quarterly Bulletin* (October 1926): 86.

17. James T. Flexner, *First Flowers of Our Wilderness* (Boston: Houghton Mifflin, 1947), 290.

18. Patent to Cornelis van der Donck, August 26, 1655. NYSA_A1880-78_VHHpt2_0045, Digital Collections, NYSA. For an earlier translation in a published document, see in Gehring, *Land Papers, 1630–1664*, 78.

19. Petition of Adriaen van der Donck, May 26, 1653. Gehring, *Correspondence, 1647–1653*, 204–205. For the 1668 sale of van der Donck's land by Elias Doughty, see Deed from Elias Doughty to Betts and Tippett, July 6, 1668, and recorded February 22, 1670. Victor H. Paltsits, ed., *Documents of the Assembly of the State of New York*, Vol. 33: 67, Part 1: Minutes of the Executive Council (Albany: State of New York, 1910), 201. The land referred to as formerly owned by "old" Youncker van der Donck is in the southern portion of Adriaen van der Donck's land, near present-day Kingsbridge. The marshy meadowlands can be visualized with the Welikia Project online, https://welikia.org/explore/mannahatta-map/.

20. Advice on Stuyvesant's Proposals, November 14, 1655. Gehring, *Council Minutes, 1655–1656*, 142.

21. Nut Island is now Governor's Island. Ibid.

22. Letter from Council of New Netherland to Director Stuyvesant at the South River, September 1655. NYSA_A1878-78_V18_0012, Digital Collections, NYSA. For an earlier translation in a published document, see Charles Gehring, trans. and ed., *Delaware Papers: A Collection of Documents Pertaining to the Regulation of Affairs on the South River of New Netherland, 1648–1664* (Baltimore: Genealogical Publishing Co., 1981), 35. Gehring, *Council Minutes, 1655–1656*, 142.

23. Advice on Stuyvesant's Proposals, November 14, 1655. Gehring, *Council Minutes, 1655–1656*, 143.

24. Letters from Council of New Netherland to Director Stuyvesant at the South River, September 1655 (second letter date blurred). Gehring, *Delaware Papers*, 36, 38.

25. Letter from Council of New Netherland to Director Stuyvesant at the South River, September 1655. NYSA_A1878-78_V18_0012, Digital Collections, NYSA. For an earlier translation in a published document, see Gehring, *Delaware Papers*, 35.

26. Advice on Stuyvesant's Proposals, November 14, 1655. Gehring, *Council Minutes, 1655–1656*, 143.

27. Melyn, "Melyn Papers," 114.

28. Ibid., 115.

29. The man was Johannes van Beek. Letter of Johannes Bogaert to Hans Bontemantel, October 31, 1655. Jameson, *Narratives of New Netherland,* 386.

30. Court Minutes of New Amsterdam, January 10, 1656, RNA_vi_bk4, n17. NYC Municipal Archives Online, Books and Manuscripts. For an earlier translation in a published document, see Fernow, *Records of New Amsterdam*, II: 8.

31. Paper Presented to the Council, January 26, 1656. Gehring, *Council Minutes, 1655–1656*, 204–205.

32. Berthold Fernow, *Minutes of the Orphanmasters of New Amsterdam, 1655–1663* (New York: Harper, 1902), 10.

33. Worker contracts June 13 and 17, 1653. Stadsarchief Amsterdam, Notarial Archive 5075, Jacob de Winter, inventory 2280, XIV.

34. Van der Donck, *Vertoogh*, 23–24.

35. Remonstrance to the States General, October 31, 1655. Gehring, *Council Minutes, 1655–1656*, 122.

36. Stuyvesant to Van der Capellen, October 30, 1655, *DRCHNY*, I: 639. Ibid.

37. Gehring, *Council Minutes, 1655–1656*, xvii; Allen W. Trelease, *Indian Affairs in Colonial New York: The Seventeenth Century* (Lincoln: University of Nebraska Press, 1997), 138–140.

38. Letter from the Council to Petrus Stuyvesant at the South River, September 1655. Gehring, *Delaware Papers*, 36. For a short discussion on tribal alliances relative to this incident, see Shorto, *Island at the Center of the World*, 280.

39. Trelease, *Indian Affairs*, 139.

40. Letter from the Directors to the Director General, December 19, 1656. Gehring, *Correspondence, 1654–1658*, 103.

41. Ibid. Trelease, *Indian Affairs*, 138.

42. Ibid.

43. Trelease, *Indian Affairs*, 147.

44. Van der Donck, *Vertoogh*, 39.

CHAPTER 16

1. "inde Massacre van Vijff en Vijftigh verlaten." Letter from Stuyvesant to the Directors at Amsterdam, June 10, 1664. NYSA_A1810-78_V15_0131. Digital Collections, NYSA. For an earlier translation in a published document, see *DRCHNY*, XIV: 550.

2. Court Minutes of New Amsterdam, January 10, 1656, RNA_v1_bk4, n17. NYC Municipal Archives Online, Books and Manuscripts. For an earlier translation in a published document, see Fernow, *Records of New Amsterdam*, II: 8.

3. Fernow, *Minutes of the Orphanmasters*, 10.

4. Charles T. Gehring and Janny Venema, eds., *Fort Orange Records, 1654–1679* (Syracuse: Syracuse University Press, 2009), 422.

5. Janny Venema, *Beverwijck: A Dutch Village on the American Frontier, 1652–1664* (Albany: State University of New York Press, 2003), 81.

6. Gehring and Venema, *Fort Orange Records, 1654–1679*, 422.

7. Fernow, *Records of New Amsterdam*, II: 203. Faded original in Court Minutes of New Amsterdam, October 30, 1656, RNA_v2_bk1, n47. NYC Municipal Archives Online, Books and Manuscripts. Nicasius de Sille was made *schout* in 1656.

8. Ibid.

9. Letter from Stuyvesant to the Directors at Amsterdam, June 10, 1664. NYSA_A1810-78_V15_0131. Digital Collections, NYSA. For an earlier translation in a published document, see *DRCHNY*, XIV: 550.

10. Charles Gehring, trans. and ed., *Council Minutes, 1652–1654* (Baltimore: Genealogical Publishing Co., 1983), 52.

11. Court Minutes of New Amsterdam, March 17, 1653, RNA_v1_bk2, n26. NYC Municipal Archives Online, Books and Manuscripts. For an earlier translation in a published document, see Fernow, *Records of New Amsterdam*, I: 71. See also chapter 1, note 10, for Ghysbrecht van der Donck.

12. Court Minutes of New Amsterdam, August 28, 1656, RNA_v1_bk2, n175. NYC Municipal Archives Online, Books and Manuscripts. For an earlier translation in a published document, see Fernow, *Records of New Amsterdam*, II: 157.

13. Hoffman, "Van der Donck-Van Bergen," 340.

14. Ibid. "Flower de luce" is a depiction of an iris, commonly referred to as fleur-de-lys and, traditionally, a symbol of French royalty.

15. "van veel druk-fouten gesuyvert." Van der Donck, *Beschryvinge van Nieuw-Nederlant* (Amsterdam: Evert Nieuwenhof, 1656), title page.

16. Blom, "Picturing New Netherland and New York," 106.

17. Blom and Looijesteijn, "Ordinary People in the New World," 207–209.

18. Proceedings of the County Court of Charles County, 1658–1666: 53, Archives of Maryland Online, 241.

19. Ibid., 229.

20. Ibid., 146–147.

21. Ibid., 261–263.

22. Ibid., 53, 248.

23. Ibid., 53, 229–231.

24. Ibid., 220; Hoffman, "Van der Donck-van Bergen," 341.

25. Proceedings of the County Court of Charles County, 1658–1666: 60, Archives of Maryland Online, 206.

26. Ibid.

27. Answer of Ex-Director Stuyvesant, October 29, 1666. NL-HaNA, Staten-Generaal, 1.01.02, inv. nummer 12564.57. For an earlier translation in a published document, see *DRCHNY*, II: 443.

28. Shorto, *Island at the Center of the World*, 296–297.

29. Answer of Ex-Director Stuyvesant, October 29, 1666. NL-HaNA, Staten-Generaal, 1.01.02, inv. nummer 12564.57. For an earlier translation in a published document, see *DRCHNY*, II: 444–445.

30. Ibid.

31. Report on the Surrender of New Netherland, October 19, 1665. NL-HaNA, Staten-Generaal, 1.01.02, inv. nummer 12564.57. For an earlier translation in a published document, see *DRCHNY*, II: 366.

32. Ibid. For an earlier translation in a published document, see *DRCHNY*, II: 368–369.

33. Remonstrance of the People, September 5, 1664. NL-HaNA, Staten-Generaal, 1.01.02, inv. nummer 12564.57. For an earlier translation in a published document, see *DRCHNY*, II: 248.

34. Ibid. For an earlier translation in a published document, see *DRCHNY*, II: 249.

35. Van Ruyven to Stuyvesant, Aug. 7, 1666. NL-HaNA, Staten-Generaal, 1.01.02, inv. nummer 12564.57. For an earlier translation in a published document, see *DRCHNY*, II: 473.

36. Paltsits, *Documents of the Assembly*, 234.

37. Ibid., 30, 197.

38. Ibid., 196–208.

39. Ibid., 199.

Chapter 17

1. Shorto, *Island at the Center of the World*, 196.

2. Nan A. Rothschild and Christopher N. Matthews, *Phase 1A–1B Archaeological Investigation of the Proposed Area for the Construction of Six Tennis Courts on the Parade Grounds of Van Cortlandt Park, the Bronx, New York*, report submitted to the City of New York Department of Parks and Recreation, n.d.; Shorto, *Island at the Center of the World*, 196.

3. De Koning, "From Van der Donck to Visscher," 5–9. Many thanks to Joep de Koning for taking time for a personal introduction to the early prints and engravings of New Netherland.

4. Shorto, *Island at the Center of the World*, 224–225.

5. Van der Donck, *A Description of New Netherland*, xviii.

6. Ada van Gastel, "Van der Donck's Description of the Indians: Additions and Corrections," *William and Mary Quarterly* (July 1990); Shorto, *Island at the Center of the World*, 137.

7. Van der Donck, *A Description of New Netherland*.

8. Oliver A. Rink, *Holland on the Hudson: An Economic and Social History of Dutch New York* (Ithaca: Cornell University Press, 1989), 164–165.

9. Jacobs, *The Colony of New Netherland*, 87–95.

10. For more on the argument for the Dutch influence on the development of New York, see Shorto, *Island at the Center of the World*.

11. Van der Donck, *A Description of the New Netherlands*, ix–xl.

12. Anderson Galleries, "The Library of Henry F. de Puy, Part One," in *Catalogue of Sale* (New York: Anderson Galleries, 1919), 118.

13. Ibid.

Bibliography

Letters, Journals, Pamphlets, Maps, Council Minutes, and Other Primary Sources

Acta Senatus. Leiden: Du Rieu, 1875.

Actorum Juridica Facultatis, Vol. 1. Universiteit Leiden Special Collections Library. Leiden.

Archief van de Notarissen ter Standplaats Amsterdam, Jacob de Winter, 5075. Stadsarchief Amsterdam.

Archief van de Staten-Generaal, 1.01.02. Nationaal Archief, The Hague.

Archieven van Senaat en Faculteiten, 1575–1877. Universiteit Leiden (ASF), Digitale Versie, 7 Oktober, 2014.

Bruce, John, ed. *Calendar of State Papers, Domestic Series, of the Reign of Charles I. 1635–1636*. London: Longmans, Green, Reader, and Dyer, 1866.

Council Minutes of New Amsterdam, Books and Manuscripts, NYC Municipal Archives Digital Archives Online, New York.

De Hooges, Antony. *De Hooges Memorandum Book*. Van Rensselaer Manor Papers Digital Collections NYSL_SC7079, New York State Library. Albany.

De Jonge, L., and A. Huijsmans. *Breda, de Korte Boschstraat, Archeologische begeleiding*. Breda: Erfgoedrapport, 2013.

De Koning, Joep. "From Van der Donck to Visscher." *Mercator's World* 5, no. 4 (July/August 2000): 1–10.

De Vries, David Pietersz. *Korte Historiael ende Journaels Aenteyckeninge van Verscheyden Voyagiens in de Vier Deelen des Wereldts-Ronde, also Europa, Africa, Asia, ende Amerika Gedaen*. 's Gravenhage: M. Nijhoff, 1911.

De Vries, David Peterson. *Voyages from Holland to America, A.D. 1632 to 1644*. Trans. Henry C. Murphy. New York: Kraus Reprint, 1853.

Dopen Wals-gereformeerd kerk, 1607–1810. Stadsarchief Breda.

Du Rieu, Willem Nicolaas. *Album studiosorum Academiae Lugduno Batavae MDLXXV– MDCCCLXXV: accedunt nomina curatorum et professorum per eadem secula.* Hagae Comitum: Apud Martinum Nijhoff, 1875.

Fernow, Berthold, trans. and ed. *The Records of New Amsterdam, 1653–1674.* 7 vols. New York: The Knickerbocker Press, 1897.

Fernow, B., ed. *Minutes of the Orphanmasters of New Amsterdam, 1655–1663, Vol. 1.* New York: Harper, 1902.

Gehring, Charles, trans. and ed. *Correspondence, 1647–1653.* New Netherland Documents Series. Syracuse: Syracuse University Press, 2000.

———. *Correspondence, 1654–1658.* New Netherland Documents Series. Syracuse: Syracuse University Press, 2003.

———. *Council Minutes, 1652–1654.* New York Historical Manuscripts Series. Baltimore: Genealogical Publishing Co., 1983.

———. *Council Minutes, 1655–1656.* New Netherland Documents Series. Syracuse: Syracuse University Press, 1995.

———. *Delaware Papers: A Collection of Documents Pertaining to the Regulation of Affairs on the South River of New Netherland, 1648–1664.* Baltimore: Genealogical Publishing Co., 1981.

———. *Land Papers, 1630–1664.* New York Historical Manuscript Series. Baltimore: Genealogical Publishing Co., 1980.

Gehring, Charles T., and J. A. Schiltkamp, trans. and eds. *Curaçao Papers, 1640–1665.* New Netherland Documents. Interlaken: Heart of the Lakes Publishing, 1987.

Gehring, Charles T., and Janny Venema, eds. *Fort Orange Records, 1654–1679.* 1st ed. New Netherland Documents Series. Syracuse: Syracuse University Press, 2009.

Hartgers, Joost. *Beschrijving van Virginia, Nieuw Nederlandt, Nieuw Engelandt, en d'Eylanden Bermudes, Berbados, en S. Christoffel.* Amsterdam: Joost Hartgers, 1651.

I. A. and G. W. C. *Breeden-Raedt aende Vereenichde Nederlandsche Provintien.* Antwerp: Francoys van Duynen, 1649.

Jameson, J. Franklin. *Narratives of New Netherland, 1609–1664.* New York: C. Scribner's Sons, 1909.

Lechford, Thomas. *Plain Dealing: or, News from New England.* Ed. J. Hammond Trumbull. Boston: J.K. Wiggin and W.P. Lunt, 1867.

Melyn, Cornelis. "Melyn Papers, 1640–1699." Collections of the New York Historical Society for the Year 1913, 97–138. New York: New York Historical Society and Jacob Melyn, 1914.

Mouw, Dirk, trans. *The Memorandum Book of Anthony de Hooges.* Albany: New Netherland Institute, 2012.

Murphy, H. C., trans. *Vertoogh van Nieu Nederland; and Breeden Raedt Aende Vereenichde Nederlandsche Provintien.: Two Rare Tracts, Printed in 1964–'50. Relating to the Administration of Affairs in New Netherland.* New York: [Baker, Godwin & Co., printers], 1854.

New York State Archives, Digital Collections. www.digitalcollections.archives.nysed.gov.

NYPL Map Warper. Viewing Map 13913. *Redraft of the Castello Plan, New Amsterdam in 1660.* Accessed December 1, 2014.

O'Callaghan, E. B., and Berthold Fernow, trans. *Documents Relative to the Colonial History of the State of New York.* 15 vols. Albany: Weed, Parsons and Company, 1856–1887.

Paltsits, Victor H., ed. *Documents of the Assembly of the State of New York,* Vol. 33: 67, Part 1: Minutes of the Executive Council. Albany: State of New York, 1910.

Proceedings of the County Court of Charles County, 1658–1666, Vol. 53. Archives of Maryland Online.

Proceedings of the County Court of Charles County, 1666–1674, Vol. 60. Archives of Maryland Online.

Pulsifer, David, ed. *Records of the Colony of New Plymouth, in New England, Volume 2.* Boston: Press of W. White, 1859.

Purple, Samuel Smith. *Index to the Marriage Records from 1639–1801 of the Reformed Dutch Church in New Amsterdam and New York.* New York: Priv. print., 1890.

Rothschild, Nan A., and Christopher N. Matthews. *Phase 1A–1B Archaeological Investigation of the Proposed Area for the Construction of Six Tennis Courts on the Parade Grounds of Van Cortlandt Park, the Bronx.* New York report submitted to the City of New York Department of Parks and Recreation, n.d.

Shattuck, M., ed., and D. Versteeg, trans. *New Netherland Papers c. 1650–1660.* A Publication of the New Netherland Research Center and the New Netherland Institute, 2011.

Van Curler, Arent. Letter of Arent van Curler to Kiliaen van Rensselaer, June 16, 1643. "Arent van Curler & the Flatts." Digital Exhibition. New Netherland Institute. https://www.newnetherlandinstitute.org.

Van Donk, Balthasar. "Bewindvoerder van de Veenhuizen venen juli 1652." Stadhouderlijk Archief: Het Archief in Tresoar, Correspondenten, abk-7, Inventaris 1.2.3.09.2.

Van den Bogaert, Harmen Meyndertsz. *A Journey into Mohawk and Oneida Country, 1634–1635: The Journal of Harmen Meyndertsz van den Bogaert.* 1st ed. Trans. and ed. Charles T. Gehring and William A. Starna. Iroquois Books. Syracuse: Syracuse University Press, 1988.

Van der Donck, Adriaen. *Beschryvinge van Nieuw-Nederlant.* Amsterdam: Evert Nieuwenhof, 1655.

———. *Beschryvinge van Nieuw-Nederlant.* Amsterdam: Evert Nieuwenhof, Second edition, 1656.

———. *A Description of New Netherland.* Ed. Charles T. Gehring and William A. Starna. Trans. Diederik Willem Goedhuys. Lincoln: University of Nebraska Press, 2010.

———. *A Description of the New Netherlands.* Ed. Thomas O'Donnell. Trans. Jeremiah Johnson. Syracuse: Syracuse University Press, 1968.

———. *Vertoogh van Nieu-Neder-Land, Wegens de Geleghentheydt, Vruchtbaerheydt en Soberen Staet desselfs.* 's Gravenhage: Michiel Stael, 1650.

Van der Donck, Adriaen, and Cornelis van Tienhoven. *Remonstrance of New Netherland, and the Occurrences There: Addressed to the High and Mighty States General of the United Netherlands, on the 28th July, 1649. With Secretary Van Tienhoven's Answer.* Trans. E. B. O'Callaghan. Albany: Weed, Parsons and Company, 1856.

Van Laer, A. J. F., ed. *Van Rensselaer Bowier Manuscripts, Being the Letters of Kiliaen Van Rensselaer, 1630–1643, and Other Documents Relating to the Colony of Rensselaerswyck.* Albany: University of the State of New York, 1908.

Van Laer, A. J. F., trans. *Council Minutes, 1638–1649.* New York Historical Manuscripts Series. Baltimore: Genealogical Publishing Co., 1974.

———. *Minutes of the Court of Rensselaerswyck, 1648–1652.* Albany: University of the State of New York, 1922.

———. *Register of the Provincial Secretary, 1638–1642.* New York Historical Manuscript Series. Baltimore: Genealogical Publishing Co., 1974.

———. *Register of the Provincial Secretary, 1642–1647.* New York Historical Manuscript Series. Baltimore: Genealogical Publishing Co., 1974.

———. *Register of the Provincial Secretary, 1648–1660.* New York Historical Manuscript Series. Baltimore: Genealogical Publishing Co., 1974.

Van Rensselaer, Kiliaen. *Brievenboek van Kiliaen van Rensselaer*, Inv. Hs–2179, Navigation and Library Collections, Het Scheepvaartmuseum. Amsterdam.

Van Rijn, Rembrandt. *The Anatomy Lesson of Dr. Nicolaes Tulp.* 1632. Oil on canvas. Mauritshuis, The Hague.

Vertrokken Lidmaten Breda, 1642–1679. Stadsarchief Breda.

Vestbrieven, 1599–1655. Stadsarchief Breda.

Volumen Inscriptionum, Catalogus Studiosorum, Academia Leydensis, 1631–1645, Universiteit Leiden Special Collections Library. Leiden.

Volumen Inscriptionum, Catalogus Studiosorum, Academia Leydensis, 1645–1662, Universiteit Leiden Special Collections Library. Leiden.

SECONDARY SOURCES

Anderson Galleries "The Library of Henry F. de Puy, Part One." In *Catalogue of Sale*, 1–134. New York: Anderson Galleries, 1919.

Bangs, Jeremy D. "Dutch Contributions to Religious Tolerance." *Church History* 79, no. 3 (September 2010): 585–613.

Banta, Theodore M., ed. *Year Book of the Holland Society of New York, 1900.* New York: Holland Society of New York.

Becker, Alfred. "Mr. Adriaen Van der Donck, the Earliest Lawyer in New York." In *Proceedings of the New York State Bar Association*, 317–331. Albany: The Argus Company, 1904.

Bielinski, Stefan. "The *Schout* in Rensselaerswijck: A Conflict of Interests." In *A Beautiful and Fruitful Place: Selected Rensselaerswijck Seminar Papers*, ed. Nancy Zeller and Charles T. Gehring et al., 3–12. Albany: New Netherland Publishing, 1991.

Blanding, Michael. *The Map Thief: The Gripping Story of an Esteemed Rare-Map Dealer Who Made Millions Stealing Priceless Maps*. New York: Gotham, 2014.

Blom, F. R. E. "Picturing New Netherland and New York: Dutch-Anglo Transfer of New World Information." In *The Dutch Trading Companies as Knowledge Networks*, ed. S. Huigen, J. de Jong, et al., 103–127. Leiden: Brill, 2010.

Blom, F., and H. Looijesteijn. "Ordinary People in the New World: The City of Amsterdam, Colonial Policy, and Initiatives from Below, 1656–1664." In *In Praise of Ordinary People*, ed. M. Jacob and C. Secretan, 203–235. New York: Palgrave Macmillan, 2013.

Burke, Thomas E. *Mohawk Frontier: The Dutch Community of Schenectady, New York, 1661–1710*. Ithaca: Cornell University Press, 1991.

Burton, Paul G. "The Antwerp Ancestry of Cornelis Melyn." *New York Genealogical and Biographical Record* 67, 157–164, 246–255. New York: New York Genealogical and Biographical Society, 1936.

Burton, Paul G. "Cornelis Melyn, Patroon of Staten Island, and Some of His Descendants." *New York Genealogical and Biographical Record* 68, 3–17, 132. New York: New York Genealogical and Biographical Society, 1937.

De Vries, Jan. *Barges and Capitalism: Passenger Transportation in the Dutch Economy, 1632–1839*. Utrecht: HES Publishers, 1981.

Deen, Femke, David Onnekink, and Michel Reinders, eds. *Pamphlets and Politics in the Dutch Republic*. Leiden: Brill, 2011.

Doty, Ethan Allen. "The Doughty Family of Long Island." *New York Genealogical and Biographical Record* 43, 312–324. New York: New York Genealogical and Biographical Society, 1912.

Easterbrook, J. "Cosmopolitanism and Adriaen van der Donck's *A Description of New Netherland*." *Early American Literature* 49, no. 1 (2014): 3–36.

Flexner, James T. *First Flowers of Our Wilderness*. Boston: Houghton Mifflin, 1947.

Frijhoff, Willem. "Director Willem Kieft and His Dutch Relatives." In *Revisiting New Netherland: Perspectives on Early Dutch America*, ed. Joyce D. Goodfriend, 147–204. Leiden: Brill, 2005.

Frijhoff, Willem. *Fulfilling God's Mission: The Two Worlds of Dominie Everardus Bogardus, 1607–1647*. Trans. Myra J. Heerspink Scholz. Boston: Brill, 2007.

Frijhoff, Willem. *Wegen Van Evert Willemsz.: Een Hollands Weeskind Op Zoek Naar Zichzelf, 1607–1647*. Nijmegen: SUN, 1995.

Gehring, Charles. *A Guide to Dutch Manuscripts Relating to New Netherland*. Albany: University of the State of New York, 1978.

———. "Wringing Information from a Drowned Princess." In *A Beautiful and Fruitful Place, Selected Rensselaerswyck Papers, Vol. 2*, ed. Elizabeth P. Funk and Martha D. Shattuck, 131–134. Albany: State University of New York Press, 2011.

Groenveld, Simon. "De Institutionele en Politieke Context." In *Van tresorier tot thesaurier-generaal: zes eeuwen financieel beleid in handen van een hoge Nederlandse ambtsdrager*, ed. J. T. de Smidt and R. M. Sprenger, 55–88. Hilversum: Verloren, 1996.

————. "New Light on a Drowned Princess—Information from London." *de Halve Maen* 74 (Summer 2001): 23–28.

Gronim, Sara Stidstone. *Everyday Nature: Knowledge of the Natural World in Colonial New York*. New Brunswick: Rutgers University Press, 2007.

Grote Kerk Breda. *The Great or Our Lady's Church Breda*. Breda.

Gysseling, M. *Toponymisch Woordenboek van België, Nederland, Luxemburg, Noord-Frankrijk En West-Duitsland (vóór 1226)*. Bouvstoffen En Studiën Voor de Geschiedenis En de Lexicografie van Het Nederlands, VI, 1–2. Brussel: Belgisch Interuniversitair Centrum voor Neerlandistiek, 1960.

Harris, Charles X. "Jacobus Gerritsen Strycker (c. 1619–1687) an Artist of New Amsterdam." *The New York Historical Society Quarterly Bulletin* (October 1926): 83–91.

Hoeven, Govert G. *Geschiedenis der Vesting Breda*. Breda: Broese, 1868.

Hoffman, William J. "An Armory of American Families of Dutch Descent: Van der Donck-Van Bergen." *New York Genealogical and Biographical Record* 67, 155–177. New York: New York Genealogical and Biographical Society, 1936.

Jacobs, Jaap. "A Hitherto Unknown Letter of Adriaen van der Donck." *de Halve Maen* 71 (Spring 1998): 1–6.

————. *The Colony of New Netherland: A Dutch Settlement in Seventeenth-Century America*. Cornell Paperbacks. Ithaca: Cornell University Press, 2009.

————. *Een zegenrijk gewest: Nieuw-Nederland in de zeventiende eeuw*. Amsterdam: Prometheus, 1999.

————. "De Frustratie van Adriaen van der Donck, Colonist in Nieuw-Nederland." *Historisch Tijdschrift Holland* 31 (1999): 74–85.

————. "Migration, Population, and Government." In *Four Centuries of Dutch-American Relations: 1609–2009*, ed. Hans Krabbendam, Cornelis A. van Minnen, and Giles Scott-Smith, 85–96. Albany: State University of New York Press, 2009.

————. *Petrus Stuyvesant, Een levenschets*. Amsterdam: Bert Bakker, 2009.

————. "To Favor This New and Growing City with a Court of Justice." *de Halve Maen* 76 (Winter 2003): 65–72.

Kleerkooper, M. M. *De boekhandel te Amsterdam voornamelijk in de 17e eeuw.* 's Gravenhage: M. Nijhoff, 1914.

Klooster, Wim. *The Dutch Moment: War, Trade, and Settlement in the Seventeenth-Century Atlantic World*. Ithaca: Cornell University Press, 2016.

Kupperman, Karen Ordahl, and Williamsburg, Virginia. *America in European Consciousness, 1493–1750*. Chapel Hill: Published for the Institute of Early American History and Culture, Williamsburg, Virginia, by the University of North Carolina, 1995.

Maika, Dennis J. "Commerce and Community: Manhattan Merchants in the Seventeenth Century." PhD diss., New York University, 1995.

Meeuwis, René, and Johan Hendriks. *Adriaen van der Donck: een Bredase burgerrechtenactivist in Nieuw-Amsterdam*. Breda: Gemeente Breda, Directie Ruimtelijke Ontwikkeling, Bureau Cultureel Erfgoed, 2009.

Merwick, Donna. *Possessing Albany, 1630–1710: The Dutch and English Experiences*. Cambridge: Cambridge University Press, 1990.

Nissenson, S. G. *The Patroon's Domain*. New York: Columbia University Press, 1937.

O'Callaghan, E. B. *Calendar of Historical Manuscripts in the Office of the Secretary of State, Albany, N.Y.* Albany: Weed, Parsons and Company, 1865.

———. *The Documentary History of the State of New York*. Albany: Weed, Parsons and Company, 1849.

———. *The History of New Netherland*. 2 vols. New York: D. Appleton and Co., 1848.

———. *The Register of New Netherland, 1626 to 1674.* Albany: J. Munsell, 1865.

O'Connor, Anahad. "After 200 Years, a Beaver Is Back in New York City." *New York Times*, February 22, 2007. Accessed April 8, 2015.

Otterspeer, Willem. *The Bastion of Liberty: Leiden University Today and Yesterday*. Trans. Beverly Jackson. Amsterdam: Leiden University Press, 2008.

Otterspeer, Willem. *Groepsportret met Dame: Het bolwerk van de vrijheid*. Amsterdam: Bakker, 2000.

Parker, Henry A. "The Reverend Francis Doughty." In *Transactions, 1904–1906*. Volume X of Publications of the Colonial Society of Massachusetts, 261–276. Boston: The Colonial Society of Massachusetts, 1907.

Parthesius, Robert. *Dutch Ships in Tropical Waters: The Development of the Dutch East India Company (VOC) Shipping Network in Asia 1595–1660.* Amsterdam: Amsterdam University Press, 2010.

Pluis, Jan, Minze van den Akker, and Ger de Ree. *Kinderspelen Op Tegels*. Assen: Van Gorcum, 1979.

Prögler, Daniela. *English Students at Leiden University, 1575–1650: Advancing Your Abilities in Learning and Bettering Your Understanding of the World and State Affairs*. Burlington: Ashgate, 2013.

Riker, James. *The Annals of Newtown, in Queens County, New-York: Containing Its History from Its First Settlement, Together with Many Interesting Facts Concerning the Adjacent Towns; Also, a Particular Account of Numerous Long Island Families Now Spread Over This and Various Other States of the Union*. New York: D. Fanshaw, 1852.

Riley, Henry T., ed. *A Dictionary of Latin and Greek Quotations, Proverbs, Maxims and Mottos*. Bohn's Classical Library. London: Bell, 1909.

Rink, Oliver A. *Holland on the Hudson: An Economic and Social History of Dutch New York*. Ithaca: Cornell University Press, 1989.

Sanderson, Eric. W. *Mannahatta: A Natural History of New York City*. New York: Abrams, 2009.

Scharf, John Thomas. *History of Westchester County: New York, Including Morrisania, Kings Bridge, and West Farms, Which Have Been Annexed to New York City*. New York: L. E. Preston & Company, 1886.

Scheurleer, Lunsingh, Theodoor Herman, and G. H. M. Posthumus Meyjes, eds. *Leiden University in the Seventeenth Century: An Exchange of Learning*. Leiden: Brill, 1975.

Shorto, Russell. *The Island at the Center of the World: The Epic Story of Dutch Manhattan and the Forgotten Colony That Shaped America.* New York: Vintage Books, 2005.

Smits, J. M. *The Making of European Private Law: Toward a Ius Commune Europaeum as a Mixed Legal System.* Antwerp: Intersentia, 2002.

Stokes, I. N. Phelps, F. C. Wieder, Victor Hugo Paltsits, Douglas C. McMurtrie, and Sidney Lawton Smith. *The Iconography of Manhattan Island, 1498–1909.* New York: R. H. Dodd, 1915.

Tepper, Michael. *New World Immigrants: A Consolidation of Ship Passenger Lists and Associated Data from Periodical Literature.* Baltimore: Genealogical Publishing Co., 1979.

Trelease, Allen W. *Indian Affairs in Colonial New York: The Seventeenth Century.* 1st Bison book print. Lincoln: University of Nebraska Press, 1997.

Van den Hout, Julie. "The Omnipotent Beaver in Van der Donck's *A Description of New Netherland*: A Natural Symbol of Promise in the New World." UC Berkeley: UC Berkeley Library. http://escholarship.org/uc/item/870174nb

Van Gastel, Ada Louise. "Adriaen van Der Donck, New Netherland and America: A Thesis in English." PhD diss., The Pennsylvania State University, 1985.

———. "Adriaen van der Donck als woordvoerder van de Nieuw-Nederlandse bevolking." In *Jaarboek Centraal Bureau voor Genealogie,* 89–107. Den Haag: Centraal Bureau voor Genealogie, 1996.

———. "Adriaen van der Donck in Rensselaerswyck: 1641–1643." *de Halve Maen* 60 (Winter 1987): 14–19.

———. "Rhetorical Ambivalence in the New Netherland Author Adriaen van Der Donck." *MELUS* 17, no. 2 (1991): 3–18.

———. "Van der Donck's Description of the Indians: Additions and Corrections." *William and Mary Quarterly* (July 1990): 411–421.

Van den Tol, Joris. "Hendrick Haecxs: Amateuristisch Lobbyen Door de WIC in de Republiek in 1647." In *Politieke Belangenbehartiging in De Vroegmoderne Nederlanden: De Rol Van Lobby, Petities, En Officiële Delegaties in De Politieke Besluitvorming,* ed. Elisabeth Geevers and Griet Vermeesch, 47–64. Maastricht: Shaker Publishing, 2014.

Van Oudheusden, Jan. *Geschiedenis van Brabant: van het hertogdom tot heden.* Zwolle: Waanders, 2004.

Venema, Janny. *Beverwijck: A Dutch Village on the American Frontier, 1652–1664.* Albany: State University of New York Press, 2003.

———. *Kiliaen van Rensselaer (1586–1643): Designing a New World.* Hilversum: Verloren, 2010.

Wilcoxen, Charlotte. "Ships and Work Boats of New Netherland, 1609–1674." In *A Beautiful and Fruitful Place: Selected Rensselaerswijck Seminar Papers,* ed. Nancy Zeller and Charles T. Gehring et al., 53–70. Albany: New Netherland Publishing, 1991.

Woltjer, J. J. *De Leidse Universiteit in Verleden en Heden.* Leiden: Universitaire Pers, 1965.

Index

Printed in the USA
CPSIA information can be obtained
at www.ICGtesting.com
LVHW090932030224
770855LV00023B/344/J